Public Policy and Politics

Series Editors: Colin Fudge and Robin Hambleton

Public policy-making in western democracies is confronted by new pressures. Central values relating to the role of the state, the role of markets and the role of citizenship are now all contested and the consensus built up around the Keynesian welfare state is under challenge. New social movements are entering the political arena; electronic technologies are transforming the nature of employment; changes in demographic structure are creating heightened demands for public services; unforeseen social and health problems are emerging; and, most disturbing, social and economic inequalities are increasing in many countries.

How governments – at international, national and local levels – respond to this developing agenda is the central focus of the Public Policy and Politics series. Aimed at a student, professional, practitioner and academic readership, it aims to provide up-to-date, comprehensive and authoritative analyses of public policy-making in practice.

The series is international and interdisciplinary in scope, and bridges theory and practice by relating the substance of policy to the politics of the policy-making process.

Public Policy and Politics

Series Editors: Colin Fudge and Robin Hambleton

PUBLISHED

Kate Ascher, *The Politics of Privatisation: Contracting Out Public Services*

Rob Atkinson and Graham Moon, *Urban Politics in Britain: The City, the State and the Market*

Jacqueline Barron, Gerald Crawley and Tony Wood, *Councillors in Crisis: The Public and Private Worlds of Local Councillors*

Danny Burns, Robin Hambleton and Paul Hoggett, *The Politics of Decentralisation: Revitalising Local Democracy*

Aram Eisenschitz and Jamie Gough, *The Politics of Local Economic Policy: The Problems and Possibilities of Local Initiative*

Stephen Glaister, June Burnham, Handley Stevens and Tony Travers, *Transport Policy in Britain*

Christopher Ham, *Health Policy in Britain: The Politics and Organisation of the National Health Service* (fourth edition)

Ian Henry, *The Politics of Leisure Policy*

Peter Malpass and Alan Murie, *Housing Policy and Practice* (fifth edition)

Robin Means and Randall Smith, *Community Care: Policy and Practice* (second edition)

Gerry Stoker, *The Politics of Local Government* (second edition)

Kieron Walsh, *Public Services and Market Mechanisms: Competition, Contracting and the New Public Management*

FORTHCOMING

Tony Green and Geoff Whitty, *The Changing Politics of Education: Education Policy in Contemporary Britain*

John Solomos, *Racial Inequality and Public Policy*

Public Policy and Politics
Series Standing Order
ISBN 0–333–71705–8 hardcover
ISBN 0–333–69349–3 paperback
(outside North America only)

You can receive future titles in this series as they are published. To place a standing order please contact your bookseller or, in the case of difficulty, write to us at the address below with your name and address, the title of the series and the ISBNs quoted above.

Customer Services Department, Macmillan Distribution Ltd
Houndmills, Basingstoke, Hampshire RG21 6XS, England.

Health Policy
in Britain

The Politics and Organisation of the
National Health Service

Fourth Edition

Christopher Ham

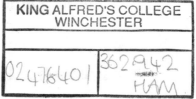

First edition 1982
Second edition 1985
Third edition 1992
Fourth edition 1999

Published by
MACMILLAN PRESS LTD
Houndmills, Basingstoke, Hampshire RG21 6XS
and London
Companies and representatives
throughout the world

ISBN 0–333–76406–4 hardcover
ISBN 0–333–76407–2 paperback

A catalogue record for this book is available
from the British Library.

10   9   8   7   6   5   4   3   2
08 07 06 05 04 03 02 01 00

Copy-edited and typeset by Povey–Edmondson
Tavistock and Rochdale, England

Printed and bound in Great Britain by
Creative Print & Design (Wales) Ebbw Vale

To Ioanna

Contents

List of Figures and Tables

Figures

Tables

Acknowledgements

The author and publishers would like to thank the following who have kindly given permission for the use of copyright material: The University of Chicago Press for a diagram from David Easton, *A Systems Analysis of Political Life*, 1965; The King's Fund for a figure from *Health Finance: Assessing the Options*, 1988; The Nuffield Trust for a table from *Who Pays For and Who Gets Health Care?*, 1998; *The Economist* for a figure from the issue of 12 December 1998; Crown Copyright material is reproduced with the permission of the Controller of Her Majesty's Stationery Office (from Department of Health, *The Government's Expenditure Plan 1998–99: Departmental Report*; Secretary of State for Health, *The New NHS: Modern, Dependable*; Secretary of State for Health, *Our Healthier Nation*; Secretary of State for Health, *A First Class Service*; Secretary of State for Scotland, *Designed to Care*; F. Drever and M. Whitehead, *Health Inequalities*; B. Botting, *The Health of Our Children*; J. Charlton and M. Murphy, *The Health of Adult Britain 1841–1994*).

Every effort has been made to contact all the copyright-holders, but if any have been inadvertently ommitted the publishers will be pleased to make the necessary arrangement at the earliest opportunity.

Preface to the Fourth Edition

This book was originally based on undergraduate and postgraduate courses I taught at Bristol University. The first edition benefited from the comments and suggestions of the students who followed those courses. I am particularly grateful to Laurie McMahon and Andrew Wall for their insights, gained during the first intake of the MSc in Public Policy Studies run by the School for Advanced Urban Studies at Bristol. I would also like to thank former colleagues at the School who commented on draft chapters, most notably Robin Hambleton, Michael Hill, Robin Means, Randall Smith and David Towell. Special mention should also be made of Ken Judge, with whom I jointly taught an undergraduate course in health policy. As editor of the series, 'Studies in Social Policy', in which the first two editions appeared, Ken encouraged me to write *Health Policy in Britain,* and as always was a constructive and critical collaborator.

The fourth edition is based on the same structure as earlier editions but has been completely revised and updated to take account of developments in health services and health policy in the 1990s. I have benefited from the advice and comments of a number of people in the Department of Health and the NHS as well as colleagues at the Health Services Management Centre at the University of Birmingham. I would particularly like to mention the assistance provided by Brigit Ayling and her colleagues in the Centre's library; the support of my assistant, Anne van der Salm; and also the work of Debbie Styer, who incorporated my new text with the original, with the last-minute help of Sue Alleyne and other colleagues. My publisher, Steven Kennedy, was even more patient on this occasion than previously.

Last but not least, I would like to thank Ioanna Burnell for her continuing support. The distractions that writing (and revising) a book inevitably creates intrudes into home life. Once again, I am pleased to dedicate the book to Ioanna.

I alone am responsible for the final text.

Solihull CHRISTOPHER HAM

Abbreviations

AHA	Area Health Authority
ASH	Action on Smoking and Health
BMA	British Medical Association
CHC	Community Health Council
CHI	Commission for Health Improvement
CIP	Cost Improvement Programme
CMO	Chief Medical Officer
CPRS	Central Policy Review Staff
CSR	Comprehensive Spending Review
DCMO	Deputy Chief Medical Officer
DGH	District General Hospital
DGM	District General Manager
DH	Department of Health
DHA	District Health Authority
DHSS	Department of Health and Social Security
DMT	District Management Team
DMU	Directly Managed Units
FHSA	Family Health Services Authority
FPC	Family Practitioner Committee
FPS	Family Practitioner Services
GHS	General Household Survey
GDP	Gross Domestic Product
GP	General Practitioner
HAS	Health Advisory Service
HCHS	Hospital and Community Health Services
HImP	Health Improvement Programme
HMC	Hospital Management Committee
HMO	Health Maintenance Organisation
JCC	Joint Consultative Committee
MAS	Management Advisory Service
MPC	Medical Practices Committee
NAHA	National Association of Health Authorities
NAHAT	National Association of Health Authorities and Trusts
NAO	National Audit Office
NICE	National Institute for Clinical Excellence
NHS	National Health Service
NHSME	National Health Service Management Executive

NHST	National Health Service Trusts
OECD	Organisation for Economic Cooperation and Development
OHE	Office of Health Economics
OPCS	Office of Population, Censuses and Surveys
PACT	Prescribing Analysis and Cost System
PCGs	Primary Care Groups
PESC	Public Expenditure Survey Committee
QALY	Quality Adjusted Life Year
RAWP	Resource Allocation Working Party
RCP	Royal College of Physicians
RGM	Regional General Manager
RHA	Regional Health Authority
RHB	Regional Hospital Board
RL	Regional Liaison
SHA	Special Health Authority
SMR	Standardised Mortality Ratio

Introduction

This book provides an introduction to health policy for students of health services in the United Kingdom. The book is concerned with both the substance of health policy and the process of health policy-making and implementation. Its aim is to introduce students to the organisation of the National Health Service (NHS), its history and development and to the way in which policies for NHS services are made and implemented in central government and in NHS bodies. The book also examines the monitoring and evaluation of health policy, and considers which groups have power over policy-making. The main concern of what follows, then, is the politics of health care: who decides, who benefits and who controls health services.

In examining health policy, the focus is not just central government, important as government is in accounting for what happens in the NHS. Rather, the book examines both the macro politics of health policy and the micro politics by reviewing the dynamics of policy-making in health bodies as well as in Westminster and Whitehall. Attention is also given to the influence of the health professions in policy-making, especially doctors, both through their involvement in committees and boards and through the power available to health professionals by virtue of their training and clinical autonomy. Put another way, if formal accounts of the organisation of government and the administration of the NHS provide the starting point of analysis, we seek to test the reality of these accounts by drawing on a wide range of studies and research evidence in the search for a fuller understanding of what actually happens in practice.

The book has been written mainly for students of social policy and administration at the undergraduate level. Other students likely to use the book are those following courses of professional training, including health service managers, health visitors. social work students and public health doctors. The contents should also be of relevance to those who provide health services, whether as members or managers of health authorities and trusts, as members of community health councils, or as civil servants in the Department of Health (DH). Many of the themes that are raised may also be of interest to the general reader seeking to appreciate the operation of the NHS and the processes of policy-making, and to an international audience concerned to understand the lessons of the NHS for other health care systems. Recognising that an introductory textbook is likely to raise as many questions as provide answers, suggestions for further reading are included at the end of the book.

One of the characteristics of contemporary debates about health policy is the strength of the views of those who participate in those debates. Controversy is the norm and opinions on what government should do to tackle the problems of the NHS are two a penny. This book endeavours to stand above these debates, reflecting the variety of views that exist in the health policy community but resisting the temptation to take sides. For readers new to this field it is important to be led into the issues that give rise to dispute as dispassionately as possible while not ignoring the conflict that exists. This is therefore not a textbook for those wanting to be persuaded of a particular point of view. Rather, it will have succeeded if the author's own values are as opaque at the end as they were at the beginning and if the reader is better informed about the terms of the debate about health policy and in a position to make up his or her mind on the issues.

When it was originally conceived, *Health Policy in Britain* was written to fill a gap between descriptive accounts of the NHS (for example, Levitt, 1979), and analytical studies which focused on a single issue (Allen, 1979), a single decision (Willcocks, 1967), or a single organisation (Eckstein, 1960). As such, it followed the model set by Brown's examination of the management of health and welfare services (Brown, 1975). Since publication of the first edition, other authors have contributed to the study of health policy, most notably Rudolf Klein through his analysis of the politics of the NHS (Klein, 1983, 1989 and 1995) and Charles Webster in both his historical and political writings (Webster, 1988, 1996, 1998). The niche that *Health Policy in Britain* occupies in an increasingly crowded field is its analysis of the dynamics of health policy at different levels and as an introduction for readers seeking a 'guide through the maze', to cite a review of an earlier edition.

The structure of the analysis

The book is organised into nine chapters. Chapter 1 examines the way in which the state has increasingly become involved in providing health services in the United Kingdom. Starting with state involvement in public health in the nineteenth century, the chapter traces the development of health insurance measures in the first part of the twentieth century and the establishment of the NHS in 1948. Particular attention is given to events after 1948, including the reorganisation of the NHS in 1974, and its subsequent restructuring in 1982.

Chapter 2 focuses on the development of health policy in the 1980s and 1990s. The chapter begins by describing the efficiency initiatives taken by the Thatcher government during the 1980s and this is followed by an account of the Ministerial Review of the NHS and the White Paper, *Working for Patients*. The process by which the White Paper was translated into law is reviewed, and the impact of the reforms is assessed.

Chapter 3 examines the policies pursued by the Blair government after the 1997 general election. The chapter begins with a review of the government's inheritance and goes on to outline the proposals in the White Paper, *The New NHS*. The structure of the NHS to emerge from the White Paper is outlined and the key features of the third way in health care reform are described.

Chapter 4 provides an introduction to contemporary issues in health policy. The sources of NHS funding and the uses to which they are put is reviewed and this leads into a summary of policies to improve health, develop health care and strengthen the link between health and social care. The process of priority-setting is then outlined and the balance between central and local responsibility discussed.

Chapter 5 considers the meaning of policy and the nature of the policy process. After identifying the main features of policy the chapter examines the organisation of central government in Britain. The functions and powers of Parliament, the Cabinet, the Prime Minister, ministers, civil servants and outside interests are explored, in order to establish the political context of health policy-making.

Chapter 6 concentrates on the workings of the Department of Health. The way in which the Department is organised is discussed, and this is followed by an examination of the various influences on health policy-making within central government. The role of pressure groups and other interests is considered, and the chapter concludes with a discussion of attempts within the DH to introduce a greater measure of analysis into the policy process.

Chapter 7 looks at the implementation of health policy, and the local influences on policy-making. A key issue here is the relationship between the DH and NHS bodies. Also significant is the position of the medical profession in the structure of management and as major resource controllers at the local level. These issues are analysed, and the extent to which national policies are implemented is discussed. The chapter also considers the ability of NHS bodies to engage in independent policy-making.

Chapter 8 focuses on monitoring and evaluation. The development of interest in this area is described and the current arrangements for monitoring and evaluation are outlined. This is followed by an assessment of the performance of the NHS in relation to health improvement and access to health care. The chapter concludes by considering the NHS in the international context.

Chapter 9 examines the distribution of power in the NHS. Through a discussion of different theories of power, the chapter asks: whose interests are served by health services? The relevance of pluralist, Marxist and structuralist theories is assessed, and issues for further research are identified. The chapter seeks to stand back from the detailed discussion of health policy in earlier chapters in order to explore the variety of over-arching approaches to understanding the development of health services and power relationships in health care.

1

The Development of Health Services and Health Policy

The National Health Service came into existence on 5 July 1948 with the aim of providing a comprehensive range of health services to all in need. One hundred years earlier the first Public Health Act was placed on the statute book, paving the way for improvements in environmental health which were to have a significant effect in reducing deaths from infectious diseases. The name of Aneurin Bevan is usually associated with the founding of the NHS, and that of Edwin Chadwick with the public health movement. However, legislation and policy are not made only or mainly by outstanding individuals. It has been said of Bevan that he was 'less of an innovator than often credited; he was at the end, albeit the important and conclusive end, of a series of earlier plans. He 'created' the National Health Service but his debts to what went before were enormous' (Willcocks, 1967, p. 104). Much the same applies to other health policy decisions. Individuals may have an impact, but under conditions not of their own making. What is more, most decisions in their final form result from bargaining and negotiation among a complex constellation of interests, and most changes do not go through unopposed. These points can be illustrated through the examples already cited.

Take the 1848 Public Health Act, for example. The main aim of the Act was to provide powers to enable the construction of water supply and sewerage systems as a means of controlling some of the conditions in which infectious diseases were able to thrive and spread. On the face of it, this was a laudable aim which might have been expected to win general public support. In fact, the Act was opposed by commercial interests who were able to make money out of insanitary conditions; and by anxious ratepayers, who were afraid of the public expense which would be involved. It was therefore only after a lengthy struggle that the Act was passed.

Again, consider the establishment of the NHS. The shape taken by the NHS was the outcome of discussions and compromise between ministers and civil servants on the one hand, and a range of pressure groups on the other.

These groups included the medical profession, the organisations representing the hospital service, and the insurance committees with their responsibility for general practitioner services. Willcocks has shown how, among these groups, the medical profession was the most successful in achieving its objectives, while the organisations representing the hospital service were the least successful. A considerable part too was played by civil servants and ministers. In turn, all of these interests were influenced by what had gone before. They were not in a position to start with a blank sheet and proceed to design an ideal administrative structure. Thus history, as well as the strength of established interests, may be important in shaping decisions. Let us then consider the historical background to the NHS.

Public health services

The most important area of state involvement in the provision of health services during the nineteenth century, in terms of the impact on people's health, was the enactment of public health legislation. Infectious diseases like cholera and typhoid posed the main threat to health at the time. The precise causes of these diseases remained imperfectly understood for much of the century, and the medical profession was largely powerless to intervene. In any event, the main reason for the decline in infectious diseases was not to be advances in medical science, but developments in the system of public health. It was these developments which provided an effective counterweight to the sorts of urban living conditions created by the industrial revolution and within which infectious diseases could flourish.

As already mentioned, it was the 1848 Public Health Act that provided the basis for the provision of adequate water supplies and sewerage systems. Behind the Act lay several years of struggle by Edwin Chadwick and his supporters. As Secretary to the Poor Law Commission, Chadwick played a major part in preparing the Commission's *Report of an Inquiry into the Sanitary Conditions of the Labouring Population of Great Britain,* published in 1842. The report, and the ever present threat of cholera, created the conditions for the Act, which led to the establishment of the General Board of Health. Subsequent progress was variable, with some local authorities keen to take action, while others held back. In practice, a great deal depended on the attitude of local interests, as the Act was permissive rather than mandatory, and the General Board of Health was only an advisory body.

Chadwick's campaign was taken forward by John Simon, first as Medical Officer to the General Board of Health, and later as Medical Officer to the Medical Department of the Privy Council, which succeeded the Board in 1858. Simon's work and the report of the Royal Sanitary Commission, which sat from 1869 to 1871, eventually bore fruit in the establishment of the Local

Government Board in 1871, and the Public Health Acts of 1872 and 1875. The 1875 Act brought together existing legislation rather than providing new powers, while the 1872 Act created sanitary authorities who were obliged to provide public health services. One of the key provisions of the 1872 Act was that local sanitary authorities should appoint a medical officer of health. These officers – whose origins can be traced back to Liverpool in 1847 – were significant figures, both in the fight against infectious diseases, and in the campaign for better health. It was mainly as a result of their activities at the local level that more concerted action was pursued.

Mothers and young children

From the beginning of the twentieth century, the sphere of concern of medical officers of health extended into the area of personal health services as the result of increasing state concern with the health of mothers and young children. One of the immediate causes was the discovery of the poor standards of health and fitness of army recruits for the Boer War. This led to the establishment by government of an Interdepartmental Committee on Physical Deterioration, whose report, published in 1904, made a series of recommendations aimed at improving child health. Two of the outcomes were the 1906 Education (Provision of Meals) Act, which provided the basis for the school meals service, and the 1907 Education (Administrative Provision) Act, which led to the development of the school medical service. It has been argued that these Acts 'marked the beginning of the construction of the welfare state' (Gilbert, 1966, p. 102). Both pieces of legislation were promoted by the reforming Liberal government elected in 1906, and the government was also active in other areas of social policy reform, including the provision of old age pensions.

At the same time action was taken in relation to the midwifery and health visiting services. The 1902 Midwives Act made it necessary to certify mid-wives as fit to practise, and established a Central Midwives Board to oversee registration. The Act stemmed in part from the belief that one of the explanations for high rates of maternal and infant mortality lay in the lack of skills of women practising as midwives. Local supervision of registration was the responsibility of the medical officer of health, whose office was becoming increasingly powerful. This trend was reinforced by the 1907 Notification of Births Act, one of whose aims was to develop health visiting as a local authority service. The origins of health visiting are usually traced back to Manchester and Salford in the 1860s, when women began visiting mothers to encourage higher standards of child care. The state's interest in providing health visiting as a statutory service mirrored its concern to regulate midwives and provide medical inspection in schools, and the importance of health visiting was emphasised by the Interdepartmental

Committee on Physical Deterioration. The 1907 Act helped the development of health visiting by enabling local authorities to insist on the compulsory notification of births. An Act of 1915 placed a duty on local authorities to ensure compulsory notification.

Arising out of these developments, and spurred on by the 1918 Maternity and Child Welfare Act, local authorities came to provide a further range of child welfare services. This involved not only the employment of health visitors and the registration of midwives, but also the provision of infant welfare centres and, in some areas, maternity homes for mothers who required institutional confinements. However, the Ministry of Health, which had been established in 1919, continued to be concerned at the high rate of maternal deaths, as the publication in 1930 and 1932 of the reports of the Departmental Committee on Maternal Mortality and Morbidity demonstrated. Particular importance was placed on the provision of adequate antenatal care. This led to an expansion of antenatal clinics, and, after the 1936 Midwives Act, to the development of a salaried midwifery service.

Health insurance

The 1911 National Insurance Act was concerned with the provision of general practitioner (GP) services. The Act was an important element in the Liberal government's programme of social policy reform, and it provided for free care from GPs for certain groups of working people earning under £160 per annum. Income during sickness and unemployment was also made available, and the scheme was based on contributions by the worker, the employer and the state.

Like other major pieces of social legislation, the Act was not introduced without a struggle. As Gilbert (1966, p. 290) has noted, 'The story of the growth of national health insurance is to a great extent the story of lobby influence and pressure groups'. Gilbert has shown how Lloyd George pushed through the Act to come into operation in 1913, but only after considerable opposition from the medical profession. The doctors were fearful of state control of their work, and of the possible financial consequences. They were persuaded into the scheme when the government agreed that payment should be based on the number of patients on a doctor's list, the capitation system, rather than on a salary, thereby preserving GPs' independence. Also, it was decided that the scheme should be administered not by local authorities, but by independent insurance committees or 'panels'. The insurance companies and friendly societies who had previously played a major part in providing cover against ill-health were given a central role on the panels. The professional freedom of doctors was further safeguarded by allowing them the choice of whether to join the scheme, and whether to accept patients. Finally, the financial fears of the profession were assuaged by the generous level of payments that were negotiated, and by the exclusion of higher-income groups from the scheme. The exclusion of these groups created a valuable source of extra income for GPs. By the mid-1940s around 21 million people or about half the population of Great Britain were insured under the Act. Also, about two-thirds of GPs were taking part. Nevertheless, the scheme had important limitations: it was only the insured workers who were covered, and not their families; and no hospital care was provided, only the services of GPs. Despite these drawbacks, the Act represented a major step forward in the involvement of the state in the provision of health services.

Hospital services

Public provision of hospitals developed out of the workhouses provided under the Poor Law. In parallel there grew up the voluntary hospital system, based at first on the monasteries and later on charitable contributions by the benevolent rich. Of the two types of institution, it was the voluntary hospitals that provided the higher standards of care. As the nineteenth century progressed, and as medicine developed as a science, the voluntary hospitals became increasingly selective in their choice of patients, paying more and more attention to the needs of the acutely ill to the exclusion of the chronic sick and people with infectious diseases. Consequently, it was left to the workhouses to care for the groups that the voluntary hospitals would not accept, and workhouse conditions were often overcrowded and unhygienic. Some of the vestiges of this dual system of hospital care can still be observed in the NHS today.

It was not perhaps surprising that workhouse standards should be so low, since one of the aims of the Poor Law was to act as a deterrent. The 'less eligibility' principle underpinning the 1834 Poor Law Amendment Act depended on the creation of workhouse conditions so unattractive that they would discourage the working and sick poor from seeking relief. The Act was also intended to limit outdoor relief: that is, relief provided outside the workhouses. In the case of medical care, this was provided by district medical officers under contract to the Boards of Guardians who administered the Poor Law. Vaccination against smallpox was one of the services for which medical officers were responsible, beginning with the introduction of free vaccination for children in 1840.

There was some improvement in Poor Law hospital services in London after the passing of the 1867 Metropolitan Poor Act. The Act provided the stimulus for the development of infirmaries separate from workhouses, and the London example was subsequently followed in the rest of the country through powers granted by the 1868 Poor Law Amendment Act. However, the establishment of separate infirmaries coincided with a further campaign against outdoor relief. This was despite the fact that in some areas public dispensaries, equivalent to rudimentary health centres, were provided for the first time. Nevertheless, the legislation which encouraged the development of Poor Law infirmaries has been described as 'an important step in English social history. It was the first explicit acknowledgement that it was the duty of the state to provide hospitals for the poor. It therefore represented an important step towards the NHS Act which followed some eighty years later' (Abel-Smith, 1964, p. 82). And as Fraser has commented, 'through the medical officers and the workhouse infirmaries the Poor Law had become an embryo state medical authority providing in effect general practitioners and state hospitals for the poor' (Fraser, 1973, p. 87).

The 1929 Local Government Act marked the beginning of the end of the Poor Law, and was a further step on the road to the NHS. The importance of the Act was that it resulted in the transfer of workhouses and infirmaries to local authorities. County councils and county borough councils were required to set up public assistance committees to administer these institutions, and were empowered to appropriate from them accommodation for the care of the sick. The intention was that this accommodation should then be developed into a local authority hospital service. Although uneven progress in this direction was made before the outbreak of the Second World War, the 1929 Act was important in placing the Poor Law infirmaries in the same hands as the other public health services which were under the control of medical officers of health. These services included not only those already mentioned, but also the provision of specialised hospitals – for example, for infectious diseases and tuberculosis – which local authorities had developed rapidly from the last decades of the nineteenth century. In addition, local authorities had a duty to provide hospitals for the mentally ill and handicapped. Local magistrates had been given the power to erect asylums under the 1808 County Asylums Act, but fear of the cost meant that the power was not widely used. The legislation was made mandatory in 1845, leading to a rapid growth in asylums thereafter. By 1930 there were 98 public asylums in England and Wales accommodating about 120 000 patients (Jones, 1972, p. 357).

Accordingly, at the outbreak of the Second World War, local authorities were responsible for a wide range of hospitals. As part of the war effort, public hospitals joined the voluntary hospitals in the Emergency Medical Service (EMS), set up to cope with military and civilian casualties and to provide some coordination of a disparate range of institutions and services. The EMS, with its regional form of organisation, provided a framework for the administration of hospital services after the war. More important, it resulted in senior members of the medical profession seeing at first hand the poor state of local authority hospitals and the smaller voluntary hospitals. At the same time, regional hospital surveys were carried out by the Nuffield Provincial Hospitals Trust, a voluntary body concerned with the quality and organisation of hospital services, and with a particular interest in the regionalisation of hospitals. The surveys were conducted in conjunction with the Ministry of Health, and provided thorough documentation of the widely varying standards which existed (hospitals for the mentally ill and mentally handicapped were not included in the surveys). The summary report of the surveys, published in 1946 as the Domesday Book of the Hospital Services, pointed to considerable inequalities in the distribution of beds and staff between different parts of the country, as well as to the lack of organisation of the service as a whole (Nuffield Provincial Hospitals Trust, 1946). It was in this sense, then, that the experience of war may be said to have created pressure for change, although what form the change should take was very much an issue for debate.

The establishment of the National Health Service

We have seen how, in a variety of ways, responsibility for the provision of health care was increasingly taken over by the state. The key legislative developments were the 1808 County Asylums Act, the 1867 Metropolitan Poor Act and the 1929 Local Government Act, all emphasising the importance of public provision of hospital services; the Public Health Acts and the legislation relating to maternal and child welfare, placing on local authorities a duty to develop environmental and later some personal health services; and the National Insurance Act, recognising the state's responsibility in relation to primary health care.

Given the *ad hoc* manner in which these developments occurred, it was not surprising that there should be calls for the coordination and consolidation of service provision. Thus the report of the Dawson Committee, set up in 1919 after the establishment of the Ministry of Health to make proposals for improving health services, recommended the provision of a comprehensive scheme of hospital and primary health care. Later reports from the Royal Commission on National Health Insurance in 1926, the Sankey Commission on Voluntary Hospitals in 1937, and the British Medical Association (BMA) in 1930 and 1938, all pointed to shortcomings in the existing pattern of services, and made various suggestions for change. These included the need for greater coordination of hospitals, and for the extension of health insurance to other groups in the population. The Royal Commission's report also suggested that health service funding might eventually be derived from general taxation instead of being based on the insurance principle.

This view was not shared by the BMA, which, in an important report from its Medical Planning Commission published in 1942, advocated the extension of state involvement in the provision of health services. The BMA suggested that health insurance should be extended to cover most of the population and that the items covered by insurance should encompass the services of hospital specialists and examinations. The same year as the BMA's report appeared saw publication of an even more influential document, the Beveridge Report on Social Insurance and Allied Services. This made wide-ranging recommendations for the reform and extension of the social security system, together with proposals for a national health service. Coming a year after the government had announced its intention to develop a national *hospital* service at the end of the war, the Beveridge Report added impetus to the movement for change.

The movement gathered momentum in subsequent years, leading to a White Paper containing proposals for a national health service in 1944, the National Health Service Act in 1946, and the establishment of the Service itself in 1948. Prolonged negotiations accompanied the birth of the Service, and these negotiations at times seemed likely to prevent the birth taking place at all (Webster, 1988). Certainly, the medical profession, as in 1911, fought strongly for its own objectives, and was successful in winning many concessions: retention of the independent contractor system for GPs; the option of private practice and access to pay beds in NHS hospitals for hospital consultants; a system of distinction awards for consultants, carrying with it large increases in salary for those receiving awards; a major role in the administration of the Service at all levels; and success in resisting local government control. The concessions made to hospital doctors led Aneurin Bevan to say that he had 'stuffed their mouths with gold' (Abel-Smith, 1964, p. 480). In fact, Bevan cleverly divided the medical profession, winning the support of hospital consultants and specialists with generous financial payments, and thereby isolating and reducing the power of GPs, who were nevertheless successful in achieving many of their aims.

Far less successful were the local authorities, who lost control of their hospitals, despite the advocacy by Herbert Morrison in the Labour Cabinet of the local government point of view. The main reason for this, apart from the opposition of the doctors, was the unsuitability of local government areas for the administration of the hospital service. As a result, Bevan – and this was one of his personal contributions to the organisation of the NHS – decided to appropriate both the local authority hospitals and the voluntary hospitals and place them under a single system of administration. Another major personal contribution made by Bevan was to persuade the medical profession that the Service should cover all of the population and not just 90 per cent as many doctors wished. Furthermore, the Service was to be funded mainly out of general taxation, with insurance contributions making up only a small part of the total finance.

This, then, is a very brief summary of the debate surrounding the establishment of the NHS. One point to note is the relative unimportance of Parliament in the debate. The policy in this case was more strongly influenced by extra-parliamentary forces, in particular by the major pressure groups with an interest in health services. As we shall argue later, these forces can be seen to comprise a health policy community within which many issues

nd agreed, either without or with only token reference to
n this sense, legislation is often little more than a record of
struck in the health policy community. There are exceptions,
ntary influence can be important, but to recognise the impor-
.... or other factors is a useful corrective to conventional textbook views of
British government and politics.

The structure of the National Health Service

The administrative structure of the NHS which came into being in 1948 was
the product of the bargaining and negotiation which had taken place in the
health policy community in the preceding years. It was therefore a representation of what was possible rather than what might have been desirable.
The structure was also shaped by the historical antecedents which have been
discussed, with the result that the Service was organised into three parts.
First, representing the closest link with what had gone before, general
practitioner services, along with the services of dentists, opticians and
pharmacists, were administered by *executive councils,* which took over from
the old insurance committees. Executive councils were appointed partly by
local professionals, partly by local authorities and partly by the Ministry of
Health, and they were funded directly by the Ministry. In no sense were
executive councils management bodies. They simply administered the contracts of family practitioners (the generic term for GPs, dentists, opticians
and pharmacists), maintained lists of local practitioners, and handled
complaints by patients.

Second, and again closely linked with the previous system of administration, responsibility for a range of environmental and personal health services
was vested in *local authorities.* These services included maternity and child
welfare clinics, health visitors, midwives, health education, vaccination and
immunisation, and ambulances. The key local officer continued to be the
medical officer of health, and funding of the services was provided partly by
central government grants and partly by local rates. A number of other
services previously administered by local authorities, most notably, hospitals,
tuberculosis services and cancer schemes, were removed from their control,
representing a substantial reduction in the role of public health departments
(Lewis, 1986).

Third, hospitals were administered by completely new bodies – *Regional
Hospital Boards (RHBs), Hospital Management Committees (HMCs),* and
boards of governors. Special status was given to the teaching hospitals – the
elite members of the old voluntary hospital system – which were organised
under boards of governors in direct contact with the Ministry of Health. This
was one of the concessions Aneurin Bevan made to the medical profession.
The vast majority of hospitals, though, came under the Regional Hospital

Figure 1.1   *The structure of the NHS, 1948–74*

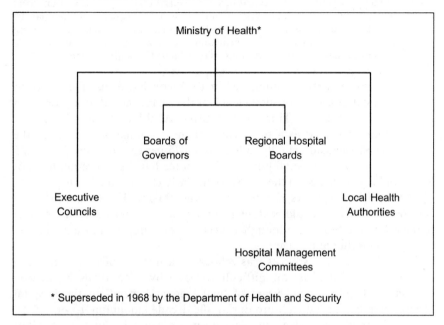

Boards, of which there were 14 in England and Wales at first, and 15 later, and Hospital Management Committees, numbering some 400 in total. RHBs were appointed by the Minister of Health, and they in turn appointed HMCs. Finance for the hospital service was passed down from the Ministry of Health through RHBs and on to HMCs. In the case of teaching hospitals, money was allocated straight from the Ministry to boards of governors. The tripartite structure of the NHS is illustrated in Figure 1.1.

The NHS between 1948 and 1974

One of the assumptions that lay behind the NHS, and which had been made in the Beveridge Report, was that there was a fixed quantity of illness in the community which the introduction of a health service, free at the point of consumption, would gradually reduce. It was therefore expected that expenditure would soon level off and even decline as people became healthier. In fact, the reverse happened. Health service spending in the years immediately after 1948 was much greater than had been allowed for in parliamentary estimates, and supplementary funding was necessary. Concern at the cost of the Service was reflected in the appointment of the Guillebaud Committee of Enquiry in 1953:

to review the present and prospective cost of the National Health Service; to suggest means, whether by modifications in organisation or otherwise, of ensuring the most effective control and efficient use of such Exchequer funds as may be made available; to advise how, in view of the burdens on the Exchequer, a rising charge upon it can be avoided while providing for the maintenance of an adequate Service; and to make recommendations. (Guillebaud Committee, 1956)

The Committee's report, published in 1956, concluded that there was no evidence of extravagance or inefficiency in the NHS. Indeed, using research carried out by Richard Titmuss and Brian Abel-Smith, the Committee showed that, expressed as a proportion of the gross national product, the cost of the Service had actually fallen from 3.75 per cent in 1949–50 to 3.25 per cent in 1953–54. If anything, the Committee felt that more money, not less, should be allocated to the NHS, particularly to make up for the backlog of capital building works needing to be undertaken. The Committee also considered that more could be done to strengthen the links between the three branches of the Service, although it was not prepared to recommend any major organisational change.

The call for extra resources was echoed by a number of individuals and organisations, and it is not difficult to see why. The 1950s have been characterised aptly as the years of 'make do and mend' in the hospital service, with capital expenditure during the decade amounting to only £100 million. Within this budget, no new hospitals could be built, and critics maintained that doctors were having to practise twentieth-century medicine in nineteenth-century buildings. This was the argument of two hospital consultants, Abel and Lewin, who in a study commissioned by the BMA and published in 1959, argued for greatly increased expenditure (Abel and Lewin, 1959). The response came in the form of the 1962 Hospital Plan, providing for an expenditure of £500 million in England and Wales in the ten years up to 1971. The key concept behind the plan was the District General Hospital (DGH), a hospital of between 600 and 800 beds providing specialist facilities for all but the rarest illnesses for a population of 100 000 to 150 000. Several completely new DGHs were to be built during the decade, while many more existing hospitals were to be upgraded to DGH standard. Thus, after a number of years of restraint, the hospital building programme witnessed a significant expansion.

The 1950s were not, however, wasted years in the hospital service. The amalgamation of local authority and voluntary hospitals soon brought results in terms of a better use of resources. The grouping of hospitals on a district basis under the control of a Hospital Management Committee, and the introduction of a system of regional planning, helped to eliminate some of the shortages and overlaps that had existed before 1948. A good example was the rationalisation of infectious diseases hospitals and the release of beds for alternative uses. Also, there was an increase in the number of medical staff employed, and the services of hospital consultants became much more widely available. Before the establishment of the NHS, most consultants worked in urban areas where there were plentiful opportunities for private practice. After 1948, the introduction of a salaried service for hospital doctors with national salary scales and conditions of service, assisted in bringing about a more even distribution of staff. At the same time, the hospital outpatient service was further developed. These were some of the advantages to accrue from a national hospital service (see Ham, 1981).

As far as general practitioners were concerned, it has been argued that 'it was general practice, sustained for 37 years by National Health Insurance and gaining substantial additional support from the new system, which really carried the National Health Service at its inception' (Godber, 1975, p. 5). A cause of concern, though, was the increasing gulf that developed between GPs and their consultant colleagues. Contact was maintained between the two branches of medical practice through a variety of mechanisms, including part-time hospital appointments for some GPs and allowing GPs direct access to hospital diagnostic facilities. But on the whole, the gulf between general practice and specialist practice widened, despite recommendations from bodies like the Guillebaud Committee that bridges should be built between the two branches of the NHS.

The most significant developments in general practice did not occur until almost twenty years after the creation of the NHS. These were the growth of health centres, and the emergence of the primary health care team. Equally important was the distribution of GPs between different parts of the country, which was overseen by the Medical Practices Committee, set up under the 1946 NHS Act. The Committee could not direct doctors to work in particular places, but it could designate areas so that well-provided areas did not improve their position at the expense of less well-provided areas. A study carried out in 1971 concluded that:

> the broad pattern of staffing needs have not changed dramatically over the last twenty to thirty years. Areas which are currently facing the most serious shortages seem to have a fairly long history of manpower difficulties, whilst those which are today relatively well supplied with family doctors have generally had no difficulty in past years in attracting and keeping an adequate number of practitioners. (Butler, Bevan and Taylor, 1973, p. 42)

In 1966 a financial inducement, a designated area allowance, was introduced to try to attract doctors to less well-provided areas, and by the 1980s the average list size of doctors practising in designated areas had steadily fallen and the proportion of the population living in such areas had also fallen significantly (Office of Health Economics, 1989). There were, however, a number of outstanding problems in relation to the quality and coverage of general practitioner services, and these are discussed further in Chapter 4.

The third branch of the Service, that provided by local authorities, developed slowly after 1948, with ambulances comprising the main element of expenditure. Care of mothers and young children, home helps and home nurses were the other major items in the local authority health budget. At the opposite end of the scale came vaccination and immunisation, and, until the second half of the 1960s, health centres, which local authorities were responsible for building. It is relevant to note that under the 1948 National Assistance Act and other legislation, local authorities also provided a range of welfare services, including old people's homes and social workers. The division of responsibility for these services and health services became a matter of increasing concern, particularly as long-term plans for both sets of services were developed in the 1960s.

The significance of the 1962 Hospital Plan has already been mentioned. A year later, the Ministry of Health published a parallel document, *Health and Welfare: The Development of Community Care*, setting out proposals for the development of local authority health and welfare services. This was much less of a national plan than the Hospital Plan. It was essentially the bringing together in one place of the ideas of local authorities for the growth of their health and welfare services. The difference between the two documents was a reflection of the greater measure of autonomy enjoyed by local authorities as compared with Regional Hospital Boards and Hospital Management Committees. Nevertheless, the Health and Welfare Plan was important in displaying publicly the directions in which local authority services were intended to develop. One point to emerge was the considerable variation in the plans of authorities, and it was hoped that comparisons would lead to the revision of plans and greater uniformity between areas. This happened to some extent, but the second revision of the Health and Welfare Plan, published in 1966, illustrated that wide differences still existed.

Both Health and Welfare Plans outlined developments in relation to four main client groups: mothers and young children, the elderly, the physically handicapped, and the mentally ill and handicapped. As far as the mentally ill and handicapped were concerned, a greater onus was placed on local authorities by the 1959 Mental Health Act, which, among other provisions, heralded a shift from hospital care to community care. The intention was that a range of community services should be developed, including homes and hostels, social clubs, sheltered workshops and social work support. The Health and Welfare Plans indicated what authorities were proposing to provide, and demonstrated that the commitment in central government to the community care policy was not always shared at the local level. Indeed, in a policy document published in 1975, the government noted that 'By and large the non-hospital community resources are still minimal . . . The failure . . . to develop anything approaching adequate social services is perhaps the greatest disappointment of the last 15 years' (DHSS, 1975a, p. 14).

A further set of ten-year plans for local authority services was prepared in 1972. In this case, the plans covered the newly established social services departments, which were created in 1971 following the report of the Seebohm

Committee. The main effect of the Seebohm reforms was to divorce those local authority health services deemed to involve mainly medical skills – such as vaccination and immunisation, and health education – from those services deemed to involve mainly social work skills – such as home helps and residential care. The former were retained by the health departments of local authorities under the control of the medical officer of health, while the latter were transferred to the new social services departments under the director of social services. The new departments comprised a range of services previously provided by the local authority welfare and children's departments, as well as some of those previously administered by the health departments. The main aims of the reforms were to integrate services which had been administered separately in the past, and to provide for the development of a comprehensive family service through the new departments.

One of the points to emerge from the Health and Welfare Plans was the commitment of local authorities to the building of health centres. For a variety of reasons, including the shortage of money and hesitancy among the medical profession, health centres did not develop in the 1950s in the way that had been envisaged by the architects of the NHS. However, local interest in health centres revived in the early 1960s, and was matched by central government attaching greater priority to health centre building. The consequence was that whereas in 1965 in England and Wales there were only 28 health centres from which 215 GPs worked, by 1989 there were 1320 in operation, with almost 8000 GPs. As a result, 29 per cent of all GPs worked in health centres, and many more worked in group practices.

Simultaneously, a greater emphasis was placed on the primary health care team, rather than on the GP working in isolation. This development was very much in line with the thinking behind the Gillie Report on *The Field of Work of the Family Doctor,* published in 1963. Although much less ambitious than either the Hospital Plan or the Health and Welfare Plan, the Gillie Report can to some extent be seen as the GPs' counterpart to these documents. The report argued for more ancillary help to be made available to GPs, and for a closer integration between GPs and other health services, particularly hospitals.

The theme of integration was taken up in a number of reports as the problem of securing coordination between the three different parts of the NHS gained increasing importance in the 1960s. The nature of the problem could be seen clearly with elderly people, who might need a short hospital stay followed by a period of convalescence and care in a local authority old people's home, and subsequent assistance at home from the GP, home help and meals-on-wheels service. In a case such as this, there was a need not only to secure close collaboration between the different professional staff involved, but also to ensure the appropriate joint planning of services. The development of long-term plans for the respective services in the early 1960s heightened this, and again pointed to the difficulty of providing a comprehensive and coordinated range of facilities within the existing system of administration, despite exhortations from central government that hospital authorities, local authorities and executive councils should plan and work together.

A second problem which had become apparent by the late 1960s was the poor quality of care provided to certain patient groups. Public attention was drawn to this issue in 1967 with publication of allegations of low standards of service provision and even the ill-treatment of elderly patients at a number of hospitals in different parts of the country (Robb, 1967). This was followed two years later by the report of the official committee which enquired into conditions at Ely Hospital, Cardiff. Ely was a mental handicap hospital, and the committee of enquiry found there had been staff cruelty to patients at the hospital. The committee made a series of recommendations for improving conditions at Ely and for preventing a similar situation arising elsewhere. Subsequently, the Department of Health and Social Security, which had been created in 1968 through the amalgamation of the Ministry of Health and the Ministry of Social Security, set aside special money to be spent on mental handicap hospitals, and this was later extended to hospitals for the mentally ill and the elderly. In addition, the Hospital Advisory Service (HAS) (in 1976 made the Health Advisory Service) was established to visit and report on conditions at these hospitals. A review of policies was also put in hand, leading to the publication of White Papers on services for the mentally handicapped in 1971, and the mentally ill in 1975. Despite these initiatives, the Ely Hospital 'scandal' was followed by further reports on conditions at other long-stay hospitals, including Whittingham, South Ockenden, Farleigh, Napsbury, St Augustine's and Normansfield, demonstrating that the process of change in what came to be known as the 'Cinderella' services was often slow, and that significant improvements were difficult to achieve (Martin, 1984).

A third problem, related to the first two, concerned the system of administrative control in the NHS. The neglect of long-stay services was not new, and had been recognised by successive Ministers of Health from the early 1950s onwards. Equally, the need for authorities to work in collaboration had been endorsed and advocated by the Ministry since the establishment of the NHS. The difficulty was in achieving and implementing these policy intentions at the local level. A variety of means of control were available to the Ministry, including circulars, earmarking funds for particular purposes, and setting up special agencies like the Hospital Advisory Service. At the same time, the bodies that were responsible locally for the administration of health services were not just ciphers through which national policies were implemented. They had their own aims and objectives, and, equally significant, they were responsible for providing services where professional involvement was strong. Doctors constitute the key professional group in the NHS, and within the medical profession some interests are stronger than others. In the hospital service it is the consultants in the acute specialties such as surgery and general medicine who have traditionally been most influential. In contrast, consultant psychiatrists and geriatricians have wielded less influence. This helps to explain why it has been difficult to shift resources in favour of services for groups like the elderly and mentally ill.

The reorganisation of the NHS

These were some of the problems which had emerged in the NHS some 20 years after its establishment. Suggestions on the best way of tackling the problems varied, but increasingly a change in the tripartite structure of the Service came to be seen as a significant part of the solution. This was the view of the Porritt Committee, a high-status body representing the medical profession, which in a report published in 1962 suggested that health services should be unified and placed under the control of area boards. The first statement of government intentions came in 1968, when the Labour government published a Green Paper which echoed the Porritt Committee's suggestion, and asked for comments on the proposal that 40 to 50 area health boards should be responsible for administering the health services in England and Wales.

One possibility was that a reorganised NHS would be administered by local government, which was itself undergoing reform at the same time. However, this was discounted in the second Green Paper, published by the Labour government in 1970. The second Green Paper put forward the idea that there should be around 90 area health authorities as the main units of local administration, together with regional health councils carrying out planning functions, and some 200 district committees as a means of local participation. These proposals were developed further in the following year by the Conservative government in the Consultative Document, which strengthened the role of the regional tier of administration and provided a separate channel for local participation in the form of community health councils. The Consultative Document, and the subsequent White Paper, also emphasised the importance of improving management efficiency in the NHS. These proposals were enshrined in the 1973 National Health Service Act and came into operation on 1 April 1974. The reorganised structure in England is illustrated in Figure 1.2.

Reorganisation had three main aims. First, it was intended to *unify* health services by bringing under one authority all of the services previously administered by Regional Hospital Boards, Hospital Management Committees, boards of governors, executive councils and local health authorities. Unification was not, however, achieved in full because general practitioners remained independent contractors, with the functions of executive councils

Figure 1.2 *The structure of the NHS, 1974–82*

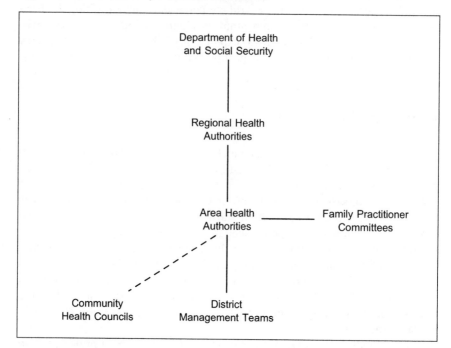

Note: This structure applied only in England. The position in the rest of the United Kingdom is explained in the text.

being taken over by family practitioner committees. Also, a small number of postgraduate teaching hospitals retained separate boards of governors.

Second, reorganisation was intended to lead to better *coordination* between health authorities and related local government services. To achieve this, the boundaries of the new Area Health Authorities were, in most parts of the country, made the same as those of one or more of the local authorities providing personal social services – the county councils in shire areas, the metropolitan district councils and the London boroughs. In addition, the two types of authority were required to set up joint consultative committees (JCCs) to facilitate the collaborative development of services.

A third stated aim of reorganisation was to introduce *better management*. In fact, important changes in the management of the hospital service had already taken place as a result of the Salmon Report on the nursing staff structure, the 'cogwheel' reports on the organisation of medical staff (so called because of the design on the cover of the reports), and the Farquharson Lang Report on the administrative practices of hospital authorities. The Conservative government particularly stressed the need to build on these changes, and one of the outcomes was *Management Arrangements for the*

Reorganised NHS, popularly known as the 'Grey Book', which set out in considerable detail the functions of each of the tiers in the new structure, as well as providing job descriptions for health authority officers. Key concepts included multi-disciplinary team working and consensus management, and the medical profession was given an explicit role in the management system. The DHSS also referred to the principle of 'maximum delegation downwards, matched by accountability upwards' to illustrate the spirit behind the new structure. Another significant aspect of the concern to improve management efficiency was the introduction of a national planning system in 1976, two years after the structural reforms (DHSS, 1976c). All of these measures were part of a wider interest within government to borrow ideas from the private sector in the hope of improving performance. It was therefore no coincidence that the new arrangements were devised with the assistance of the management consultants, McKinsey & Co. Ltd. But the changes also reflected the particular concern in the NHS, discussed earlier, to find a more effective means of pursuing national priorities at the local level, and of shifting resources in favour of neglected groups.

The reorganised National Health Service

Thus, after almost 26 years, the NHS underwent a major organisational change. Within the new structure, Regional Health Authorities (RHAs) took over from Regional Hospital Boards, with somewhat wider responsibilities and slightly modified boundaries. The members of RHAs were appointed by the Secretary of State for Social Services, and their main function was the planning of health services. Beneath RHAs there were 90 Area Health Authorities (AHAs) in England, and their members were appointed partly by RHAs, partly by local authorities, and partly by members of the non-medical and nursing staff. The AHA chairman was appointed by the Secretary of State. Some AHAs contained a university medical school and teaching hospital facilities, and were designated as teaching areas. AHAs had planning and management duties, but one of their most important functions was to develop services jointly with their matching local authorities. Both RHAs and AHAs were supported by multi-disciplinary teams of officers, Alongside each AHA was a Family Practitioner Committee (FPC) which administered the contracts of GPs, dentists, pharmacists and opticians. FPC members were appointed by the AHA, local professionals and local authorities. Finance for health authorities and FPCs was provided by the Department of Health and Social Security. Most areas were themselves split into health districts, each of which was administered by a district management team (DMT), which in practice became the lowest tier of the Service. At district level were located Community Health Councils (CHCs), introduced as part of the reorganised structure to represent the views of the public to health authorities. There were around 200 Community Health Councils in England.

It is pertinent to note that somewhat different arrangements were made in Wales, Scotland and Northern Ireland, which until reorganisation had had similar structures to those existing in England. The Welsh reorganisation bore the closest resemblance to that of England, the main exception being the absence of RHAs in Wales, where the Welsh Office combined the functions of a central government department and a regional authority. The differences were rather greater in Scotland, where again there was no regional tier of administration. Instead, the Scottish Office dealt directly with 15 health boards, a majority of which were divided into districts. There was no separate system of administration for family practitioner services, and the Scottish equivalent of CHCs were called Local Health Councils. In Northern Ireland, there were four health and social services boards, in direct contact with the DHSS (Northern Ireland), and each of the boards was split into a number of districts. As their name indicated, these boards were responsible for personal social services as well as health services. What is more, as in Scotland, there was no separate system of administration for family practitioner services. District Committees performed the function of CHCs.

These, then, were the administrative changes brought into being in 1974. However, almost before the new system had had the chance to settle down, the reorganised structure became the subject of attack from a number of quarters (Webster, 1996). Criticism centred on delays in taking decisions, the difficulty of establishing good relationships between administrative tiers, and the widespread feeling that there were too many tiers and too many administrators. In fact, the DHSS acknowledged in evidence to the House of Commons Public Accounts Committee that there had been an increase of 16 400 administrative and clerical staff as a result of reorganisation, although some of these staff had previously worked in local authority health services, while others were recruited to the new Community Health Councils (Public Accounts Committee, 1977, p. xvii).

Research on the operation of the new structure pointed to other problems, including the unexpectedly high cost of reorganisation, both in terms of finance and, more particularly, of the impact on staff morale (Brown, 1979). These issues were the subject of analysis and review by the Royal Commission on the NHS, which was established in 1976 at a time of considerable unrest in the NHS. The unrest stemmed from industrial action by various groups of health service workers, and discontent in the medical profession with the government's policy of phasing out private beds in NHS hospitals. The Commission was asked 'To consider in the interests both of the patients and of those who work in the National Health Service the best use and management of the financial and manpower resources of the National Health Service' (Royal Commission on the NHS, 1979), and it reported in 1979. In its report, the Commission endorsed the view that there was one tier of administration too many, and recommended that there should be only one level of authority beneath the region. A flexible approach to change was advocated, and the Commission pointed out that structural reform was no panacea for all of the administrative problems facing the NHS. Other conclusions in a wide-ranging survey were that Family Practitioner Committees should be abolished, and Community Health Councils should be strengthened.

It fell to the Conservative government which took office in May 1979 to respond to the report. In *Patients First*, a consultative paper published at the end of 1979, the government announced its agreement with the proposal that one tier of administration should be removed, and suggested that District Health Authorities should be established to combine the functions of the existing areas and districts. *Patients First* also stated that Family Practitioner Committees would be retained, and that views would be welcomed on whether Community Health Councils would still be needed when the new District Health Authorities were set up (DHSS, 1979a). The Government's final decisions on the main aspects of reorganisation were published in July 1980 (DHSS, 1980a). In large part, they endorsed the *Patients First* proposals, and in addition announced that Community Health Councils would remain in existence, though their functions would be reviewed.

The result was the creation of 192 District Health Authorities (DHAs) in England. DHAs came into operation on 1 April 1982, and within districts emphasis was placed on the delegation of power to units of management. Detailed management arrangements varied considerably, with some units covering services in districts as a whole, such as psychiatric services, while others were limited to a single large hospital. Health authorities were expected to establish management structures within overall cost limits set by the DHSS, and in 1983 it was estimated that the amount spent on management in the NHS had fallen from 5.12 per cent of the total budget in 1979–80 to 4.44 per cent in 1982–83, representing a saving of £64 million. Apart from the reduction in administration, the main change wrought by the reorganisation was the loss in many parts of the country of the principle of coterminosity between health authorities and local authorities. Equally significant was the announcement in November 1981 that Family Practitioner Committees (FPCs) were to be further separated from the mainstream of NHS administration and given the status of employing authorities in their own right. This change was brought into effect by the Health and Social Security Act 1984 and FPCs achieved their independent status on 1 April 1985. In addition, a number of Special Health Authorities were established. Their main responsibility was to run the postgraduate teaching hospitals in London. The structure of the NHS in England after 1982 is shown in Figure 1.3.

In the rest of the United Kingdom different changes were made, reflecting the different administrative structures existing in Scotland, Wales and

Figure 1.3 *The structure of the NHS, 1982–91*

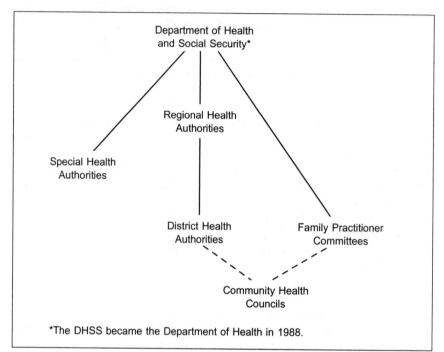

Department of Health
and Social Security*

Regional Health
Authorities

Special Health
Authorities

District Health
Authorities

Family Practitioner
Committees

Community Health
Councils

*The DHSS became the Department of Health in 1988.

Note: The structure applied only in England. The position in the rest of the United Kingdom is explained in the text.

Northern Ireland. In Wales the main change was the abolition of the district level of management, and the establishment in its place of a system of unit management on a similar basis to that developed in England. In Scotland, a varied approach was pursued initially, some health boards deciding to abolish the district tier, others opting to retain it. However, in 1983 the Secretary of State for Scotland announced that all districts would be abolished and that they would be replaced by a system of unit management from 1 April 1984. As in England and Wales, the importance of delegating power to the local level was stressed. The same principle of delegation applied in Northern Ireland, where the basic structure of health and social services boards was retained. Within boards, district teams were superseded by unit management arrangements.

Conclusion

This chapter has provided an overview of the development of state involvement in the provision of health services in the United Kingdom. It has set out the historical context for discussions in the rest of the book on the dynamics of health policy formulation. Already, however, some key questions about health policy have been raised, if not answered, and they can be summarised as follows:

- First, we have noted the importance of focusing on negotiation and bargaining in the policy community in seeking to understand and explain the detailed processes of health policy-making. In particular, our preliminary analysis has highlighted the significance of identifying the key pressure groups and of examining their interaction with policy-makers. This issue is discussed further in Chapter 6.
- Second, we have noted that there may sometimes be a gap between the intentions of policy-makers and what happens in practice. This was considered in relation to the continued neglect of 'Cinderella' services, and the failure to develop adequate community-based services for the mentally ill. These examples draw attention to the importance of policy implementation, which is examined further in Chapter 7.
- A third question concerns the relationship between policy-makers and service providers. A factor of major significance in the NHS is the position occupied by doctors as service providers and their concern to retain control over their own work. We have seen how the medical profession has fought strenuously to keep its independence, most especially in the campaign by GPs to be independent contractors rather than salaried employees. Hospital doctors have been equally concerned to maintain their autonomy even though they are in a salaried service. As the DHSS acknowledged in evidence to the House of Commons Expenditure Committee, 'the existence of clinical freedom undoubtedly reduces the ability of the central authorities to determine objectives and priorities and to control individual facets of expenditure' (Expenditure Committee, 1971). The concept of clinical freedom therefore poses peculiar difficulties for policy-makers seeking to change patterns of resource allocation. It also raises central questions about the power structure in the NHS, questions to which we return in later chapters.
- Related to this, a fourth issue not addressed directly so far but of crucial importance, concerns the relationship between health services and society. In other words, what purposes are served by health services, and what is the significance of the dominant position occupied by the medical profession? These issues are rarely discussed explicitly in books on health services and health policy. Instead, implicit assumptions are often made about the benevolent motives underlying state involvement in the provision of health services. Thus, the NHS is viewed as a great social experiment, and as a concrete expression of the development of more humane attitudes to disadvantaged groups in society. In short, the Service is seen as one of the main planks in the welfare state.

In contrast to the last point above, recent writings from Marxist and political economy perspectives have questioned the benevolence of the NHS, and have pointed to the way in which health services help to reproduce labour power and maintain a healthy workforce. Marxists also emphasise the crucial role played by doctors in individualising problems which may have social causes. According to this line of analysis, health services and their operation cannot be understood in isolation from the class structure of society. These are key issues which are considered in the final chapter of the book.

2

Health Policy under Thatcher and Major

If health policy between 1948 and 1982 was characterised by successive adjustments to the original design of the NHS and a focus on fine tuning its administrative structure, in the following 15 years events took a different turn. The election of the Conservative government under Margaret Thatcher in 1979, coupled with the emergence of major funding pressures, led to the consideration of more radical alternatives. Of particular importance was the introduction of the reforms set out in the White Paper, *Working for Patients*, published in 1989 (Secretary of State for Health and others, 1989a). These reforms in turn followed from the introduction of general management and the implementation of a range of efficiency initiatives. The aim of this chapter is to trace the development of health policy from Thatcher to Major, and in the process to examine the various influences on policy-making and implementation

Increasing NHS efficiency

In reviewing the evolution of health policy in the 1980s and 1990s, it is essential to understand the economic and political context in which the NHS developed. The oil crises of the mid-1970s brought to a halt the rapid expansion of public services and public expenditure that had characterised the postwar era. The Labour government in power at the time was forced to introduce much tighter economic policies bringing it into conflict with its traditional support base in the trade unions and marking the beginning of the end of the corporatist style of politics that had dominated British government in the 1960s and 1970s. These changes were accelerated by the Conservative government elected in 1979 which challenged the prevailing Keynesian orthodoxy and pursued a programme involving the privatisation of state-owned enterprises, reductions in some forms of taxation and controls over public spending. One of the consequences for the NHS was that budgets grew much more slowly than had previously been the case, and attention shifted from the use of increases in resources made available by government to ways of deploying existing budgets more efficiently. As the 1980s wore on, the consensus that had prevailed on health policy broke down and bargaining between government and pressure groups gave way to conflict over plans to introduce market principles into the NHS.

During the first half of the 1980s the main focus of government policy was how to make the NHS more businesslike and efficient. In this respect, health policy illustrated the emergence of what came to be known as the new public management (Hood, 1991) and the priority attached by the Thatcher government to achieving value for money in the use of public resources. The challenge for the government was to find a way of squeezing more services out of existing budgets at a time when NHS expenditure was growing more slowly than in the past (Bloor and Maynard, 1993) and when demands were increasing because of the ageing population, advances in medical technology and rising patient expectations. The quest for efficiency within the NHS was not new but it became a high political priority in this period and dominated policy debates (Klein, 1995).

In the case of the NHS, the Thatcher government did not come to power in 1979 with a comprehensive and coherent programme of reform. Rather, it introduced a series of policies intended to increase efficiency, and the relationship between these policies was not always apparent. Although the effect was to bring to an end the period of incremental adaptation that had been characteristic of the postwar consensus on the NHS, it was difficult to detect at any stage a clear plan guiding the changes that were made. As Webster has commented:

> The Thatcher reforms represented a long-drawn-out sequence of changes, amounting to a process of continuous revolution, in which the end result was not predictable at the beginning, and indeed the whole process of policy-making was akin to a journey through a minefield, advances being made in an erratic manner, as dictated by the exigencies of political opportunism. (Webster, 1998, pp. 143–4)

Nowhere was this better illustrated than in relation to the wide range of efficiency initiatives launched during the 1980s. One such initiative was a requirement that health authorities should generate efficiency savings every year, which was intended to release funds from existing budgets to support new service developments. Efficiency savings were renamed 'cost improvement programmes' in 1984, and by the end of the decade it was estimated that these programmes had achieved annual savings of almost £1 billion in the hospital and community health services in England. Second, a series of Rayner scrutinies were conducted along the lines of those carried out in the civil service by Sir Derek (later Lord) Rayner and his staff. Rayner was brought in from the retail chain Marks and Spencer to advise the government in 1979 and the approach which bears his name was first applied to the

NHS in 1982. The scrutinies were carried out by NHS managers and areas examined included transport services, recruitment advertising and the collection of payments due to health authorities under the provisions of the Road Traffic Act. One of the most controversial studies concerned the use of residential accommodation for NHS staff where it was estimated that up to £750 million could be saved through the sale of property.

Third, performance indicators were developed during 1982 and were first published in the following year. The indicators covered clinical services, finance, manpower and estate management and enabled health authorities to compare their performance with what was being achieved elsewhere. The information used readily available statistics and included variables such as cost per case, length of stay and waiting lists. Ministers emphasised that the indicators were a starting point for a district's assessment of performance and not its conclusion, with health authorities expected to investigate areas in which performance was apparently exceptional and to take remedial action.

Fourth, in 1983 health authorities were asked to test the cost-effectiveness of catering, domestic and laundry services by inviting tenders for the provision of these services from their own staff and from outside contractors. It was estimated that the first round of competitive tendering achieved annual savings of £110 million with most of these savings deriving from contracts won in-house by health authority staff (Social Services Committee, 1990). Some authorities extended competitive tendering to other services such as engineering maintenance and building maintenance.

Fifth, in 1988 the income-generation initiative was launched. This was designed to explore ways in which health authorities could generate additional resources. A total of £10 million was yielded in the first year through schemes such as income from private patients, car parking charges, and the use of hospital premises for retail developments. In addition to these initiatives, a number of other policies were pursued including reductions in manpower, a review of arrangements for audit, and an enquiry into land and property.

Making the NHS businesslike

Of all the policies pursued during this period, the introduction of general management following the Griffiths report of 1983 had the most significance in the longer term. This report was produced by a small team led by Roy Griffiths, deputy chairman and managing director of the Sainsbury's supermarket chain. Griffiths and his team were asked by the Secretary of State for Social Services to give advice on the effective use of manpower and related resources in the NHS. In the event, Griffiths interpreted this briefly broadly, offering in the space of a succinct report a fundamental critique of NHS management and its failure to ensure that resources were used either efficiently or with the needs of patients in mind. Specifically, the report identified the absence of a clearly defined general management function as the main weakness of the NHS, commenting:

> Absence of this general management support means that there is no driving force seeking and accepting direct and personal responsibility for developing management plans, securing their implementation and monitoring actual achievement. It means that the process of devolution of responsibility, including discharging responsibility to the Units, is far too slow. (Griffiths Report, 1983, p. 12)

Accordingly, the report recommended that general managers should be appointed at all levels in the NHS to provide leadership, introduce a continual search for change and cost improvement, motivate staff and develop a more dynamic management approach. At the same time, the report stated that hospital doctors 'must accept the management responsibility which goes with clinical freedom' (p. 18) and participate fully in decisions about priorities. Another key proposal was that the management of the NHS at the centre should be streamlined and strengthened through the establishment of a Health Services Supervisory Board and an NHS Management Board, with the Chairman of the Management Board being drawn from outside the NHS and the civil service. The report did not attempt to offer a comprehensive analysis of management arrangements in the NHS but rather a series of recommendations for immediate action. As the team concluded:

> action is now badly needed and the Health Service can ill afford to indulge in any lengthy self-imposed Hamlet-like soliloquy as a precursor or alternative to the required action. (p. 24)

This advice was heeded by the Secretary of State who, in welcoming the report, announced that he accepted the general thrust of what the team had to say. Subsequently, the Supervisory Board and Management Board were established within the DHSS, and the government asked health authorities to appoint general managers at all levels in the Service. A phased programme of implementation was planned, beginning with the identification of regional general managers followed by general managers at unit and district levels. Table 2.1 shows the background of general managers appointed in the first round and illustrates that the majority at all levels were administrators from within the NHS. The government also endorsed the Griffiths report's view that doctors should be involved in management and that they should be given responsibility for management budgets. To this end a number of demonstration projects were established and in 1986 management budgeting was superseded by the resource management initiative. The change in terminology signalled a shift in emphasis away from the development of a budgeting system in isolation towards an approach in which doctors and

Table 2.1   *Background of general managers, 1986*

	Administrators	Doctors	Nurses	Other NHS	Outside NHS	Total
Regional general managers	9	1	1	1	2	14
District general managers	113	15	5	17	38	188
Unit general managers	322	97	63	16	44	542

Source: Hansard (1986).

nurses took on more responsibility for the management of resources as a whole.

Research evidence indicated that the impact of these changes was mixed. In the DHSS, the Supervisory Board was largely invisible and did not provide the leadership that the Griffiths report had envisaged. The Management Board was more prominent, particularly in leading the implementation of general management and resource management. However, its role initially excluded involvement in the development of policy which continued to be the responsibility of the Department's Policy Group (see Chapter 6). This meant that the Board's influence was limited and its first chairman, Victor Paige, became increasingly frustrated at political interference in his work, resigning from his post in 1986. Griffiths' own assessment was that the changes made at the centre were 'half hearted in their implementation' (Griffiths, 1992, p. 65) and did not succeed in introducing the clarity he and his team had sought.

At a local level, the impact of general management varied with some studies arguing that managers had gained influence in relation to doctors and others maintaining that change had been minimal (Harrison, 1994). In relation to resource management, an evaluation of experience in the demonstration projects indicated that some progress had been made in involving doctors and nurses in management but much remained to be done and the process of change could not be rushed (Packwood, Keen and Buxton, 1991). In reality, the most important effect of the Griffiths report was to lay the foundations for the introduction of the internal market in 1991. This was because the appointment of what became a cadre of chief executives within the NHS helped to clarify management arrangements and created a group of staff who were largely receptive to the policies that were being pursued. Coupled with the greater involvement of clinicians in management that followed from the introduction of resource management, general management enabled the Thatcher government to implement the most radical changes to the NHS since its inception. We now examine the genesis of these changes and their impact in the 1990s

Dealing with the funding crisis

As the 1980s wore on, a widening gap emerged between the money provided by the government for the NHS and the funding needed to meet increasing demands. This is illustrated in Figure 2.1 which compares actual spending, spending adjusted to include cash-releasing cost improvements, and target spending based on the government's own estimate of the resources needed to fund the demands of an ageing population, advances in medical technology, and rising patient expectations. By 1987–88, the cumulative shortfall in the hospital and community health services since 1981–82 amounted to £1.8 billion, even after allowing for the recurrent savings from cost improvement programmes. For 1987–88 alone, expenditure was almost £400 million below its target level (King's Fund Institute, 1988).

The impact of cumulative underfunding became particularly apparent during the course of 1987. In the autumn of that year, many health authorities had to take urgent action to keep expenditure within cash limits. A survey conducted by the National Association of Health Authorities reported that authorities were cancelling non-urgent admissions, closing wards on a temporary basis, and not filling staff vacancies in order to cope with financial pressures (NAHA, 1987). In the face of a developing crisis in the funding of hospital services, the British Medical Association called for additional resources to help meet the funding shortfall. And in an unprecedented move, the presidents of the Royal Colleges of Surgeons, Physicians and Obstetricians and Gynaecologists issued a joint statement claiming that the NHS had almost reached breaking point and that additional and alternative financing had to be provided (Ham, Robinson and Benzeval, 1990).

The government responded in two ways. First, in December 1987, ministers announced that an additional £101 million was to be made available in the UK to help tackle some of the immediate difficulties that had arisen. Second, Prime Minister Thatcher decided to initiate a far-reaching review of the future of the NHS. The decision was revealed in an interview on the BBC TV programme, Panorama, in January 1988 and it was made clear that the results would be published within a year. The Prime Minister established a small committee of senior ministers chaired by herself to undertake the review and the committee was supported by a group of civil servants and political advisers (Timmins, 1995). In a departure from established consultative processes, pressure groups like the BMA were not involved and the analysis of options for change was confined to a small group at the core of government. The leaders of the BMA at the time have subsequently described their exclusion from the policy process (Lee-Potter, 1997).

At the time the Ministerial Review was announced, there was widespread speculation that the government would use the opportunity of a crisis in

Figure 2.1 *Hospital and community health services: trends in spending, targets and shortfalls*

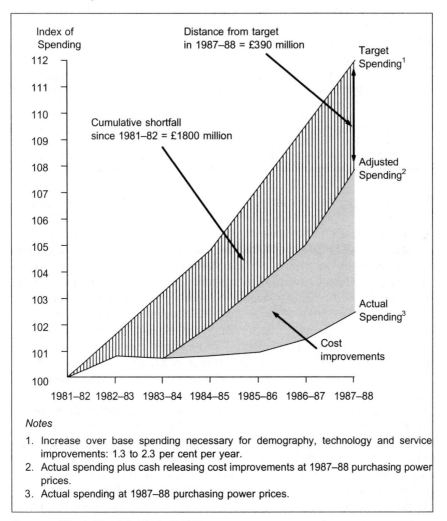

Notes
1. Increase over base spending necessary for demography, technology and service improvements: 1.3 to 2.3 per cent per year.
2. Actual spending plus cash releasing cost improvements at 1987–88 purchasing power prices.
3. Actual spending at 1987–88 purchasing power prices.

Source: King's Fund Institute (1988).

health service financing to examine radical alternatives to the NHS. In fact, a working party had been set up to assess alternative financing methods in the early years of the Thatcher government. The working party was composed of representatives from the DHSS, the Treasury, and the Health Departments of Wales, Scotland and Northern Ireland, together with two specialist advisers with experience of the private health sector. The working party's report was submitted to ministers at the beginning of 1982. Although the report was not published, the Secretary of State, Norman Fowler, announced in July 1982 that the government had no plans to change the system of financing the NHS largely from taxation.

As Fowler notes in his memoirs, the government reached this conclusion because the working party found:

> Every country in Europe was facing an explosion in demand for health care; every country in Europe was spending substantial public resources upon health; and in many ways our centrally run, centrally funded system was the most effective in controlling costs. There was no inherent cost advantage in moving over to an entirely new financing system and it was also clear that whatever system was chosen, taxation would still have to finance a giant share of the service. The unemployed, the poor, the chronically sick and disabled and of course children would need to be covered by public money. (Fowler, 1991, p. 184)

Notwithstanding this conclusion, the Chancellor of the Exchequer called for a review of spending on the welfare state after the re-election of the Thatcher government in 1983. The outcome of the review was a Green Paper on public expenditure and taxation in the 1990s. Coming after the leak of a confidential report from the Central Policy Review Staff, which set out various options for reducing government spending, including a switch to private insurance for health services, the Chancellor's action prompted speculation that alternative methods of financing the NHS might again be under serious consideration. In practice, the Green Paper did not put forward detailed suggestions for particular expenditure programmes, but the government did argue that it was necessary to decide what could be afforded in terms of public expenditure and then set expenditure plans consistent with that decision.

In the absence of any specific proposals to change the basis of health services financing, ministers pursued a policy of achieving greater efficiency in the NHS and encouraging the development of private insurance and private provision alongside the NHS. The result was a considerable expansion in the number of people covered by private health insurance schemes and in the role of private health care providers. By 1989, the number of people in the UK covered by private insurance totalled over 6 million, around 11 per cent of the population. The growth in the number of subscribers was particularly rapid in the period 1979–81 and it began increasing again towards the end of the 1980s. In the main, private insurance includes cover for a limited number of services, in particular non-urgent surgery for conditions such as hernias and varicose veins, and the majority of subscribers are in group schemes, especially those provided by companies as fringe benefits.

Paralleling the expansion of private insurance has been an increase in the number of beds provided in private hospitals. These hospitals are run by non-profit-making organisations such as Nuffield Hospitals, and by for-profit groups. The 1980s witnessed strong growth among the for-profit sector and by 1988 there were around 200 private and voluntary hospitals in England, providing 7 per cent of all acute beds. These hospitals treated approximately 8 per cent of all inpatients and carried out about 17 per cent of all elective surgery (National Audit Office, 1989). As Nicholl and colleagues have shown, the proportion of waiting-list operations done privately increased from one-eighth in 1981 to one-sixth in 1986, with an even higher proportion being performed in London and the South East. In 1986, over one-quarter of hip replacement operations were done privately (Nicholl, Beeby and Williams, 1989).

In tandem with the growth of private acute hospitals there was a rapid expansion in private residential and nursing home provision for elderly people and other vulnerable groups. This expansion was stimulated by a change in the supplementary benefit regulations in 1983 which enabled people being cared for in private and voluntary homes to receive higher levels of financial support from the state. This financial incentive led to a considerable increase in the number of places available in the private sector. As a consequence, public expenditure in this area rose from £10 million in 1979 to £1000 million by the end of the decade. The other area in which private contributions increased was in relation to charges for NHS treatment. In the main, this involved increases in existing charges for prescribed drugs, dental care and opthalmic services. The effect was to raise the share of total NHS income from these sources although their overall contribution remained less than 5 per cent of the total budget.

In making these comments, it is important to recognise the diversity of the private sector and the wide range of services it encompasses. These include not only acute hospitals and nursing homes but also hospices, convalescent homes, screening, complementary or alternative medicine, and non-prescribed drugs (Maxwell, 1987). In some cases, the role of the private sector is marginal, in other cases it is indispensable. What is clear is that in the decade following the report of the Royal Commission on the NHS private health care moved from a relatively insignificant position to become a key component in the overall pattern of health services provision in the UK. In 1989 it was estimated that private and voluntary hospitals and nursing homes supplied 15 per cent of all UK hospital-based treatment and care by value (Laing, 1990).

Working for Patients

It was against the background of a tightly constrained public sector and a growing private sector that the Ministerial Review of the NHS was initiated. Although the Review was conducted in private, a large number of organisations and individuals took the opportunity to publish their own views on the direction the Review should take. Initially, much of the debate centred on alternative methods of financing health services. A variety of proposals were put forward, including suggestions for raising supplementary sources of finance for the NHS, increasing and extending patient charges, encouraging the further growth of private insurance, and switching from taxation to social insurance as the main source of funds for the NHS.

As the Review progressed, it became clear that there was little enthusiasm for a major change in how the NHS was financed. The reasons for this included support for taxation as the principal method of funding and recognition that the alternatives all had drawbacks and might not help in addressing the problems that gave rise to the Review. In other words, the same factors identified by Norman Fowler as precluding a move to private insurance in the early 1980s again served to maintain the status quo. This was confirmed by the Chancellor of the Exchequer at the time of the Review who has recalled in his memoirs:

> we looked . . . at other countries to see what we could learn from them; but it was soon clear that every country we looked at was having problems with its provision of medical care. All of them – France, the United States, Germany – had different systems; but each of them had acute problems which none of them had solved. They were all in at least as much difficulty as we were, and it did not take long to conclude that there was surprisingly little that we could learn from any of the other systems. To try to change from the Health Service to any of the other sorts of systems in use overseas would simply be out of the frying pan into the fire. (Lawson, 1992, p. 616)

As the financing debate took a back seat, greater attention was paid to how resources could be used more efficiently through changes to the delivery of health services. Of particular importance was the proposal that hospitals should compete for resources in an internal market. This proposal had originally been advocated by Alain Enthoven in 1985 (Enthoven, 1985) and it was taken up and developed by right-wing think-tanks such as the Adam Smith Institute and the Centre for Policy Studies. The debate about delivery also included proposals to make doctors more accountable for their performance and to involve doctors more effectively in management. In parallel, suggestions were put forward for strengthening the management of health services by building on the introduction of general management.

During the Review, the Prime Minister decided to split the DHSS into two and to move the Secretary of State, John Moore, to the Department of Social Security. This decision was prompted by the difficulty experienced by Moore in managing one of the biggest government departments, and the need to ensure that health issues received the undivided attention of a senior minister at a time of critical importance for the government. Before his departure, Moore indicated that he intended to pursue a path of evolutionary reform, and this was reinforced by the appointment of Kenneth Clarke as the new Secretary of State for Health. Clarke took up his post in July 1988, and he played a major part in the preparation of the White Paper, *Working for Patients*, which was published in January 1989 (Secretary of State for Health and others, 1989a).

In the White Paper, the government announced that the basic principles on which the NHS was founded would be preserved. Funding would continue to be provided mainly out of taxation and there were no proposals to extend patient charges. Tax relief on private insurance premiums was to be made available to those aged over 60, apparently at the Prime Minister's insistence (Lawson, 1992), but the significance of this was more symbolic than real. For the vast majority of the population, access to health care was to be based on need and not ability to pay. The main changes in the White Paper concerned the delivery of health services. These changes were intended to create the conditions for competition between hospitals and other service providers, through the separation of purchaser and provider responsibilities and the establishment of self-governing NHS trusts and GP fundholders.

As well as these changes, the White Paper aimed to strengthen management arrangements. In the new Department of Health (DH), this was to be achieved by appointing a Policy Board and NHS Management Executive in place of the Supervisory Board and NHS Management Board. At a local level, the composition of health authorities was to be revised along business lines. Managers would sit as members of authorities for the first time and would be joined by a small number of non-executive directors appointed for their personal contribution and not because they were drawn from designated organisations. Similar changes were planned for the family practitioner services, involving the replacement of Family Practitioner Committees by Family Health Services Authorities (FHSAs). The new authorities would appoint general managers, thereby following the example of DHAs and RHAs, and these managers would sit as members of the authorities alongside four members drawn from the health professions, five other non-executives and a chairman. The government proposed that the non-executive members of RHAs, DHAs and FHSAs should be paid in order to attract able people to serve in this capacity.

Another important aim of the White Paper was to make doctors more accountable for their performance. In part, this was to be achieved by general managers playing a bigger part in the management of clinical activity. This included participating in the appointment of consultants, in drawing up job plans for each consultant, and in deciding which consultants should receive distinction awards (increases in salary intended to reward clinical excellence). In addition, new disciplinary procedures would be introduced for hospital doctors to enable disciplinary matters to be dealt with expeditiously. Considerable emphasis was also placed on the involvement of doctors and nurses in management through an extension of the resource management initiative, and on making medical audit a routine part of clinical work in both general practice and hospitals.

The reform of primary care and community care

Although *Working for Patients* included important recommendations affecting primary care, in the main it was concerned with hospital services, particularly acute hospital services. In view of the origins of the Review in a crisis of funding in hospitals, this was hardly surprising. Nevertheless, in parallel with the Review, the government developed equally far reaching proposals for the future of primary care and community care. The primary care changes stemmed from a consultative document issued in 1986 and a White Paper, *Promoting Better Health*, published in 1987 (Secretary of State for Social Services and others, 1987). The stated aims of the changes were to raise standards of health and health care, to place greater emphasis on health promotion and disease prevention, and to offer wider choice and information to patients. A key element in the changes was the introduction of new contracts for GPs and dentists.

The contract for GPs, which was published at the same time as *Working for Patients*, included provision for health checks for new patients, three-yearly checks for patients not otherwise seen by a GP, and annual checks of patients aged 75 or over. In addition, targets were set for vaccination, immunisation and cervical cancer screening, encouragement was given to the development of health promotion clinics and the provision of minor surgery, and GPs were expected to become more closely involved in child health surveillance. Other features of the new GP contract included extra payments for doctors practising in deprived areas, additional money to employ practice staff and improve practice premises, and a request that practices produce an annual report and information leaflets for patients. The procedure through which patients change their doctors was also simplified. Overall, the proportion of a GP's income that derives from capitation payments was increased from 46 per cent to 60 per cent. This was designed to act as an incentive to GPs to provide services demanded by patients. The new contract came into operation in April 1990.

In the case of family dentists, the new contract emphasised the need for dental care to include preventative work as well as restorative treatment. Regular patients would be entitled to more information about their treatment in a treatment plan, emergency cover arrangements, and replacement of certain restorations which failed within a year. As far as children were concerned, dentists were to receive a capitation payment for each child instead of being paid by item of service for treatment given. Part of the cost of these changes was met by introducing a charge for adult dental examinations and by removing most adult eye tests from the NHS. The new contract for dentists came into operation in October 1990.

The government's plans for the future of community care were developed in response to a report prepared by Sir Roy Griffiths in 1988 (Griffiths Report, 1988). The community care White Paper, *Caring for People*, published in 1989, contained the government's proposals (Secretary of State for Health and others, 1989b) which in large part endorsed the recommendations of the Griffiths Report. Local authorities would be given the lead responsibility in the planning of community care and would be required to prepare community care plans in association with NHS authorities and other agencies. It was expected that local authorities would become enablers and purchasers, coordinating the provision of care in different sectors, and providing some services directly themselves.

These changes would go hand in hand with new funding arrangements. Under these arrangements, there would be no incentive to admit people to private and voluntary residential provision with the bill being paid by the Department of Social Security. Instead, the income support available to people in need of assistance from public funds would be the same whether they lived at home or in voluntary or private sector residential care. In this way, it would be possible to target more effectively public support of people in residential care.

Implementing the reforms

The proposals set out in *Working for Patients* aroused strong feelings on all sides. Opposition to the government's proposals was led by the medical profession. The British Medical Association launched a fierce campaign, and this was directed as much against the new contract for GPs as against the programme set out in the White Paper. Organisations representing patients shared many of the concerns of the medical profession as did bodies speaking for other staff groups. There was more support for the reforms from managers and health authorities, although the timetable for implementing some of the changes was widely perceived to be unrealistic. Despite opposition, the government's large majority in Parliament meant that the NHS and Community Care Bill received the Royal Assent in June 1990. The determination of the Secretary of State, Kenneth Clarke, was particularly important in this process.

In comparison with the NHS reforms, the discussion of the changes to community care provoked much less controversy. The Griffiths Report had attracted considerable support at the time of its publication and the fact that the government accepted most of the recommendations of the Report helped to smooth the process of reform. The one major concern about the changes was whether local authorities would be allocated enough money to develop adequate services in the community. This issue was complicated by the reform of local government finance with the community charge or poll tax replacing domestic rates in 1990. Mainly because of this, the government decided to delay implementation of the changes to community care until 1993.

Figure 2.2 *The structure of the NHS in England, 1991–96*

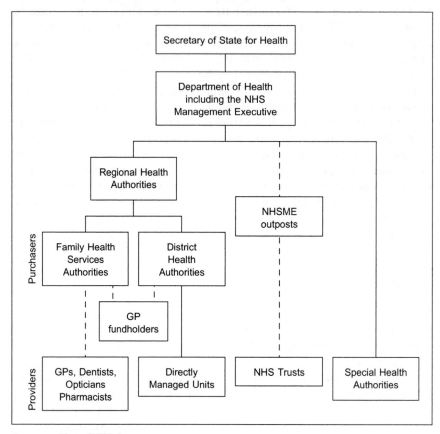

Source: Ham (1997a).

The structure of the NHS in England as it emerged from these changes is illustrated in Figure 2.2. In the rest of the UK similar changes were implemented, although the timetable for reform in both Scotland and Northern Ireland was somewhat slower than in England and Wales. There were also detailed differences in the composition of health authorities in each country.

At the heart of the reforms was a shift from an integrated system in which DHAs both held the budget for health care and managed hospital and community health services, to a contract system in which responsibility for purchasing and provision was separated. This was achieved by the creation of entirely new organisations, self-governing NHS trusts, to manage services thereby enabling DHAs to focus on purchasing health care for the populations they served. Alongside DHAs, GP fundholders purchased a limited range of services for their patients, the budgets they received being deducted from the resources allocated to DHAs. Under these arrangements, DHAs and GP fundholders negotiated contracts with NHS trusts to provide services, and these contracts (or service agreements as they were often known) specified the cost, quantity and quality of care expected by purchasers. One of the purposes of separating responsibility for purchasing and provision was to stimulate competition between providers in what was often referred to as an 'internal market'. Through competiton, the Thatcher government argued that there would be a strong incentive to increase efficiency within the NHS and to enhance responsiveness to patients.

Responsibility for overseeing implementation of the reforms was vested in the NHS Management Executive working on behalf of ministers. The NHS Management Executive continued to be located within the Department of Health but increasingly it took on the role of head office of the NHS and its separation from the rest of the Department was reinforced by its relocation from London to Leeds in 1992. Unlike the NHS Management Board, which had been chaired by a minister after the resignation of Victor Paige (p. 31), the NHS Management Executive was led by a former health service manager, Duncan Nichol, who adopted a style of working in which NHS staff were closely involved in the implementation process. The position of the NHS Management Executive within the Department became stronger over time with ministers relying on its support in ensuring that the reforms to the NHS were implemented smoothly. To assist it in this task, the NHS Management Executive established a number of regional outposts to oversee the performance of NHS trusts.

Implementation of *Working for Patients* differed from previous reorganisations in that the reformed structure was not put in place on a single appointed day. Rather, implementation was phased in in recognition of the complexity of the changes and political anxieties about their feasibility. This was particularly apparent in the case of the two major organisational innovations contained within the reforms, NHS trusts and GP fundholders, whose numbers increased every year between 1991 and 1996 (see Table 2.2).

Table 2.2 *The implementation of GP fundholding and NHS trusts*

	NHS trusts	GP fundholders
1991	57	306
1992	99	288
1993	136	600
1994	140	800
1995	21	560
1996	–	1200

Figures are for number of new entrants each year in England.

At the outset, there was some uncertainty about the degree of interest there would be in NHS trusts and fundholding in view of the strength of opposition to *Working for Patients* on the part of the medical profession. In the event, a combination of commitment by general managers, the leadership provided by the NHS Management Executive, and financial incentives that made it attractive for managers and doctors to put themselves forward meant that support for these innovations was greater than expected.

In the course of implementation, the proposals in *Working for Patients* were progressively modified to enable all NHS providers to seek trust status (not just acute hospitals with over 250 beds as the White Paper had specified) and to encourage smaller as well as bigger general practices into fundholding. These developments were possible because the broad framework set out in the White Paper omitted many of the details of how the internal market would operate in practice, and what details there were changed in the light of debate and experience. Further guidance was given in a series of working papers issued after publication of *Working for Patients*, but to a considerable extent it was left to NHS staff to make the reforms work on the ground. The contrast with the 1974 reorganisation of the NHS which derived from a highly detailed design developed by the DHSS could not have been greater.

This reflected the speed with which *Working for Patients* was produced, the absence of any coherent proposals on the part of those involved in the Ministerial Review, and a concern to avoid more radical alternatives because of the risk of unpopularity . The consequence of these gaps in the government's thinking was that Ministers and civil servants were 'making it up as they went along' (Timmins, 1995, p. 467). This also meant that managers and health service professionals were left to discover the importance of the separation of purchaser and provider roles, NHS trusts, GP fundholding and contracts in the process of implementation. In some respects, therefore, national policy was shaped by the local response as well as vice versa. To be sure, on certain issues the Department of Health did publish prescriptive guidance which appeared at odds with the emphasis on the devolution of responsibility within the internal market, but in many areas policy was made on the hoof as part of an emergent strategy (Ham, 1997a).

An example which illustrates this is the development of GP fundholding. Initially, the rules specified that only practices with 11 000 patients or more would be eligible to apply to become GP fundholders in England. This limit was subsequently reduced to 7000 patients, then to 5000 and eventually to 3000 patients. In the process, various options were offered to GPs ranging from a limited version of the scheme known as community fundholding, through standard fundholding, to total purchasing. The last of these options emerged from four pilot projects initiated within the NHS, and the experience of these projects led the Department of Health to establish 50 total purchasing schemes in England in 1996. In parallel, DHAs developed a number of approaches to GP commissioning including locality groups and commissioning forums. What started as two models of purchasing in this way evolved into a complex mosaic (Smith *et al.*, 1997) as the proposals set out in *Working for Patients* were adapted and amended through a series of iterations between the NHS Management Executive and managers and doctors at a local level.

Alongside the phased approach to change and the emphasis on an emergent strategy, implementation was affected by the changing political context. Even before the reforms were launched in April 1991, Margaret Thatcher had had doubts about whether they would work and she asked a number of businessmen to assess the state of readiness within the NHS (Timmins, 1995). Despite their advice that the reforms were unlikely to succeed, Kenneth Clarke persuaded the Prime Minister to allow him to proceed, although with a general election imminent strenuous efforts were made to ensure that change was introduced in a planned fashion. In the code language favoured by ministers and civil servants, the emphasis was placed on a 'steady state' and a 'smooth take off' for the reforms in order to avoid hospitals running into financial difficulties as a result of the operation of the internal market in the run up to the election. The risks were perceived to be particularly great in London where purchasers had an incentive to move contracts and resources from relatively expensive teaching hospitals in inner London to providers with lower costs. Partly in anticipation of problems arising, in 1991 the government appointed Professor Sir Bernard Tomlinson to lead an inquiry into the future of health services in London and to make recommendations.

The example of London is instructive. It illustrates that the signals thrown up by the market were joined with an independent review in an attempt to secure an orderly process of change. Additional funds were made available to the Thames regions to assist hospitals in financial difficulty, and applications from four hospitals to become NHS trusts were put on hold in 1993 until the outcome of the Tomlinson inquiry and the government's response were known. At the same time, at least one health authority in London was instructed not to move contracts to an alternative provider to avoid introducing further instability into the organisation of services (Ham, 1997a). Outside London these issues were handled less through Tomlinson-style inquiries than by health authorities working with each other and with providers to plan the changes in provision that the market necessitated. Whatever the preferred approach, the outcome was the same: the internal market became a *managed* market in which competition and planning went hand in hand.

By intervening to determine the future of health care in London and other areas, ministers were acknowledging the realities of a health service in which the ultimate responsibility for decisions rested with them. Yet, in so doing, they ran the risk of weakening the competitive incentives designed to drive down costs and raise standards. This applied particularly to NHS trusts

whose freedoms as self-governing organisations were increasingly constrained by central guidance from the Department of Health. As one of
the civil servants most closely involved in this process has observed:

> . . .ministers and the centre are finding it difficult to reconcile devolved
> accountability with the demand for detailed monitoring created by parliamentary
> interest in operational issues. In consequence, the centre is drawn into a whole
> range of issues, from hospital catering standards to the freedom of speech of
> hospital staff that it once expected to leave to the discretion of local management.
> The dilemma is that without substantial operating freedom, Trust management
> cannot be expected to produce a better performance than the old directly managed
> units, but that with such freedom there is bound to be a diversity of behaviours and
> performance. The existence of outliers is then seen – by the press, auditors and
> politicians – as a cause for central regulation. (Smee, 1995, p. 190)

In practice, market management and regulation developed in an *ad hoc*
manner and it was not until the end of 1994 that national guidance was
published (DH, 1994). This guidance drew on experience within the NHS in a
practical example of national policy being shaped by experience of implementation. Issues covered included provider mergers, purchaser mergers,
managing change where providers were in difficulty, and collusion, the
emphasis being placed on using regulation to promote competition wherever
possible. In the event, the guidance had little influence in practice, coming
too late to change ways of working that were already established and to alter
the imperatives facing politicians in circumstances where providers were
threatened with closure or major change of use. This was again exemplified
by the position in London with the government accepting in principle the
recommendations of the Tomlinson report that major service reconfigura-
tions were required but subjecting many of these recommendations to further
detailed scrutiny and in the process moderating the impact of the market.

It was partly for this reason that ministers changed their approach to the
presentation of the changes, describing their policies as a programme of
management reforms and not an internal market. This was associated with an
emphasis on the need for partnership between purchasers and providers and
the use of long-term service agreements in place of annual contracts. The
shortcomings of contracting under the reforms were highlighted in a number
of reports (National Audit Office, 1995) with block contracts predominating
and offering little advantage to providers over the global budgets they
replaced. Under the terms of block contracts patients tended to follow the
money rather than vice versa by being referred to the NHS trusts where
contracts had been placed. This meant that the incentives to improve
performance built into the reforms were weakened. As we discuss below,
the most comprehensive assessment of the impact of the reforms argued that
it was the failure to provide sufficiently strong incentives that accounted for
the limited evidence of change during this period (Le Grand, Mays and

Mulligan, 1998). The other side of the same coin is that political intervention and government directives continued to be more important than competitive markets and financial incentives in shaping the direction of the NHS.

The impact of the reforms

In assessing the impact of the reforms, it is as well to remember the title of the White Paper from which they derive. *Working for Patients* may have been a response to the funding problems facing the NHS at the end of the 1980s, but its declared purpose was to improve services to patients. In this it was following the lead set in the Griffiths report on general management which was critical of the failure of the NHS to develop a customer orientation and which recommended that greater attention should be given to surveying the experience of users and making services more responsive to their needs. The emphasis on patients was maintained after John Major replaced Margaret Thatcher as Prime Minister in 1990 with publication of the *Patient's Charter* which set out a range of rights and standards and provided the basis for the development of performance tables showing how NHS trusts compared in areas such as waiting times and cancelled operations.

In taking stock of progress in implementing the reforms, ministers maintained that increases in the number of patients treated provided a clear indication that patients were benefiting, although independent analysts pointed out that these increases were probably the result of substantial increases in funding for the NHS between 1990 and 1993 rather than due to the reforms *per se*. Ministers also used reductions in the longest waiting times for treatment to argue that the NHS was becoming more responsive. While the evidence on waiting times was stronger than in relation to the number of patients treated, critics contended that patients waiting under a year for their operations were waiting longer to enable the government to deliver its promise in the *Patient's Charter* that no patient should wait longer than two years. Other assessments were equally inconclusive with the British Social Attitudes' survey reporting in 1994 that levels of dissatisfaction with the NHS had fallen at the same time as the Health Services Commissioner or Ombudsman criticised the record of the NHS in responding to patient complaints and argued that the more fragmented structure introduced as a consequence of the reforms had made it more difficult to coordinate the provision of care. Later evidence from the British Social Attitudes Survey confirmed the concerns of the Health Services Commissioner with figures from 1996 indicating the highest ever level of reported dissatisfaction with the NHS (Judge, Mulligan and New, 1997).

Researchers have offered a variety of judgements on the impact of the internal market experiment. The most comprehensive early assessment detected relatively few changes in the first stages of implementation and argued that more time was needed to reach an informed judgement (Robinson and Le Grand, 1994). A more positive assessment was made by the Organisation for Economic Cooperation and Development (1994a) which found much to commend in the changes that had been introduced, highlighting fundholding in particular as an example of success, and pointing to encouraging early results from the performance of NHS trusts. These conclusions were challenged by Bloor and Maynard (1994) who pointed to the inadequacies of the evidence on which they were based. In a separate review, Maynard and Bloor (1996) argued that the success of the reforms had been mixed, a view supported by Klein (1995) in his assessment.

The most thorough analysis of the evidence to date has concluded that overall little change – positive or negative – can be detected (Le Grand, Mays and Mulligan, 1998). This analysis systematically reviewed the findings from a large number of research studies, seeking to assess the impact of the reforms under five broad headings: efficiency, equity, quality, choice and responsiveness and accountability. Like other researchers, these authors emphasised the difficulty of separating the effects of the reforms from other changes in policy occurring at the same time and from increases in NHS funding. Given this caveat, they noted some evidence of improvements in efficiency, indications that equity was affected adversely by the differential access achieved by GP fundholders, no evidence that trust status had an impact on quality, minimal change to choice and responsiveness, and no real difference in accountability arrangements. As we noted earlier, the main explanation of these findings offered by these authors is that the incentives contained within the internal market were too weak. Le Grand and colleagues emphasised that their analysis was concerned primarily with *measurable* change, and they added that there was some evidence of cultural change as a result of the reforms which may not have been adequately captured in the research studies they reviewed.

In relation to cultural change, the findings of Ferlie and colleagues lend support to the argument that *Working for Patients* did have an impact on roles and relationships within the NHS (Ferlie, Ashburner, Fitzgerald and Pettigrew, 1996). Among the changes reported by these researchers was a reorientation of hospital specialists towards GPs and some evidence that the influence of managers and of clinicians in management roles was increasing. Other research pointed in a similar direction with evidence that some GP fundholders had made significant changes in the provision of services to patients, albeit with the important qualification that a majority of GPs holding budgets had not used their powers to alter established arrangements (Audit Commission, 1996). In the case of NHS trusts, peformance was again variable with examples of innovation arising out of the management freedoms available to trusts occurring in parallel with minimal or no change in other contexts.

Figure 2.3 *The structure of the NHS in England, 1996–99*

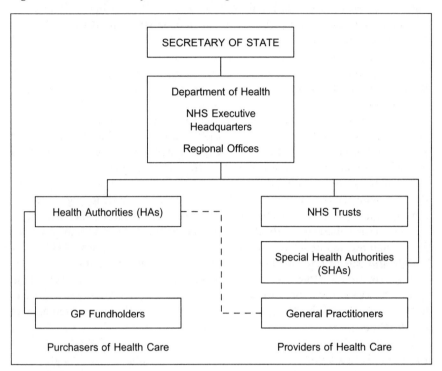

Source: NHSE.

These findings echo the author's own assessment based both on research into the reforms and experience of working with a wide range of NHS bodies throughout this period (Ham, 1997a). What this indicated was that the traditional influence of providers, especially those located in acute hospitals, was challenged by health authorities in their new purchasing role and by GP fundholders. As a consequence, more attention was given to public health issues, a development that was reinforced by the publication of a national health strategy for England (see chapter 4). Primary care also received higher priority as health authorities and fundholders undertook a reassessment of established expenditure patterns. This included GPs offering extra services in their practices and in some cases hospital specialists seeing patients in the community on an outreach basis. The impact on resource allocation may have been at the margins (Klein, Day and Redmayne, 1996) but the change in behaviour and culture was nevertheless tangible. The cause of this was less the operation of the internal market, which as we have seen was tightly constrained, than the reorientation of purchasers to populations and patients. Put another way, the separation of purchaser and provider responsibilities altered the organisational politics of the NHS leading to changes in the balance of power both within the medical profession and between doctors and managers.

Streamlining the structure

As implementation of the reforms progressed, it became apparent that a contract-based system was more expensive to administer than the integrated system it replaced. The scale of increase in management costs was difficult to quantify with precision, although one estimate suggested that the reforms had resulted in an additional expenditure of £1.5 billion on management. Much of this increase derived from the need to employ staff to negotiate and monitor contracts and to supply information to purchasers and providers. Ministers responded by establishing a review of functions and manpower in 1992 which started as an examination of the respective roles of RHAs and NHS Management Executive regional outposts in England, but turned into a comprehensive assessment of management arrangements at all levels. This became necessary because, in the spirit of an emergent strategy, it was clear that the structure of the NHS was no longer in tune with the requirements of the reforms.

The outcome was a decision to merge the functions of RHAs and the regional outposts in eight regional offices of the renamed NHS Executive. In addition, the roles of DHAs and FHSAs were combined in unified health authorities and action was taken to reduce management costs. Taken together, these changes amounted to nothing less than a further reorganisation of the NHS, and the new structure is illustrated in Figure 2.3. Subsequently, an efficiency scrutiny set out a number of ways in which paperwork and regulation could be reduced, including moving towards longer-term contracts or service agreements (NHS Executive, 1996). In making this proposal, the scrutiny was reflecting developments already occurring within the NHS, illustrating once again the extent to which national policy was shaped during the course of implementation.

To return to the starting point of this chapter, the reorganisation of the NHS that took place in 1996 and the organic nature of the reforms lend support to Webster's observation that developments in health policy under Margaret Thatcher and John Major involved a continuous revolution. Yet, unlike Webster, it is not necessary to subscribe to the view that ideological imperatives were the main driving force (1998, pp. 142–8) behind the reforms to explain what happened. As Klein (1995, p. 176) has suggested, there are at many different ways of telling the story of *Working for Patients* and its aftermath, ranging from a response to the changing state of the economy to an exercise in policy learning. All versions of the story put politicians at the heart of the reform of the NHS, but other influences were also at work. What is clear is that the evolution of health policy in the 1980s and 1990s sheds further light on the dynamics of the policy process and in the conclusion we draw out the main lessons.

Conclusion

In this chapter we have seen how changes in the economic context in which the NHS functions and in political debate exerted a significant influence on health policy. The election of a Conservative government under Margaret Thatcher and the adoption by the government of policies to control public expenditure and achieve greater efficiency in public services led to radical reforms to the NHS. The incremental pattern of policy development that dominated the first 30 years of the NHS was replaced by the implementation of changes that were neither the product of political consensus nor the outcome of bargaining between government and pressure groups. This is a reminder of the need to seek explanations of the development of health policy beyond the health sector, a theme we return to in later chapters.

One of the most striking observations on health policy in this period is that a government with a parliamentary majority was able to drive through changes in the face of strong opposition. This testifies to the power of the executive in the British system of government and shows that even unpopular policies can be implemented if the government has the political will to do so. The involvement of Prime Minister Thatcher in the most radical of these policies undoubtedly contributed to this as did her adherence to the school of conviction politics. Yet Margaret Thatcher was not alone in this regard as the determination of Kenneth Clarke to face down the medical profession amply demonstrated. To this extent, health policy during the 1980s and 1990s showed that ministers matter and make a difference.

The corollary is that the power of even the most well-placed pressure groups may not always be sufficient to defeat proposals put forward by ministers. This lesson emerges not just from the failure of the British Medical Association and other groups to stop the government proceeding with the implementation of *Working for Patients*, but also from the inability of doctors to prevent the imposition of a new contract for GPs in 1990. In both instances, ministers overcame resistance to their policies and were not afraid to risk unpopularity in the process. The established rules of conduct in the health policy community were suspended (although not abandoned), and in place of bargaining and negotiation with key groups ministers decided among themselves what they wanted to do and acted accordingly. Notwithstanding this, pressure groups were closely involved in the implementation of policy and on many issues apart from *Working for Patients* and the new contract for GPs they continued to exert influence.

Finally, it is clear that the implementation of policy feeds back into policy-making, making it difficult to draw hard and fast distinctions between these activities. This is particularly evident from experience in the 1990s when doctors and managers in the NHS shaped the implementation of *Working for Patients* and in so doing influenced how national policy itself developed. A number of examples of this have been identified in this chapter, indicating how the broad framework set out in *Working for Patients* was adapted and refined in practice. In this respect, the impact of political ideology was modified by managerial pragmatism and judgement of what was likely to be acceptable to the public and the health professions.

3

New Labour and the NHS

The election of a Labour government under Tony Blair in 1997 brought to an end 18 years of Conservative government under Margaret Thatcher and John Major and appeared to offer the prospect of a return to quieter times for the NHS. In practice, this was not to be as the Blair government developed its own policies for the modernisation of the NHS and in the process published proposals which were just as radical as those contained in *Working for Patients*. These proposals centred on what ministers described as a 'third way' of reform, different from both the internal market of the Thatcher government and the application of centralised planning by previous Labour governments. The aim of this chapter is to analyse this third way and to explore variations in its application to different parts of the United Kingdom at a time when the devolution of power opened up increasing differences of approach between England, Northern Ireland, Scotland and Wales.

The inheritance

The way in which successive Conservative Health Ministers changed the language used to present their reforms by placing less emphasis on competition and more on partnership was noted in the previous chapter. This change was initiated as early as 1991 when the then Secretary of State for Health, William Waldegrave, explained in an interview that the NHS market:

> isn't a market in a real sense . . . it's competition in the sense that there will be comparative information available. It's not a market in that people don't go bust and make profits and all that, but it's using market-like mechanisms to provide better information. (quoted in Smith, 1991, p. 712)

Waldegrave's comments were echoed by his successor Virginia Bottomley in a 1995 speech reviewing the development of the reforms. Like Waldegrave, Bottomley emphasised the importance of competition by comparison and she argued for a:

. . . long-term and strategic view. A great deal can and will be achieved through the purchaser/provider system. As that relationship matures, I want to see greater use of longer-term contracts between health authorities, fundholders and NHS Trusts . . . The new NHS requires a strategic oversight . . . There are many issues . . . where it is important to take a broad view. The implementation of our strategy for developing cancer services is just one example of where we shall achieve a long-term goal by working together within the framework offered by the new NHS. (Bottomley, 1995, p. 7)

Bottomley's replacement, Stephen Dorrell, also played down the role of markets in health care and focused instead on using what he described as the *management reforms* to increase efficiency and raise standards. In his view, there was a need to encourage collaboration between purchasers and providers and long-term relationships, in part because of the policy of reducing management costs. Dorrell's position was expressed most clearly in a White Paper on the NHS published in 1996, restating the government's commitment to the founding principles of the NHS, and outlining a future in which priority would be given not to the development of the market but to information and information technology, professional development and managing for quality (Secretary of State for Health, 1996). Viewed in retrospect, the White Paper was an important stepping stone between the application of market principles in the early 1990s and the explicit rejection of these principles at the end of the decade.

Yet if competition and markets were words that rarely crossed the lips of politicians, experience within the NHS was more variable. The development of partnership-working and long-term contracts evolved in parallel with continuing and in some cases increasingly competitive behaviour on the part of purchasers and providers. This was apparent in the movement of contracts by purchasers between providers, and the efforts of NHS trusts to increase their income by attracting contracts from purchasers in the NHS and the private sector. To this extent, there was a dissonance between the policy message articulated in government, and practice within the NHS. Put another way, with the competitive genie out of the bottle, politicians experienced difficulties in squeezing it back in, at least in those parts of the NHS where there was both scope for competition and an inclination to use the levers that had been introduced to bring about improvements in performance.

With competition out of favour among Ministers, a new policy agenda began to emerge in the latter stages of the Major government. This owed less to a belief in market forces than a desire to use the organisational changes brought about by *Working for Patients* to achieve other objectives. Specifically, the separation of purchaser and provider roles refocused attention on the public health agenda as health authorities developed strategies for meeting the needs of the populations they served in line with the national health strategy published by the government (see Chapter 4). There was also increasing interest in primary care as the shift in the balance of power that resulted from *Working for Patients* turned the spotlight on services in the community and ways in which these services might be strengthened. The other main strand in the new policy agenda was the establishment of a research and development programme for the NHS, including the encouragement given within the programme to evidence-based health care. None of these policies was in place at the time *Working for Patients* was published, but all rose to prominence as a consequence of the reforms.

The emphasis placed on public health, primary care and evidence based health care and the shift away from competition had the effect of narrowing the differences between the Thatcher government and the Labour Party. In reality, the common ground between the Conservatives and Labour became larger as a result of movement on both sides. From a position of outright opposition to the internal market in 1989, the Labour Party came to acknowledge that there had been some benefits from the changes contained within *Working for Patients* while promising to reverse those elements of the changes which it disliked. This was evident in the first restatement of Labour's policy published in 1995, *Renewing the NHS* (Labour Party, 1995), which accepted the value of the separation of purchaser and provider responsibilities, although as a means of ensuring that providers were held to account for their performance rather than a vehicle for promoting competition. *Renewing the NHS* also proposed to abolish GP fundholding because of its expense and inequity and to replace it with a system of GP commissioning. And, consistent with developments already taking place, Labour announced that annual contracts would be replaced by longer-term comprehensive health care agreements.

These proposal were taken a stage further in 1996 in a speech given by Labour's shadow Secretary of State for Health, Chris Smith. The speech outlined eight guiding objectives behind Labour's policy:

1. resources should be allocated equitably so that health care is available on the basis of need;
2. there was a need to improve the quality of care at all levels in the NHS;
3. the cost of administration and management had to be cut to the minimum necessary to meet the NHS's fundamental aims;
4. NHS-funded services should continue to be provided by the NHS;
5. there was a need for a clearer national framework for service priorities;
6. there was value in separating health commissioning from responsibility for delivering health care;
7. it was essential to have a system that gave all GPs and other primary health care professionals a voice in shaping health services; and
8. greater accountability and transparency was needed for the planning and funding decisions made by health authorities, hospitals and GPs.

Particular emphasis was placed on replacing fundholding with local commissioning groups of GPs covering populations of between 50 000 and 150 000 people. These groups would control resources for their patients leaving health authorities free to concentrate on strategic commissioning. Smith claimed that Labour's plans were quite different from the internal market established by the Conservatives and the approach favoured by Labour in the past in that they rejected both 'a top-down system that is run and decided by consultants and executives', and 'a market system based on hundreds of thousands of individual transactions all happening in uncoordinated and frequently contradictory fashion'. Instead the plans represented 'a third and better alternative: a devolved system, where decisions are taken close to the patient, but within a broader strategic structure that promotes equity and efficiency' (Smith, 1996). Notwithstanding the rhetoric and the characteristic desire of politicians to distance themselves from their opponents, Smith's words contained clear echoes of those uttered by Virginia Bottomley in 1995 and illustrated the extent of convergence of thinking on the future of the NHS.

The willingness of the Labour party to accept some of the policies initiated by its political opponents was symptomatic of the changes to Labour's approach that occurred throughout the 1990s. Having lost four general elections in succession, the Labour party undertook a fundamental review of its programme and developed a series of proposals in different areas of public policy designed to make it more attractive to the electorate. These proposals drew on the philosophy of leaders like Tony Blair and were distinctive both in the acceptance that some of the changes made under the Thatcher and Major governments should be supported and in the rejection of policies associated with what became known as old Labour. It is this that helps to explain why the election of the Blair government in 1997 did not entail a return to the *status quo ante*, but rather a further period of reform in which the organisation of the NHS was altered yet again. Put another way, health policy in the late 1990s was shaped by the changing face of British politics with developments in the NHS paralleling changes made in other sectors such as education and social care.

The new NHS

On its arrival in office the Blair government had developed the outlines of its approach to the NHS but this approach was much stronger in relation to the principles that should guide change than the detail of how to convert these principles into practice. It was also the case that the new government was clearer about what it was opposed to – the fragmentation of the NHS market – than what it was for. This reflected frequent changes among Labour Party shadow health ministers and continuing internal debates between the modernisers who were willing to accept some of the changes initiated by the Thatcher government and the traditionalists who were much more sceptical and whose influence was still important. The first six months of the new government were therefore taken up with elaboration of the policy position articulated by the Labour party in opposition, and it was not until December 1997 that the government's proposals were published.

The White Paper setting out these proposals, *The New NHS*, identified six principles behind the government's plans:

- to renew the NHS as a genuinely national service
- to make the delivery of health care against these new national standards a matter of local responsibility
- to get the NHS to work in partnership
- to drive efficiency through a more rigorous approach to performance and by cutting bureaucracy
- to shift the focus onto quality of care so that excellence is guaranteed to all patients
- to rebuild public confidence in the NHS

The White Paper went on to state:

> In paving the way for the new NHS the Government is committed to building on what has worked but discarding what has failed. There will be no return to the old centralised command and control system of the 1970s. . . But nor will there be a continuation of the divisive internal market system of the 1990s. . . Instead there will be a 'third way' of running the NHS – a system based on partnership and driven by performance. (Secretary of State for Health, 1997, p. 10)

This statement and others in the White Paper indicated that the Blair government was at pains to distance itself from both Conservative policies towards the NHS and the approach of previous Labour governments. In this respect, developments in health policy mirrored those across government as a whole, with 'new Labour' seeking to carve out a niche in the marketplace of political ideas that was both distinctive and electorally attractive. The 'third way' was used to describe the position that was adopted and many of the initiatives taken in relation to the NHS found echoes in the reform of other public services like education and social care.

The central and recurrent description of the government's stance *in The New NHS* White Paper was 'new', with the modernisation of the NHS identified as the main objective. Ministers emphasised that they were adopting a pragmatic approach based on the belief that 'what counts is what works' (p. 11). It was for this reason that the White Paper included a commitment to retain what it described as 'the separation between the planning of hospital care and its provision' (p. 12) as well as the decentralisation of responsibility for operational management to NHS trusts and the priority attached to primary care. Indeed, in relation to primary care, the government announced that while fundholding *per se* would be abolished, it wanted to extend the principles of fundholding to all family doctors and community nurses through a system of primary care groups. Equally important, the White Paper included a clear commitment to bring an end to what was left of the market and to promote collaboration and partnership. In this sense it was seeking to 'go with the grain' (p. 11) of developments already underway, for example by moving towards longer-term service agreements and further reducing the paperwork and bureaucracy associated with annual contracting.

The Blair government's approach was eclectic as well as being pragmatic. Whereas the Thatcher government's reforms were based on a single core idea – the use of the market to improve NHS performance – the White Paper included a number of different mechanisms to increase efficiency and to enhance responsiveness (Ham, 1999). For example, there was a return to greater central involvement in the NHS in the aspiration to develop a 'one nation NHS' (p. 55), and to reduce variations in performance through the development of national service frameworks and the creation of agencies like the National Institute for Clinical Excellence. In parallel, the White Paper placed considerable emphasis on the freedom available to GPs and others in the new primary care groups to make decisions on the use of resources at a local level and to bring about improvements in services for patients.

Similarly, ministers pointed out that their plans included a wide range of incentives for NHS staff to increase efficiency and raise standards alongside the use of sanctions to penalise poor performance. The incentives focused on the flexibilities available to primary care groups to move resources around and to redeploy savings; the sanctions on new arrangements for visiting hospitals and other providers through the proposed Commission for Health Improvement, and the threat of intervention by ministers and civil servants in the event of performance failures. The eclectic nature of the government's approach was particularly apparent in the framework for performance management set out in the White Paper which demonstrated that in future performance would be assessed not only in relation to efficiency (the preoccupation of the Thatcher and Major governments), but also to health improvement, fair access, effective delivery, patient experience and health outcome (see Chapter 8).

In putting forward these proposals, ministers explained that they represented a ten-year programme for the modernisation of the NHS. The aim was to encourage 'evolutionary change rather than organisational upheaval' (p. 5) and in the process to address weakness in the system the government had inherited. This entailed shifting the focus to integrated care for patients as a reaction against the fragmentation of the market, and out of a concern to promote continuity of care and collaboration between different agencies and staff. Although not primarily about the funding of the NHS, the White Paper included a commitment to continue paying for health care through taxation and to increase spending on the NHS in real terms every year. In making this commitment, the government emphasised that it expected to see 'major gains in quality and efficiency' (p. 15), including quicker and more convenient access to services through a reduction in waiting lists for treatment and the application of information technology to deliver services in different ways.

The new structure

Figure 3.1 illustrates the structure of the NHS in England as it emerged from the White Paper. As this shows, health authorities were at the heart of the new NHS, the White Paper setting out their functions as:

- assessing the health needs of the local population, drawing on the knowledge of other organisations;
- drawing up a strategy for meeting these needs, in the form of a Health Improvement Programme, developed in partnership with all the local interests and ensuring delivery of the NHS contribution to it;
- deciding on the range and location of health care services for the Health Authority's residents, which should flow from, and be part of, the Health Improvement Programme;
- determining local targets and standards to drive quality and efficiency in the light of national priorities and guidance, and ensuring their delivery;
- supporting the development of primary care groups so that they can rapidly assume their new responsibilities;
- allocating resources to primary care groups; and
- holding primary care groups to account.

In addition, health authorities have continuing responsibilities in relation to public health, including the surveillance, prevention and control of communicable disease.

The White Paper emphasised that health authorities would give strategic leadership at a local level with a particular focus on developing health improvement programmes (HImPs) in conjunction with NHS bodies, local authorities and other partner organisations. HImPs were intended to be local health strategies and a means of translating national targets for the improvement of health and health services into practice. Health authorities were also given a major role in the development and support of primary care groups (PCGs). This included establishing groups and helping them take on more responsibility for commissioning and service provision, thereby freeing up health authorities to concentrate on their strategic functions. PCGs are held

Figure 3.1   *The structure of the new NHS*

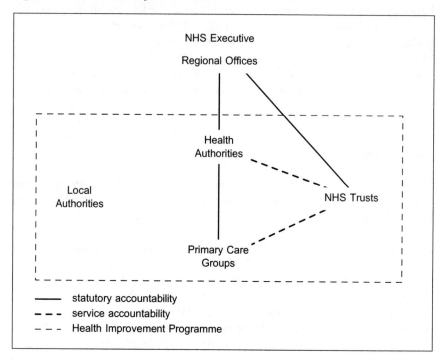

NHS Executive

Regional Offices

Health
Authorities

Local
Authorities

NHS Trusts

Primary Care
Groups

——— statutory accountability
- - - service accountability
– – – Health Improvement Programme

Source: Secretary of State for Health (1997).

to account to health authorities through annual accountability agreements which provide the framework for monitoring and performance review.

The number and configuration of PCGs was determined locally by health authorities in discussion with GPs and others involved in primary care, subject to the approval of regional offices. In the event, 481 groups were set up in England in April 1999 serving populations ranging from 46 000 to 257 000. Each PCG is run by a board comprising four to seven GPs, one or two community or practice nurses, one social services nominee, one lay member, one health authority non-executive, and the group's chief executive. PCG chairs are almost invariably GPs and are supported by a small management team. While membership of PCGs is a requirement for all GPs, there is flexibility over the degree of responsibility they wish to assume. This is illustrated in Figure 3.2 which shows the intended movement of PCGs from advisory bodies at level one to freestanding agencies known as primary care trusts accountable for commissioning care and providing community services for the population at level four. All PCGs were initially established at levels one or two, and expressions of interest were invited from groups wishing to take on further responsibilities from April 2000.

Figure 3.2 *Levels of primary care groups*

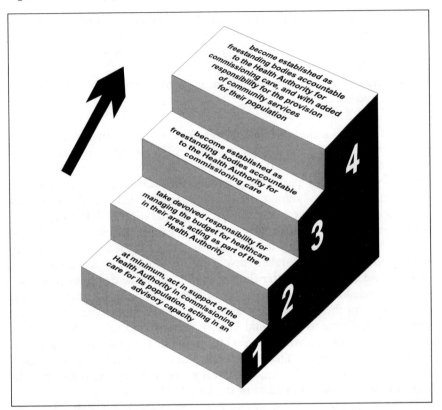

become established as
freestanding bodies accountable
to the Health Authority for
commissioning care, and with added
responsibility for the provision
of community services
for their population

become established as
freestanding bodies accountable
to the Health Authority for
commissioning care

take devolved responsibility for
managing the budget for healthcare
in their area, acting as part of the
Health Authority

at minimum, act in support of the
Health Authority in commissioning
care for its population, acting in an
advisory capacity

Source: Secretary of State for Health (1997).

Guidance issued after publication of the White Paper contained further details on the functions of PCGs, and three core functions were identified:

1. To improve the health of their community by:

   - addressing the health needs of the population;
   - promoting the health of the population; and
   - working with other organisations to deliver effective and appropriate care.

2. Develop primary and community health services through:

   - clinical governance to develop high quality primary and community services;
   - professional development, education and training; and
   - investing in improving primary care services.

3.   The commissioning of secondary care services:

- over time, take on responsibility for commissioning the majority of hospital services;
- develop appropriate mechanisms and structures to commission services; and
- seek long-term investment in care by developing NHS service agreements.

NHS trusts were the other main organisations in the structure that was developed by the Blair government. While many of the responsibilities of trusts continued as before, the government underlined its expectation that trusts would work in partnership with health authorities in the spirit of collaboration that lay behind the changes. To this end, health authorities were expected to involve trusts fully in the preparation of HImPs and they were given reserve powers to ensure that capital investment and new consultant medical staffing decisions of trusts did not cut across the strategy set out in HImPs. In parallel, new statutory duties for partnership and quality were created, the latter finding expression in the emphasis placed on clinical governance. Under these duties, chief executives of trusts are held accountable for the quality of the services they provide, and the White Paper proposed that each trust should establish a sub-committee chaired by a senior clinician to lead work on quality. In parallel with the proposals for a National Institute for Clinical Excellence and a Commission for Health Improvement, the introduction of clinical governance indicated the commitment to put quality at the heart of the new NHS.

It was significant that the structure set out in the White Paper included local authorities alongside NHS bodies. This reflected the concern in the government's plans to break down barriers between agencies and to encourage partnerships not only within the NHS but more widely. The consultative document on public health published early in 1998 underlined this concern with its proposal that HImPs should be the means of translating national health targets into action, and that health action zones should be established in which NHS bodies would come together with local authorities and others to tackle the root causes of ill-health and develop new ways of involving local people (Secretary of State for Health, 1998a). In addition, provision was made for local authority chief executives to participate in meetings of the health authority and subsequent proposals on partnership-working and social services went further to suggest ways in which barriers to joint working might be removed through changes to the statutory framework. The consultative document on public health also announced that the government intended to place a duty on local authorities to promote the economic, social and environmental well-being of their area.

Implementation

Taken together, these proposals amounted to a further period of radical change within the NHS. Although ministers emphasised that the proposals were to be implemented gradually over a ten-year period, the continuous revolution initiated by the Thatcher government was perpetuated under the Blair government which showed no wish to slow the process of change. A further similarity with the reforms that followed from *Working for Patients* was that *The New NHS* set out a broad framework rather than a detailed blueprint. The guidance that was issued after publication of the White Paper filled in many of the gaps but, as with the Thatcher reforms, there was scope for NHS bodies to take the framework developed by the government and adapt it in the process of implementation.

The establishment of primary care groups was the most important innovation made by the government and signalled a clear commitment to maintain the move towards a primary-care-led NHS initiated by the Conservatives. Indeed, by involving all GPs in commissioning and offering the opportunity to primary care groups to take on the management of community health services and to become primary care trusts, the government was taking the Conservatives' reforms a good deal further and was holding out the prospect of an NHS in which doctors and nurses in primary care would exercise increasing influence. The decision to give PCGs control of up to 90 per cent of the budget and to unify different elements in the budget, thereby allowing resources to be transferred between hospitals and the community, was particularly important, creating an incentive for as much work as possible to be done in primary care and to reduce the use of hospital services. In pursuing this approach, the government was seeking, in the words of the White Paper, to 'align clinical and financial responsibility' (p. 9), drawing on the experience of fundholding and extending this to primary care as a whole.

The proposals on public health and health improvement were also significant. Although previous governments had given priority to these issues, the commitment of the Blair government was indicated by the appointment of the first Minister for Public Health and by the focus on the role of health authorities in improving the health of the population and not just developing local health services. The decision to maintain the separation between planning and service provision was motivated by a concern to avoid health authorities being drawn into the management of services, thereby enabling them to concentrate on the public health agenda. Similarly, the proposal to give PCGs responsibility for commissioning most health services for their patients was intended to free up health authorities to assess the health needs of the populations they served and to make a reality of the national health strategy at a local level. In this sense, health authorities were expected to become public health agencies, leading the development of local health strategies and harnessing the contribution of different agencies in so doing. Publication of the Acheson Report on inequalities in health in 1998 underlined the importance of this role by demonstrating the persistence of variations in health on class, gender and ethnic lines. As the report made clear, action to tackle these inequalities hinged on the contribution of not only the NHS but also other public and private agencies whose decisions impacted on health, and health authorities had a pivotal role in coordinating this action (Acheson Report, 1998). This was reinforced by innovations such as health action zones and the priority attached to partnership-working with agencies outside the health sector.

As far as health services were concerned, the attention given to the quality of care in the government's plans emerged as a particularly high priority. Again, improving quality was not a new policy objective, but the combination of strong political commitment and a series of incidents which highlighted failures of performance meant that the momentum behind this objective was of a different order than under other governments. This was illustrated by publication of a document, *A First Class Service*, setting out the government's plans in detail and explaining the link between the various initiatives that had been set in train (Secretary of State for Health, 1998b). Figure 3.3 shows the role of the National Institute for Clinical Excellence and national service frameworks in establishing standards; the place of clinical governance in ensuring the delivery of these standards at a local level; and the contribution of the Commission for Health Improvement and other mechanisms in monitoring delivery. The significance of these initiatives lay in recognition that self-regulation by the health professions was no longer sufficient to ensure consistently high standards, and that new mechanisms were needed to promote quality within the NHS.

One of the themes linking these changes was the concern to reduce variations in performance. The extent of variations in NHS performance was emphasised in *The New NHS* White Paper and was reiterated in relation to health outcomes in the Acheson Report and in relation to quality in *A First Class Service*. The policies of the Blair government were designed to reduce these variations primarily by seeking to change behaviour rather than changing the structure of the NHS. Of course, structural change did occur following publication of the White Paper, but the reforms that followed from *The New NHS* were unlike those that occurred in the 1974 and 1982 reorganisations when introducing a new structure was the central objective of government policy. The Blair government sought to bring about changes in behaviour through a variety of mechanisms, including new forms of regulation, the use of information to compare performance, the application of incentives, and the further development of peer review among health professionals.

Figure 3.3 *A framework for quality*

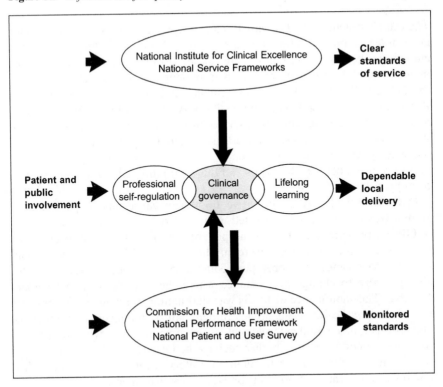

Source: Secretary of State for Health (1998b).

As we noted earlier, it was this eclectic mixture of instruments that made up the 'third way' and that constituted new Labour's alternative to the use of competition to improve performance. In reality, notwithstanding the rhetoric of politicians, the market did not entirely disappear under the government's plans. The residue of competition was most evident in the commitment to collect and publish data on the comparative performance of providers. It was also apparent in the ability of PCGs to move services from one provider to another as a last resort if improvements in performance could not be achieved in other ways. This meant that there was still a degree of 'contest-ability' in the new NHS, a word used by Labour politicians to describe their plans in opposition if not in government. The form that competition took under the Blair government may have been different from that envisaged by the architects of the Thatcher reforms but it was closely related to the position adopted by Conservative Health Ministers in the run up the 1997 general election with the emphasis on competition by comparison and on the need for collaboration alongside the market.

Integrated care

The establishment of PCGs was in many ways the cornerstone of the Blair government's policy. The rationale behind PCGs was that they would empower GPs, community nurses and others to bring about improvements in health and health services for their patients in the process of moving 'beyond fundholding'. By aligning clinical and financial responsibility in PCGs, ministers sought to create an incentive for health professionals and managers to tackle weaknesses in service provision and to overcome some of the obstacles of previous arrangements when budgets were divided into separate compartments. Of particular importance was the opportunity to move resources between hospitals and the community where this was seen to be appropriate.

PCGs also included an incentive to review variations in performance among GPs in that groups operated within a fixed budget and the decisions of GPs on prescribing, referrals and patient treatment had an impact on the PCG as a whole. Ministers were in this way establishing a mechanism intended to promote not only peer comparison and peer review, but also peer pressure to change performance where this was deemed to be unacceptable. The significance of PCGs was that action to reduce variations was to be taken by health professionals rather than by managers or politicians. Only if this failed would external regulation come into play whether through the involvement of existing bodies such as the General Medical Council and the Audit Commission, or through the intervention of newly-established institutions like the Commission for Health Improvement.

The wider significance of PCGs was that they signalled a further move towards a system of clinically managed care in which the staff in day to day contact with patients became the main agents of change. In this respect, there were parallels with the work of health maintenance organisations (HMOs) which have led the development of managed care in the United States. Key features of HMOs include an emphasis on the prevention of illness and the provision of information to patients to encourage self-care; the promotion of quality through the adoption of clinical guidelines and protocols; the use of nurses and other health care professionals in place of doctors where appropriate; and the encouragement given to doctors from different backgrounds to work together in networks as part of multispecialty groups. The opportunity available to PCGs to become primary care trusts (PCTs) held out the prospect of a 'one-stop shop' model of service delivery in which all but the most highly specialised forms of care would be offered by PCTs. Not only this, but also the pilot projects initiated under the 1997 Primary Care Act (see Chapter 4) suggested that GPs in PCTs might choose to be salaried rather than independent contractors, and indeed that nurses might take on some of the functions traditionally performed by doctors.

The establishment of PCGs and PCTs were examples of the Blair government's aim of developing integrated care. By bringing together the services of primary care teams and those of nurses and other staff working in the community services, and by linking the provision of care with a large measure of responsibility for commissioning, these new organisations were an attempt to overcome the fragmentation of previous arrangements. The development of national service frameworks along the lines of the Calman-Hine (1995) proposals for cancer services was motivated by a similar concern. The unanswered question was whether these initiatives would eventually lead to the full range of services coming together in vertically integrated trusts. *The New NHS* White Paper indicated that this was not the government's intention, at least initially, leading to speculation that the alternative would be to promote 'virtual' integration between trusts with continuity of care being assured through the adoption of national service frameworks and explicit care pathways, linked to a set of incentives which encouraged integration, rather than the creation of organisations responsible for managing all services. Government proposals for promoting partnerships suggested that the involvement of social care in these arrangements would assist the drive towards integration.

To make these points is to underline not only the radicalism of the plans set out in *The New NHS*, but also the time needed to make them work in practice. This was reinforced by experience with some of the forerunners of PCGs in the form of the total purchasing projects initiated under the Conservatives and the GP commissioning pilots set up by Labour on coming into office. Evidence from evaluations into total purchasing and GP commissioning indicated the difficulty of achieving effective involvement by all GPs, the demands placed on lead GPs and the importance of providing management support in enabling improvements in services to be achieved (Mays, Goodwin, Killoran and Malbon, 1998; Regen, Smith and Shapiro, 1999). Indeed, at a time when the support of GPs for the government's proposals was variable, there were doubts about the willingness of the most important participants in PCGs to play a full part in the new arrangements.

Despite reassurances from ministers, continuing concerns existed among GPs that they were being asked to take responsibility for unpopular rationing decisions and that resources for the development of primary care would be diverted into secondary care. GPs were also concerned that they would not have sufficient influence in PCGs under the proposals set out in the White Paper. Following negotiations between the government and the BMA, ministers made a number of concessions to GPs about their plans for PCGs, demonstrating that the influence of pressure groups was still important even in the aftermath of the Thatcher and Major governments. In this respect, the established rules of conduct in the health policy community illustrated their resilience, indicating in the process that politicians may have regained influence in the development of policy but they remained dependent on the support of key groups to make policy work in practice

The comprehensive spending review

The New NHS White Paper was published at the mid-point of the comprehensive spending review (CSR) initiated by the Blair government on coming into office. The purpose of the review was to take stock of public expenditure as a whole and the balance between spending programmes in the light of the government's election commitments. Although the government allocated extra resources to the NHS during the course of the review, it was not until its completion in July 1998 that the implications for the NHS were made public.

The significance of the CSR was threefold. First, it resulted in education and health receiving significant increases in expenditure at a time when lower priority was attached to other spending programmes. Second, the CSR was based on plans for three years rather than the usual period of one year. And third, the additional resources allocated by the government were intended to produce specified improvements in performance. The watchwords of the White Paper which announced the results of the CSR were 'money for modernisation' and 'investment for reform' in recognition that ministers expected public services to become more efficient, equitable and responsive as a result of the commitment made by the government (Chancellor of the Exchequer, 1998).

To ensure that this happened, departments were required to negotiate public service agreements with the Treasury setting out performance targets for different services. In the case of the NHS, the CSR led to a planned increase in expenditure of £21 billion between 1999 and 2002. This amounted to an annual increase of 4.7 per cent in real terms. The targets to be achieved with this money included the reduction of waiting lists by 100 000 to fulfil the promise made by the Prime Minister before the election. The public service agreement subsequently negotiated with the Treasury set out a range of other targets. These included objectives relating to the national health strategy, the policy of improving quality and access, and the emphasis on primary care. Consistent with the CSR and the priority attached by the Blair government to partnership working, a number of targets included a commitment to collaboration between the NHS and other agencies.

The increases in expenditure that resulted from the CSR appeared to relieve some of the pressure within the NHS and to provide a response to analysts who pointed to increasing evidence of rationing of services to argue that the commitment to a universal and comprehensive NHS was no longer sustainable. Yet on closer inspection, the priority attached to the NHS was not as impressive as first appeared, in part because the increase of £21 billion was calculated by adding together the extra spending planned over three years, and in part because pay awards made to NHS staff in 1999 eroded the value of the real-terms increase assumed in the CSR White Paper. The claim of both Conservative and Labour governments in their respective 1996 and

1997 White Papers on the future of the NHS that rationing was unnecessary and that there was no reason to believe that the NHS could not cope with the demands of demography, technology and rising expectations appeared increasingly untenable. This was underlined by the difficulty experienced by the Blair government in achieving its target of reducing waiting lists, dealing with the pressures of emergency hospital admissions during the winter months, and finding the resources to pay for new drugs and medical technologies.

The last of these points was illustrated by the debate over the use of Viagra, a drug for the treatment of male impotence which became available in 1998. Because of concerns about the cost of Viagra and the impact on other NHS priorities, the government announced that it would not be used immediately within the NHS and it sought expert advice on how it should be rationed. Subsequently, the Secretary of State for Health issued guidelines proposing that Viagra should be prescribed within the NHS only in specified circumstances. This provoked a highly critical reaction from the medical profession and resulted in debate in the media about priorities within the NHS. At a time when it was known that other drugs were about to became available with consequences that were likely to be similar, arguments about rationing received renewed attention. These arguments were reinforced by legal judgements that the NHS was liable to pay for the costs of continuing care for patients who were previously thought to fall within the remit of local authority social services departments and increasing gaps in the availability of dental care within the NHS. These are issues we discuss further in the following chapter.

Northern Ireland, Scotland and Wales

Health policy and the organisation of the NHS in Northern Ireland, Scotland and Wales have always differed from England in some respects, and the election of the Blair government took this a stage further. In particular, the establishment of a Scottish parliament and a Welsh assembly with powers over services like the NHS hold out the prospect of increasing divergence of approaches in the constituent parts of the United Kingdom. This was evident even before the creation of these new legislative bodies with the publication of White Papers in Scotland and Wales setting out proposals for change which departed in important ways from the structure planned for the NHS in England.

In the case of Scotland, the White Paper, *Designed to Care*, proposed the establishment of primary care trusts bringing together all services other than acute care. Within primary care trusts, local health care cooperatives of GPs would have the option of taking some responsibility for budgets as would GPs choosing not to join a cooperative. Figure 3.4 illustrates the structure of

Figure 3.4 *The structure of the NHS in Scotland*

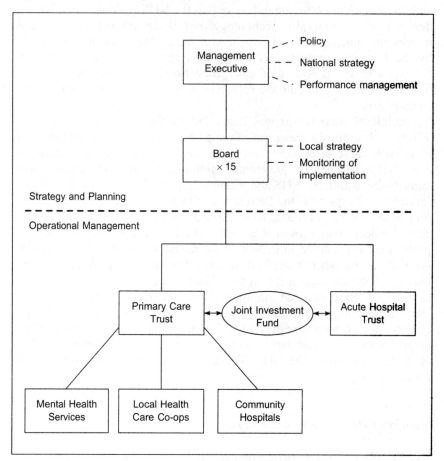

Source: Secretary of State for Scotland (1997).

the NHS in Scotland following these changes, indicating a distinction between the strategic and planning roles of Health Boards and the operational management responsibility of trusts. As in England, an important objective in Scotland is the development of integrated care, and joint investment funds are intended to facilitate integration between primary care trusts and acute trusts.

The White Paper for Wales, *NHS Wales: Putting Patients First*, differed from the English White Paper in proposing the establishment of local health groups instead of primary care groups. These were set up on a coterminous basis with local authorities and as subcommittees of health authorities.

Initially, the White Paper indicated that local health groups would be advisory bodies but would take on greater responsibility for commissioning services over time. Unlike in Scotland and England, there were no plans to move quickly to primary care trusts, although the White Paper noted that this might happen in the longer term. The configuration of NHS trusts in Wales was reviewed in parallel with debate on the White Paper and as a result the number of trusts was reduced significantly. Similar changes took place in Scotland as part of the move towards acute trusts and primary care trusts.

The position in Northern Ireland was reviewed in the consultation document *Fit for the Future*, whose proposals reflected the unique features of Northern Ireland, in particular the integration of health and social care, and the uncertainty surrounding the future of political arrangements in the province in the context of the plans to set up an assembly. Two options were outlined in the consultation document, the first following the approach set out in England and centring on the establishment of primary care groups, the second entailing the creation of local care agencies which would comprise primary care partnerships to commission care and trusts to manage services. Under both options, it was proposed that the structure of health and social services should be streamlined to reduce the number of organisations involved and to simplify the management of services. A paper published in 1999 set out the results of consultation on *Fit for the Future* and proposed that 5 health and social care partnerships should take over the functions of both the health and social services boards and fundholders, and that the number of trusts should be halved.

The devolution of power to Scotland and Wales and plans to change the system of government in Northern Ireland raised the issue of regional devolution in England and its potential impact on the NHS (Hazell and Jervis, 1998). This arose most immediately in the case of London with plans for an elected mayor having implications for the NHS even though health services did not formally come within the province of local government in London. Elsewhere, the establishment of regional development agencies raised questions about the relationship between the NHS and other parts of government, not least in view of the concern to achieve closer integration between different public services. Although the establishment of elected regional assemblies was not on the agenda of the Blair government during its first term, the prospect that this might happen opened up a debate that was resolved at the time of the creation of the NHS when the views of Aneurin Bevan that the NHS should be established as a national service under separate administrative agencies carried the day against Herbert Morrison's argument that local government control was the preferred option (see Chapter 1). At the time, Bevan acknowledged that putting the NHS under elected authorities was an option for the future and the constitutional radicalism of the Blair government appeared to make this a real possibility.

Conclusion

In this chapter we have described the policies of the Blair government towards the NHS. In the process we have noted the strong element of continuity between the latter stages of the Conservative government and the approach pursued by the new Labour government. There were of course differences between politicians but these were much less significant than might have been expected in view of the debate that took place on *Working for Patients* a decade earlier. Continuity was born out of convergence which resulted from movement on both sides. The third way pursued by the Blair government incorporated important elements of the reforms initiated by the Thatcher and Major government and was facilitated by the retreat on the part of Conservative politicians from the pro-market policies of the early 1990s. It also illustrated the extent of the change that had occurred within the Labour Party itself involving the development of policies to modernise public services as a whole and not just the NHS.

To this extent, the evolution of health policy in the 1990s indicates the influence of learning in the policy process. On the one hand, Conservative ministers adjusted course in the light of experience and feedback on what was working and what was not working in the implementation of *Working for Patients*. On the other hand, Labour politicians were willing to take a pragmatic approach, emphasising that 'what counts is what works' and avoiding the temptation to engage in knee-jerk opposition to policies initiated by their opponents. The scope for learning extended to the implementation of *The New NHS* which like *Working for Patients* provided a broad framework only and offered the opportunity for policy to be shaped and remade as it was carried into action.

To make this point is to underline the argument of Heclo (1974) and others that policy-making is both an arena in which there is bargaining between different interests and a focus for puzzling about ways of tackling social problems. The balance between bargaining and puzzling varies between issues and over time, and in the case of health policy in Britain the political struggles of the late 1980s and early 1990s gave way to a greater degree of analysis and reflection as the decade wore on. To be sure, there remained disagreements between the government and pressure groups about the detail of policy and to some degree the direction of change, but after the sound and fury that greeted *Working for Patients* these disagreements were relatively unimportant. Having emphasised the politics of policy-making in the previous chapter, the emphasis on learning in this chapter draws attention to another important aspect of the policy process.

While the changes to the organisation of the NHS initiated by the Blair government were being implemented, the debate about NHS funding and rationing simmered in the background and occasionally flared up into open disputes, as in the debate about Viagra. This debate was not new but it assumed particular intensity in this period as the ability of the NHS to continue providing universal and comprehensive services came under scrutiny. To understand the context of this debate we now go on to review long-term trends in the funding of the NHS and the way in which rationing occurs.

4

Contemporary Issues in Health Policy

The aim of this chapter is to describe the development of health policy and to summarise key issues in the funding and provision of health care. The chapter begins with an analysis of trends in NHS expenditure and an assessment of the sources of funding and its distribution. This leads into a discussion of current policy issues in relation to public health, health care and social care. The chapter concludes with a review of priority-setting or rationing.

The growth of NHS expenditure

One of the assumptions made in the Beveridge Report was that expenditure on health services would decline once the backlog of ill-health which was thought to exist in the community had been eradicated by the introduction of a health service free at the point of use. This assumption turned out to be false, and far from declining expenditure increased steadily in the years after the establishment of the NHS. As Table 4.1 shows, whereas in its first full year of operation the Service cost £437 million to run, by 1996 expenditure in the United Kingdom had risen to an estimated £42 billion. Over the same period the real cost of the NHS increased fivefold, and the NHS share of total public expenditure rose from 11.8 per cent in 1950 to an estimated 14.5 per cent in 1996.

These increases were necessary to enable the NHS to meet the demands created by changes in demography, technology and society. Analysts of health services pointed out that there was not a fixed quantity of disease, as the idea of a backlog of ill-health implied, but rather there was potentially infinite demand (Thwaites, 1987). This was because of the greater use of services by elderly people and their increasing numbers in the population; the opportunities for diagnosis and treatment opened up by developments in medical technology; and the emergence of a new generation of service users

Table 4.1 *NHS expenditure UK, 1949–96*

Calendar year	Total (£m)	Total NHS cost at 1949 prices (£m)
1949	437	437
1954	564	453
1959	826	547
1964	1 190	687
1969	1 791	870
1974	3 944	1 153
1979	9 046	1 275
1984	16 553	1 502
1989	25 491	1 772
1994	40 195	2 207
1996	42 155	2 220

Source: OHE (1997)

with higher expectations of the standard of care to be provided. Although the importance of these factors varied from year to year and were difficult to quantify, taken together they added to the pressures confronting the NHS and helped fuel the increase in expenditure over time. Another way of expressing this increase is shown in Figure 4.1 which illustrates the share of the gross domestic product consumed by the NHS rising from 3.5 per cent in 1949 to nearly 6 per cent in 1996.

The size of the NHS budget is shaped by the state of the economy and government decisions on the priority to be attached to different spending programmes. High rates of growth in the 1960s and early 1970s gave way to lower increases in the late 1970s and 1980s. This change was stimulated by escalating oil prices which fuelled inflation and caused successive governments to take action to control public expenditure. One of the mechanisms used was cash limits which capped expenditure on most areas of NHS spending and imposed a strict financial discipline on those responsible for running services. The election of the Thatcher government in 1979 meant that spending continued to be tightly controlled as monetarist policies began to bite. The government gave priority to achieving economic prosperity through privatisation and competition, and social policy expenditure was subjected to close scrutiny. A strong emphasis was placed on using expenditure on public services like the NHS more efficiently, and we noted in Chapter 2 the wide range of efficiency initiatives launched during this period. The purse strings were subsequently loosened as more money was allocated to the NHS between 1990 and 1993 to ease the introduction of the proposals set out in *Working for Patients*. Growth rates were then much lower until the election of the Blair government in 1997 and the comprehensive spending

Figure 4.1   *Cost of NHS as percentage of GDP*

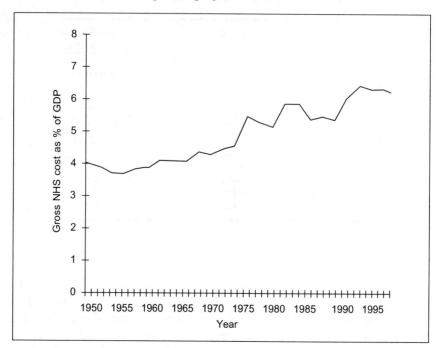

Source: OHE (1997).

review initiated by the government which from 1999 resulted in a return to the higher increases experienced in the early 1990s (see Chapter 3).

Alongside public expenditure on health care, private spending accounts for around 15 per cent of total health care expenditure. Private expenditure is made up of the charges paid by patients for NHS prescriptions, dental care and ophthalmic services, as well as spending on services that are provided privately. The latter may be paid for out of pocket or under the terms of private medical insurance. Over 6 million people or around 11 per cent of the population are covered by private medical insurance in the United Kingdom. The number of people with insurance has increased steadily throughout the lifetime of the NHS and expansion was particularly rapid in the early 1980s. The majority of subscribers are in group schemes, especially those offered by companies as fringe benefits, and the main services provided are outpatient appointments with specialists and quicker access to non-urgent surgery than is available within the NHS.

International comparisons show that expenditure on health care in the United Kingdom as a proportion of gross domestic product is lower than in many other developed countries. This is illustrated in Figure 4.2. Analysis of variations in health service expenditure between countries indicates that levels of spending are closely related to levels of national income and that the

Figure 4.2 *International comparison of expenditure on health care, 1996*

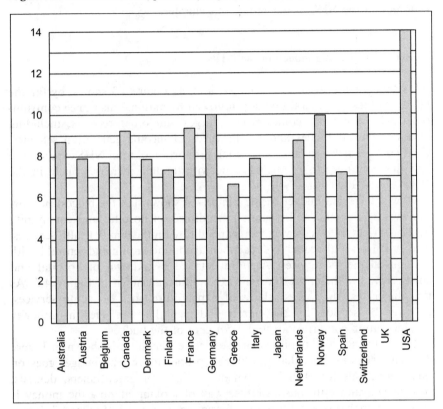

Source: OECD (1998).

United Kingdom spends more or less what would be expected given the pattern of economic development in the postwar period. The main difference between the United Kingdom and other countries is in the composition of health service spending, with private expenditure making up a smaller proportion of the total in the United Kingdom than the average for OECD countries. This has led some commentators to argue that the funding pressures under which the NHS operates should be addressed by encouraging private expenditure to increase to the levels found elsewhere.

Whatever the merits of these arguments, it is clear that the NHS is an effective mechanism for controlling expenditure on health care. The corollary is that this may create problems, as when a series of years of expenditure constraint require staff in the NHS to cut back or delay the provision of services in order to balance their budgets. This is precisely what happened in 1987, and the funding crisis in that year forced the Thatcher government to set up its review of the NHS. These funding pressures reappeared in the mid-1990s and were accompanied by debates about the rationing of health services and the denial of treatment to patients. We consider the challenge of rationing in the NHS at the end of this chapter.

Raising and spending money in the NHS

NHS funds come from three sources, and, as Figure 4.3 shows, by far the largest of these is general taxation followed by national insurance contributions. The remainder comes from charges and other receipts, including income from land sales and the proceeds of income generation schemes. Charges have always comprised a small proportion of total NHS expenditure and this continues to be the case, notwithstanding increases made in the 1980s and 1990s.

How is the NHS budget spent? Figure 4.4 shows that the biggest proportion went on capital and current expenditure on hospital and community health services followed by current expenditure on the family health services. The remainder is allocated to departmental administration and central health and miscellaneous services. A more detailed breakdown of hospital and community health services current expenditure is shown in Figure 4.5. As this illustrates, the largest share of expenditure goes on acute services, followed by services for the elderly and mental health. Health authority administration comprises around 4 per cent of the budget.

The distribution of family health services expenditure is shown in Figure 4.6. This demonstrates that the biggest proportion of the budget goes on pharmaceuticals followed by payments to general practitioners, dentists, pharmacists and opticians. Another way of looking at how the money is spent is to analyse expenditure by different age groups. As Figure 4.7 shows, expenditure is particularly high at the time of birth and among older people. The rising trend of expenditure with age explains why the ageing population adds to the demands facing the NHS.

Staff salaries and wages are the largest single item of expenditure in the NHS as a whole, comprising around two-thirds of the total. Table 4.2 provides a breakdown of directly employed staff in different groups, and as the table shows, nurses and midwives comprise almost half of all staff. As well as these directly employed staff, 27 000 general practitioners, 16 000 dentists, 10 000 retail pharmacists and 6000 opticians work as independent contractors.

While almost all of the NHS budget is allocated according to a weighted capitation formula, some resources are set aside for specific purposes. Earmarking funds in this way has been used by the Blair government to ensure that priority is given to particular services and needs. The NHS modernisation fund established by the government includes money to cut waiting lists, improve primary care, develop drug advisory services, support health action zones, and invest in information technology initiatives.

Figure 4.3 *Sources of NHS finance, 1997–98*

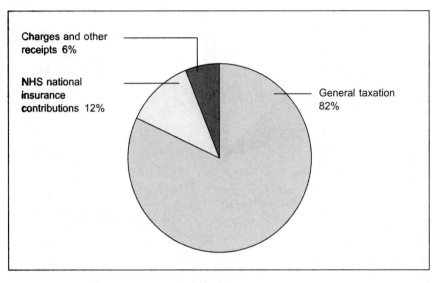

Charges and other
receipts 6%

NHS national
insurance
contributions 12%

General taxation
82%

Source: DH (1998a).

Figure 4.4 *Distribution of NHS budget, 1997–98*

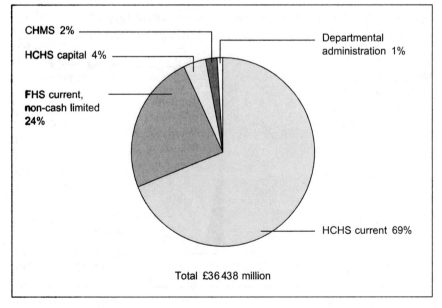

CHMS 2%

HCHS capital 4%

FHS current,
non-cash limited
24%

Departmental
administration 1%

HCHS current 69%

Total £36 438 million

Source: DH (1998a).

Figure 4.5 *Distribution of hospital and community health service expenditure 1995–96*

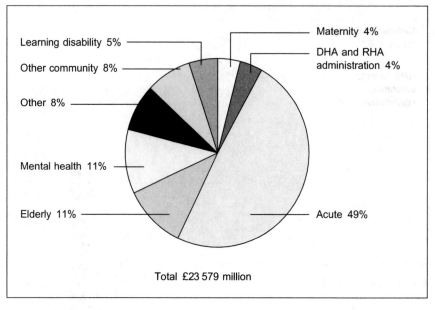

Source: DH (1998a).

Figure 4.6 *Distribution of family health services expenditure 1996–97*

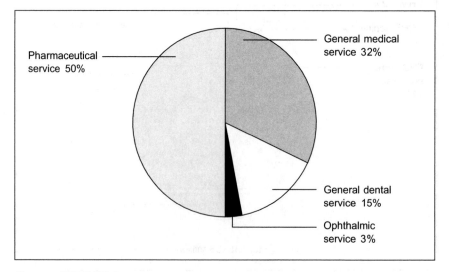

Source: DH (1998a).

Figure 4.7 *Distribution of hospital and community health services expenditure by age group 1995–96*

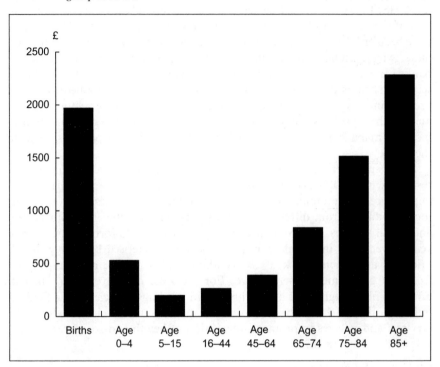

Source: DH (1998a).

Table 4.2 *NHS directly employed staff, 1996, England (WTEs)*

	Number	%
Nurses, midwifes and health visitors	335 300	44
Medical and dental	56 800	7
Scientific, therapeutic and technical	99 000	13
Healthcare assistants	16 800	2
Support staff	70 100	9
Administration and estates	167 400	22
Ambulance	15 100	2
Other	3200	0.5
Total	763 800	

Note: percentages may not total 100 due to rounding
Source: DH (1998a).

NHS capital expenditure has traditionally been provided and controlled by the Treasury in the same way as current expenditure. In the first decade of the NHS, funds for capital development were limited and only on publication of the Hospital Plan in 1962 did this change. More recently, NHS trusts have been encouraged to seek resources through the private finance initiative under which public sector capital projects are paid for via money loaned by banks. Initially, the private finance initiative was used for minor NHS schemes such as car parks and incinerators, but it is now applied to major projects including the rebuilding of entire hospitals. Private sector involvement in these projects encompasses not only the provision of capital, but also facilities management and the development of services in partnership with the NHS.

The Department of Health gives guidance to the NHS on the use of resources in circulars, White Papers and related documents. Of particular importance is the annual guidance on planning and priorities which brings together advice from different sources to set out priorities for both health and social services. The content of this guidance and its format varies from year to year, but in recent years it has been characterised by a long list of priorities and often a lack of clarity about which are the most important from the government's perspective. For the sake of convenience, current priorities may be grouped under three main headings: policies in the field of public health and health improvement; policies to develop health care services; and policies to promote integration of health and social care. Each will be discussed in turn.

Public health and health improvement

The priority attached to health improvement since the mid-1970s reflects the rediscovery of public health and recognition that factors like poverty, employment and housing are often more important than health care services in reducing morbidity and premature mortality. The new public health (Ashton and Seymour, 1988) draws on analysis of historical improvements in health and incorporates the findings of research into contemporary health problems to highlight both the limits of modern medical intervention and the need to tackle the causes of illness, whether these are found in the environment or in people's behaviour. Evidence that the health of the population in Northern Ireland, Scotland and Wales is poorer than in England, even though expenditure on health services is higher in these countries, reinforces the need for action outside the health sector to improve health. The healthy cities programme promoted by the World Health Organisation in 1985 gave practical expression to the new public health at an international level and underlined the importance of intersectoral action and the development of healthy public policies across government.

Policies to improve health under the NHS have a long history. In 1976 the DHSS published a consultative document entitled *Prevention and Health: Everybody's Business* (DHSS, 1976d) which noted that improvements in health in the previous century had resulted largely from the public health movement rather than specific medical interventions, and argued that further gains were dependent on people taking care of themselves by changing their lifestyle. Individuals were urged to stop smoking, take more exercise and adopt an appropriate diet in order to reduce the risk of ill-health and death. These views were reiterated in a White Paper on *Prevention and Health*, published a year later (DHSS, 1977a), and a series of other publications gave advice on issues such as safety during pregnancy, eating for health and avoiding heart attacks.

A rather different approach was taken in the Black Report on *Inequalities in Health*, published in 1980. This report resulted from the deliberations of a working group set up to assemble information about differences in health status among the social classes and factors which might contribute to these differences. Following a comprehensive review of the available data, the working group concluded 'we wish to stress the importance of differences in material conditions of life' (Black Report, 1980, p. 357) in explaining social class inequalities in health. On this basis, the working group made a series of recommendations for reducing inequalities, in particular emphasising the importance of factors outside the NHS. Among its proposals were the suggestion that child benefit should be increased, an infant care allowance introduced, housing conditions improved, and free school meals made available to all children. The Thatcher government was not persuaded by the analysis and recommendations of the Black Report, and it was not until almost 20 years later that the Report was taken seriously by policy-makers (see Chapter 8).

In the United Kingdom during the 1980s, particular attention was paid to the development of policies to limit the spread of HIV/AIDS. Earmarked funds were set aside to support work in this field with priority being given to preventing HIV/AIDS through changes in behaviour and the provision of information to the public about risk factors. This emphasis on changes in lifestyle was also reflected in the work of the Health Education Authority, the body responsible at a national level for campaigns to improve health. The Authority initiated programmes on cigarette smoking, alcohol abuse and healthy eating, including the 1987 'Look After Your Heart' campaign. In parallel, the Thatcher government put forward proposals for preventing illness by strengthening the role of GPs, dentists and other providers of primary care (Secretary of State for Social Services and others, 1987). As we noted in Chapter 2, this included the implementation of new contracts for GPs and dentists which contained incentives to encourage health checks, vaccination and immunisation, screening, health promotion, and preventative dentistry.

The need for a concerted approach to illness prevention was highlighted in the Acheson Report of 1989 which focused on the role of health authorities. In response, the government asked each health authority to appoint a director of public health whose task included producing an annual report on the health of the population, coordinating the control of communicable disease, and developing policies on prevention. A number of authorities used this opportunity to set targets for health improvement drawing on the strategy *Health for All by the Year 2000* published by the World Health Organisation (WHO). The approach adopted by the WHO was also influential in the preparation of a national health strategy for England. The White Paper entitled *The Health of the Nation* (Secretary of State for Health, 1992) set targets for the improvement of health in five key areas including HIV/AIDS. A Cabinet Committee was appointed to oversee implementation of the strategy in government as a whole, while at a local level health authorities through their directors of public health were expected to work with other agencies to counteract the conditions which give rise to ill-health and to attach higher priority to prevention within the NHS. An analysis of the implementation of the White Paper demonstrated that there was often a gap between the intentions of policy-makers and what happened in practice (DH, 1998b) and we return to examine implementation in Chapter 7.

The Health of the Nation was superseded by the consultation paper *Our Healthier Nation,* issued by the Blair government shortly after coming into office. Although similar in some respects to *The Health of the Nation,* the consultation paper differed in placing greater emphasis on the social, economic and environmental causes of illness and in explicitly acknowledging the importance of inequalities in health. *Our Healthier Nation* identified two aims of the health strategy, namely:

> To improve the health of the population as a whole by increasing the length of people's lives and the number of years people spend free from illness. To improve the health of the worst off in society and to narrow the health gap. (Secretary of State for Health, 1998a, p. 5)

It went on to propose a national contract for better health in which government, local communities and individuals would work in partnership to improve health. As Table 4.3 shows, the contract set out action by different agencies and the consultation paper also identified three settings for action: schools, workplaces and neighbourhoods. In relation to targets, *Our Healthier Nation* again differed from *The Health of the Nation* by proposing four priority areas instead of five, and by restricting the number of targets to be pursued. Specifically, the consultation paper suggested the following aims for the year 2010:

- *Heart Disease and Stroke*: to reduce the death rate from heart disease and stroke and related illnesses amongst people aged under 65 years by at least a further third;

- *Accidents*: to reduce accidents by at least a fifth;
- *Cancer*: to reduce the death rate from cancer amongst people aged under 65 years by at least a further fifth;
- *Mental Health*: to reduce the death rate from suicide and undetermined injury by at least a further sixth.

No targets were set for reducing health inequalities as the Acheson inquiry into health inequalities was still in progress at the time *Our Healthier Nation* was published. When the results of the Acheson inquiry were made available at the end of 1998 they not only confirmed the analysis of the Black Report

Table 4.3 *A contract for health*

Government and national players can:	*Local players and communities can:*	*People can:*
Provide national coordination and leadership	Provide leadership for local health strategies by developing and implementing Health Improvement Programmes	Take responsibility for their own health and make healthier choices about their lifestyle
Ensure that policy-making across Government takes full account of health and is well-informed by research and the best expertise available	Work in partnerships to improve the health of local people and tackle root causes of ill-health	Ensure their own actions do not harm the health of others
Work with other countries for international cooperation to improve health	Plan and provide high quality services to everyone who needs them	Take opportunities to better their lives and their families' lives, through education, training and employment
Assess risks and communicate those risks clearly to the public		
Ensure that the public and others have the information they need to improve their health		
Regulate and legislate where necessary		
Tackle the root causes of ill-health		

Source: Secretary of State for Health (1998a).

but also found that in some respects inequalities had widened in the intervening period (Acheson Report, 1998). It was expected that the White Paper on the health strategy planned for publication in 1999 would take account of these findings in setting out the government's revised targets.

Alongside the priorities set out in *Our Healthier Nation*, two other areas – smoking and drugs – have been singled out for action. In a White Paper on smoking published in 1998, the government set out a wide range of measures designed to cut the number of people smoking by 2010. Although rejecting a ban on smoking in public places, the White Paper included plans to develop smoking cessation clinics, restrict tobacco advertising and protect young people and children. In the case of drugs, the Blair government appointed a so-called 'drugs czar' to coordinate action across government as a whole to reduce drug misuse and the harm which results. Part of the NHS modernisation fund was earmarked for drug advisory services to enable the NHS to contribute to this process.

The potential for achieving further health improvement is illustrated by international comparisons of health status. What these comparisons show is that health in the United Kingdom has improved significantly in the last century but still lags behind that of other countries. This is illustrated in Figure 4.8 which shows life expectancy at birth for men and women in EU countries. While England achieves better results than some other countries, France, Italy and Sweden perform consistently better. Similar differences exist in relation to specific causes of premature death such as cancers and heart disease. Taken together with evidence on variations in health within the United Kingdom, these statistics help to explain why public health has received increased attention among policy makers.

Health care

Policies to develop health care services encompass a wide range of initiatives. In recent years these have included the development of policies in relation to cancer services, maternity care, primary care and waiting lists. Underpinning many of these policies is a concern to raise standards of health care provision and to improve access and convenience. Publication of the *Patient's Charter* in 1991 exemplified this concern and was the first attempt since the establishment of the NHS to define the rights of patients and the standards of service they should expect from the NHS (DH, 1991). The *Patient's Charter* was one of a series of charters published by the Major government as part of its policy to improve the performance of public services and it reflected recognition among policy-makers of the importance of rising public expectations of the NHS.

Table 4.4 summarises the standards and guarantees in the *Patient's Charter* including additions contained in the enlarged and updated version

Figure 4.8 *Expectation of life at birth, EU, 1995*

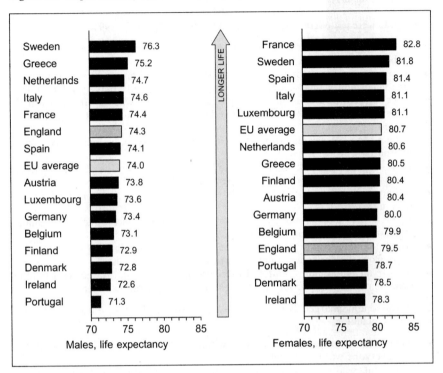

Source: Secretary of State for Health (1998a).

published in 1995. As this shows, particular emphasis was placed on reducing waiting times for hospital treatment. A maximum waiting time of 18 months was promised for inpatient treatment and 26 weeks for the first outpatient appointment. A maximum waiting time of 12 months was also set for coronary artery bypass grafts. Performance tables setting out how providers were performing on a number of the *Patient's Charter* standards were published beginning in 1994, and over time greater attention was given to measures of clinical performance alongside indicators of access and responsiveness.

The focus on clinical performance in the *Patient's Charter* was one element in the policy of improving the effectiveness of NHS services initiated by the DH in 1993. This policy incorporated work on clinical audit stemming from *Working for Patients*; the adoption of clinical guidelines to ensure the more effective delivery of health care; and the establishment of the health technology assessment programme to evaluate the costs and effectiveness of both new and established technologies. Work on health technology assessment formed the largest body of research within the NHS research

Table 4.4   *The Patient's Charter*

Ten rights were included in the *Patient's Charter* published in 1991:

- to receive health care on the basis of clinical need, regardless of ability to pay;
- to be registered with a GP;
- to receive emergency medical care at any time through a GP or through the emergency ambulance service and a hospital accident and emergency department;
- to be referred to a consultant, acceptable to a patient, when a GP thinks this is necessary, and to be referred to a second opinion if a patient and GP agree this to be desirable;
- to be given a clear explanation of any treatment proposed, including any risks or alternatives;
- to have access to health records, and to know that those working for the NHS are under a legal duty to keep their contents confidential;
- to choose whether or not to take part in medical research or medical student training;
- to be given detailed information on local health services, including quality standards and maximum waiting times;
- to be guaranteed admission for treatment by a specific date no later than two years from the day when a patient is placed on a waiting list;
- to have any complaint about NHS services investigated and to receive a full and prompt written reply from the chief executive or general manager.

The updated and enlarged *Patient's Charter* published in 1995 set out new rights and standards including:

- 90 per cent of outpatients to be seen within 13 weeks for their first appointment and everyone within 26 weeks;
- all patients waiting for an operation to be guaranteed admission for treatment no later than 18 months from the day of being placed on a waiting list;
- a three to four-hour standard for 'trolley waits' in accident and emergency departments, to be reduced to two hours from April 1996;
- urgent home visits by community nurses within four hours and for non-urgent patients within two days.

---

and development programme whose aim was to promote evidence-based health care. Initiatives supported through the research and development programme included the United Kingdom Cochrane Centre and the NHS Centre for Reviews and Dissemination. One of the purposes of these initiatives was to provide NHS decision-makers with advice and information about clinical effectiveness, which was intended to ensure that resources were used on interventions of benefit to patients.

The policy of improving effectiveness was given added impetus following the election of the Blair government in 1997. The government's plans for raising standards and promoting quality built on the initiatives already in place and led to the establishment of the National Institute for Clinical Excellence (NICE) and the Commission for Health Improvement. The role of NICE is to produce authoritative national guidance on the use of new and existing technologies, while the Commission for Health Improvement has the job of scrutinising standards and advising on action needed to strengthen quality. The work of these new institutions is supported by the development of national service frameworks setting out national standards and models for services such as coronary heart disease and mental health. In addition, a framework of clinical governance was introduced to strengthen existing systems for quality control. The priority attached to these issues by the Blair government was in part a response to evidence of failures of clinical performance within the NHS, and a concern to underpin self-regulation within the medical profession with other mechanisms of quality assurance.

The government also gave priority to policies designed to improve access and convenience within the NHS. Of particular significance was the reduction of waiting lists for hospital treatment in the light of the pledge made by the Prime Minister when in opposition to cut the number of people on waiting lists by 100 000. Extra resources were allocated to implement this pledge and a national waiting-list action team was established to ensure delivery of the target that had been set. The emphasis on access and convenience was seen too in the establishment of a number of pilot projects to introduce booked admission systems in place of waiting lists and to test out a 24-hour telephone nurse helpline known as NHS Direct. In addition, an annual survey of patient and user experience was set up to provide regular feedback on how well the NHS was serving its customers. A related initiative was the encouragement given to the use of new technologies to improve access to care, as in the more widespread application of telemedicine within the NHS.

Policies on primary care had as one of their aims making services more responsive to patients and more appropriate to their needs. The position of primary care as the first point of contact for patients and the gateway to hospital and specialist services has long been seen as a strength of the NHS. This position was reinforced by the 1965 Doctors' Charter and the new contract for GPs that followed in 1966. Subsequent developments focused on the extension of group practice and primary care teams and the improvement of premises. Notwithstanding these developments and the improved distribution of family doctors around the country, the Royal Commission on the NHS highlighted a number of weaknesses in primary care, including the poor quality of services in certain declining inner city areas (Royal Commission on the NHS, 1979). Many of these weaknesses persist and there continue to be concerns about variations in standards and performance.

Only with the 1997 Primary Care Act have powers been created to encourage new approaches to be developed. These centre on a series of pilot projects, including the employment of salaried family doctors and nurse-led schemes. The Act emerged from a process of consultation and debate started under the Major government and it was passed into law with the support of Opposition parties. Its main significance is in offering greater flexibility and choice in the provision of primary care. This entails the continuation of independent contractor status for GPs who prefer this option, and the ability to negotiate local personal medical services contracts for GPs who wish to do so. Alongside changes to arrangements for providing cover for GPs in the evenings and at weekends, often involving the creation of cooperatives in which doctors support each other in delivering services out of hours, the Primary Care Act pilots open up a new chapter in the development of primary care. This involves not only the choice of different kinds of working arrangements but also the emergence of new primary care organisations.

Many of these organisations build on initiatives taken in the light of *Working for Patients*. The establishment of GP fundholding and GP commissioning in different forms marked a move away from the GP practice as the principal form of primary care organisation to the establishment of multifunds, total purchasing projects, locality commissioning groups, out-of-hours cooperatives and related agencies. The effect was to break down the isolation of individual doctors and practices and to encourage increased collaboration. This was reinforced by the setting up of GP commissioning pilots under the Blair government, and subsequently the introduction of primary care groups across the NHS in England. The GP practice continues to be of fundamental importance in these arrangements, but increasingly practices are working within a local framework of primary care and in so doing are comparing their approach with that of peers. As an example, variations in the use and cost of pharmaceuticals are being examined by the new primary care organisations as part of a shift towards managed primary care.

Policy on acute hospital services has developed in a piecemeal fashion and with the exception of waiting lists has not received the same attention as policy in other areas. The organisation of acute services was first addressed systematically in the 1962 Hospital Plan which set out a vision of a network of district general hospitals (DGHs) serving populations of 100 000 to 150 000, and each containing between 600 and 800 beds. The programme of hospital building that occurred after the Plan resulted in the building of many completely new DGHs and the upgrading of several existing hospitals to DGH standard. The Bonham Carter Report of 1969 (Central Health Services Council, 1969) proposed that even larger DGHs should be built to serve bigger populations but these proposals were not accepted. Instead, policy moved in favour of smaller DGHs supported by community hospitals (DHSS, 1980b). Despite this, the changing pattern of medical staffing in hospitals, with junior doctors spending more time undergoing training, consultants playing a bigger part in the delivery of services, and specialisation requiring a larger number of consultants to work together to offer the full range of services to a high standard, threatened the viability of smaller DGHs and led to moves to link and integrate services at adjacent hospitals (Ham, Smith and Temple, 1998).

Changing patterns of use of acute services have resulted in more patients being treated in fewer beds. This has been made possible by advances in medical technology, including the increased use of day surgery, developments in anaesthetics, and the use of new drugs. The average length of stay of patients in acute hospitals has fallen as a consequence and NHS hospitals typically operate with high levels of bed occupancy and little spare capacity. This has caused problems in recent years, especially during the winter months when increases in emergency admissions have put pressure on a system already working close to its limits. In some cases this has meant patients having to wait on trolleys until beds have become available. Policy on acute services has sought to deal with this by allocating additional resources to assist with winter pressures and by encouraging the development of alternatives to hospital care in the community and in nursing homes. The government has also acted to increase the provision of intensive care facilities as rising demands have exposed inadequacies in capacity.

Developments in health care technology will result in further changes to the delivery of services. Of particular importance are developments in molecular biology which are leading to increased understanding of the genetic contribution to disease. This is opening up new opportunities for the diagnosis of illness and in the longer term may enable effective treatments to be developed. Advances in technology will also increase the possibilities for self-care as individuals and families take more responsibility for their health. Through the use of the Internet and other information sources, patients are likely to become more assertive users of services, challenging the power of health professionals and seeking to become partners in care. Policy initiatives like NHS Direct, a nurse-led telephone helpline and source of advice, indicates that these possibilities are already resulting in changes in service provision.

Looking further ahead, it is possible to identify the way in which developments in technology will increase the scope for services to be provided outside hospital (Warner and Riley, 1994). This will entail not only a shift to home based care but also enhanced primary care and a move of services into the community. When hospital treatment is needed, the length of stay will continue to fall as greater use is made of alternatives such as patient hotels, nursing homes, and hospital at home schemes. The establishment of primary care groups and trusts can be seen as a way of facilitating these developments. Acute hospitals will continue to play an important part in the delivery of services to patients but the opportunities to substitute other forms of care means that their role will change significantly.

In two areas, maternity services and cancer services, government has set out policies at a national level on how it wishes to see services develop. Maternity services policy follows the recommendations of the *Changing Childbirth* report which advocated a move towards woman-centred care. This placed the emphasis on information, choice and flexibility, and implementation was supported through a series of development projects. Policy on cancer services derives from the Calman-Hine report which set out a framework for commissioning high quality cancer care (Calman-Hine, 1995). The central proposal of this report was that care should be organised at three levels – primary care, cancer units and cancer centres – linked together to offer a network of appropriate services to patients. The Calman-Hine report is seen by the government as a model to be followed in other areas as national service frameworks are developed as part of the drive to raise standards within the NHS. Alongside maternity services and cancer services, proposals have been issued for the commissioning of highly specialised services to enable these services to be provided at appropriate centres.

Health and social care

Policies on health and social care over the last 40 years have focused particularly on the expansion of care in the community. In the case of elderly people and people with mental illness, learning difficulties and physical disabilities, there has been a move away from providing care in hospitals and residential institutions to offering support in the home and in home-like settings. Implementation of this policy has pointed up the importance of effective joint planning between the NHS and local authorities who are responsible for social care services. Successive governments have placed high priority on the integration of health and social care but with the exception of Northern Ireland, where these services are the responsibility of a single agency, progress in achieving integration has been variable.

In the case of people with mental illness, the 1959 Mental Health Act signalled the intention to develop community-based services, spurred on by developments in the treatment of mental illness and in social attitudes which made it possible to begin the run down of the large old psychiatric hospitals or asylums which had been the main source of care until that point. The White Paper, *Better Services for the Mentally Ill* (DHSS, 1975), continued this trend and encouraged the integration of hospital services for people with mental illness in DGHs. The White Paper also included norms for the provision of services by local authorities, encompassing day centres, hostels and long-stay accommodation. In practice, public expenditure restrictions served to slow the development of these services, and the availability of comprehensive mental health care remained uneven. This again demonstrated the gap between the intentions of policy and implementation.

The care programme approach developed in the 1990s was intended to ensure that health and social care needs were assessed systematically and agreed services provided. This was supplemented by guidance on the components of care the government expected to be offered to people with mental illness. In view of concerns about patients discharged from hospital without adequate support, supervised discharge was introduced in 1996 to provide more control over certain categories of patients considered to pose risks either to themselves or the community. The rapid succession of policy initiatives in this period culminated in publication of a White Paper, *Modernising Mental Health Services*, in 1998 setting out the Blair government's plans for the future. The White Paper highlighted the failures of the community care policy and indicated that additional resources would be provided not only to address these failures but also to fund extra beds. To this extent, the White Paper recognised the need for a range of services to be available to people with mental illness and it reflected both public and political recognition of the continuing role of hospitals in the treatment of mental illness.

Policies for people with learning difficulties have undergone significant change following the White Paper, *Better Services for the Mentally Handi-capped*, published in 1971 (DHSS, 1971). The main objective of the White Paper was to bring about a reduction of about one-half in the number of hospital beds provided for mentally handicapped people (as they were known at the time), and to expand local authority services in the community. Standards in hospital were also to be improved to overcome the deficiencies noted in the Report of the Committee of Enquiry into Ely Hospital, Cardiff (Ely Report, 1969) which found evidence both of the neglect of patients and their abuse. A review published in 1980 indicated progress in meeting these objectives and proposed an even greater reduction in hospital provision and the need for care to be provided in smaller units (DHSS, 1980c). The review went on to stress the importance of developing local authority services and integrating these services with those provided by health authorities. These developments were taken further by the increasing emphasis placed on enabling people with learning difficulties to live an ordinary life in the community through supported living programmes and similar initiatives. In recognition that social care is often more important for people with learning difficulties than health care, in some parts of the country health authorities and local authorities have agreed to pool budgets, with local authorities taking the lead responsibility for the commissioning of these services.

Services for elderly people were last subject to a major policy review in 1981 (DHSS, 1981b), and since then have been through a series of changes driven largely by shifting policies in respect of public funding of care in private and voluntary sector residential and nursing homes. These changes centred on the availability of resources through the social security budget to pay for care in these homes during the 1980s. Expenditure increased rapidly, reaching £2.5 billion a year by 1993, and it was partly in response to this that the government acted to cap spending and to make local authorities the lead agencies in arranging social care. The shift in policy was also stimulated by a desire to move resources away from residential and nursing home provision by giving local authorities greater flexibility to develop home care and other services in line with the recommendations of the Griffiths Report on community care (see Chapter 2). In implementing these changes, the government transferred resources from the social security budget to local authorities and it indicated that it expected services to be purchased from providers in the independent sector rather than to be provided directly by local authorities.

One of the consequences of the growth of social security spending and the contribution of the independent sector was that the role of the NHS in the provision of care declined significantly, focusing mainly on acute services rather than long-term or continuing care. This happened by default rather than design and it represented a major shift in policy that was never debated or agreed (Audit Commission, 1997). As a result, people above a certain income level were required to pay themselves for continuing care instead of having access to such care in the NHS. In 1994 the Health Service Commissioner or Ombudsman upheld a complaint from the wife of a man suffering brain damage who argued that the NHS should have provided continuing care to her husband. This led the DH to issue guidance to health authorities and local authorities asking them to develop local policies and eligibility criteria on continuing care and indicating that health authorities in some areas would need to increase expenditure on these services to enable the NHS to meet its obligations in the light of the Ombudsman's judgement.

The election of the Blair government resulted in the establishment of a Royal Commission to explore options for the future funding of long-term care against a background of increasing dissatisfaction with the progressive shift of responsibility from the public to the private sector. The Royal Commission reported in 1999 with the majority recommending that all nursing and personal care in care homes, and all personal care in people's own homes, should be provided free. The provision of accommodation and food would be means tested and it was estimated that the cost of making these changes would be around £1 billion initially. The minority on the Commission dissented from these proposals, arguing that they would involve the use of public funds to support better-off members of society at the expense of those most in need. Instead, the minority proposed that the existing rules on means testing should be relaxed and nursing care only should be free. For its part, the government promised to consider the report of the Royal Commission in formulating its own proposals for change. This was widely interpreted as indicating a reluctance to accept the recommendations of the Commission majority.

A theme that runs through discussion of policies for all these priority groups is the importance of joint planning and provision between the NHS and local government in making a reality of community care. A series of reports over the years have reviewed arrangements for integration and have made proposals for strengthening links between services. Of particular importance were the arrangements for joint planning and joint finance put in place in the 1970s. While some progress has been made in achieving better integration, political, professional and organisational differences have not facilitated joint approaches, and more radical proposals for change such as placing health and social care under the control of a single agency have been considered but rejected. The most recent policy document to address these issues similarly maintains that 'Major structural change is not the answer' (DH, 1998c, p. 5), and instead proposes to remove the barriers to joint working by introducing new powers to enable pooled budgets, the establishment of lead commissioners and the development of integrated provision.

One small but notable innovation that occurred in 1998 was the publication for the first time of guidance on national priorities to both health services and social services. The guidance was an indication of the commitment of the government to break down the 'Berlin Wall' between health and social care, and it set out priorities for each service as well as areas in which a joint approach was required. To return to the starting point of this chapter, one of the features of this guidance was the long list of priorities identified and the difficulty of determining which were the most significant. Although there has been a move during the 1990s on the part of successive governments to be more disciplined in their advice on priorities, there remains an underlying problem of priority overload and a tendency on the part of politicians to add to the demands placed on NHS bodies rather than to limit these demands.

Priority-setting

The need to set priorities was highlighted by the Royal Commission on the NHS which noted:

> the demand for health care is always likely to outstrip supply and . . . the capacity of health services to absorb resources is almost unlimited. Choices have therefore to be made about the use of available funds and priorities have to be set. (Royal Commission on the NHS, 1979, p. 51)

Priority-setting is not new and in the first phase of the NHS debate centred on the adequacy of the funding made available by the government and the decision to introduce charges for some services. As time went, the lengthening of waiting lists for hospital treatment came to exemplify rationing by delay and there was also evidence that doctors rationed access to specialist services such as dialysis for the treatment of kidney failure (Halper, 1989). The latter example illustrates the more general point that NHS rationing tended to be implicit and a matter of clinical judgement rather than a process that occurred out in the open. Only in the 1970s when expenditure constraints began to bite and growth rates slowed did governments address the issue of priority-setting systematically.

The high point of priority-setting at a national level occurred in 1976 when the Labour government published a consultative document on *Priorities* setting out quantified targets for the development of different services (DHSS, 1976b). In the following year there was a retreat from this approach with the White Paper, *The Way Forward* (DHSS, 1977b), indicating in broad terms, as illustrative projections only, the kinds of developments that might occur. This process was taken to its logical conclusion in *Care in Action* (DHSS, 1981c), the first statement on priorities produced by the Thatcher government, which gave a general account of government policies for different services and client groups, and argued that priority-setting was a matter for local decision and local action. Notwithstanding a return to greater central involvement in the running of the NHS in subsequent years, the emphasis on local responsibility for priority-setting was reiterated in later guidance, the circular on planning guidelines issued in 1988, for example, stating that wide variations in the circumstances of individual health authorities meant that the pace of change in major services would not be the same throughout the NHS.

The reluctance of governments to take a lead in setting priorities derives from the political costs involved in taking unpopular decisions. This was illustrated by the response to the 1976 *Priorities* document and the opposition of groups representing services identified as low priorities to the approach taken by the government. In these circumstances, it is not surprising that politicians prefer to pass responsibility to health authorities or seek to mask the effects of their policies. As Klein (1995) has observed, the diffusion of blame is an enduring feature of the NHS and helps to explain why decision-makers at a local level are given the responsibility of making choices between different services. Similarly, politicians may resort to subterfuge and evasion in reconciling limited budgets and growing demands. The withdrawal of long-term care from the NHS through a series of incremental decisions (see above) is a clear illustration of this, demonstrating how care may be rationed even in the absence of public debate. Restrictions on the availability of dental services within the NHS indicate a different kind of approach, with care that was once seen as part of the core of NHS provision being withdrawn as a consequence of dissatisfaction on the part of dentists with NHS terms and conditions. In this case, the failure of the government to respond to the decision of dentists in some areas to no longer offer to provide services within the NHS meant that dental care *de facto* became a private service in these areas.

In relation to services other than long-term care and dentistry, local responsibility for priority-setting results in variations between areas in the availability of services within the NHS. This has become known as 'rationing by postcode'. Access to care then depends on where people live and this has raised questions about the claim of the NHS to be a national service in which care is available on the basis of need. Examples include the priority attached to new drugs such as beta interferon for the treatment of multiple sclerosis, and access to services like infertility treatment. In both of these cases there are variations between areas reflecting differences between health authorities in the importance given to competing claims on the use of resources. The decision of the Blair government to establish the National Institute for Clinical Excellence and to develop national service frameworks may over time reduce these variations and promote greater consistency in service provision, but for the foreseeable future the emphasis placed on local responsibility for decision-making suggests that differences in access will be the norm. The only exceptions will be in those few areas of policy – like the reduction of waiting lists – which are such high political priorities that wide local variation is deemed to be politically unacceptable.

How then do health authorities arrive at decisions on priorities? Research evidence indicates that local decisions are shaped by inherited commitments and by bargaining between different interests. National guidance on priorities plays a major part in this process and account is also taken of the views of local people and the preferences of providers. The outcome tends to involve incremental adjustments to existing budgets rather than major changes of direction as health authorities spread resources around in seeking to reconcile the demands placed upon them (Ham, 1993; Klein, Day and Redmayne, 1996). Decisions are informed by the application of techniques and evidence on cost-effectiveness, but it is the judgement of local policy-makers and their weighing of different claims that is decisive. Put another way, priority-setting is an arena in which the politics of the NHS are played out at a local level and in Chapter 7 we explore further the dynamics of the micro politics of health care.

In the absence of explicit priority-setting at a national level, clinicians continue to be closely involved in rationing. Both hospital doctors and GPs make decisions in their daily work which shape the allocation of resources, whether this involves the prescribing of drugs, or decisions on whether to refer patients for a specialist consultation or an operation. The unofficial concordat between the government and the medical profession, based on government deciding on the budget that can be afforded and doctors determining how this budget should be used (Klein, 1995), has survived the first 50 years of the NHS, but appears increasingly fragile as the medical profession and its representatives put pressure on government to increase the available resources in order to reduce the difficulties involved in rationing decisions by clinicians, and as politicians seek to constrain doctors' discretion by developing guidelines for the use of services. And in circumstances in which deference to medical views is declining and there is a greater willingness on the part of patients and their relatives to challenge decisions with which they disagree, it seems only a matter of time before the United

Kingdom follows the example of other countries and acknowledges the need for priorities to be established openly at a national level, notwithstanding the political costs that may be incurred. In this respect, the creation of institutions like the National Institute for Clinical Excellence may be seen as an attempt to square the circle in that it creates the opportunity for priority-setting decisions to be taken explicitly and nationally while continuing to distance politicians from these decisions.

Conclusion

In this chapter we have described the development of health policy and summarised key issues in the funding and provision of health care. We have noted that the size of the NHS budget is shaped by the state of the economy and government decisions on priorities between spending programmes. Periods of growth have been interspersed with years of relative famine as economic imperatives and political bargaining have combined to determine the allocation of resources to different sectors.

Policies for specific services have been developed in relation to public health and health improvement, health care, and health and social care and evidence indicates that there has often been a gap between aspiration and achievement. Responsibility for reconciling the many priorities identified by government and allocating resources between competing claims rests with health authorities. Clinicians are also involved in rationing and there is a continuing tension between the role of doctors in deciding on the treatment of individual patients and the attempt by managers and politicians to influence priorities at a national and local level. The existence of clinical judgement exerts a considerable influence on the policy process and this is a theme to which we shall return in later chapters.

The paradox of a national health service in which NHS bodies and doctors play a major part in resource allocation is explained by the political costs involved in explicit priority-setting at a national level, and the quest for alternative ways of diffusing blame and avoiding accountability. This point has not been lost on health authorities and the medical profession, hence the clamour for government to take a lead on these issues. In the next phase of development, primary care groups will be expected to take a greater responsibility in priority-setting, and already there are signs that GPs may be unwilling to ration care between patients. The major unresolved question is the balance that will be struck between the role of these groups and the guidance emerging at a national level from NICE and other sources.

5

The Policy-making Process
in Central Government

The aim of this chapter is to offer a framework for thinking about policy and the policy process. The chapter begins with a definition of policy and goes on to describe the systems model which has been developed as a way of analysing and studying the policy process. The limitations of such a model are noted and the need to draw on other perspectives is highlighted. The rest of the chapter discusses the organisation of British government including the role of Parliament, the Prime Minister and Cabinet, ministers and civil servants, government departments and pressure groups. The chapter concludes by noting the changes that have occurred to the organisation of government and those that are planned, in particular the move to devolve power within the United Kingdom.

What is policy?

Although many writers have attempted to define policy, there is little agreement on the meaning of the word. It is therefore tempting to follow Cunningham and argue that 'policy is rather like the elephant – you recognise it when you see it but cannot easily define it' (quoted in Smith, 1976, p. 12). Attractive as this interpretation is, it may be worth spending a little time clarifying the meaning of policy, and the different ways in which it has been used.

A useful starting point is the work of David Easton, who has argued that political activity can be distinguished by its concern with 'the authoritative allocation of values' within society (Easton, 1953, p. 136). Easton uses values in a broad sense to encompass the whole range of rewards and sanctions that those in positions of authority are able to distribute. Values are allocated by means of policies, and for Easton 'A policy . . . consists of a web of decisions and actions that allocate . . . values' (Easton, 1953, p. 130). A number of points can be made about this definition.

First, Easton argues that the study of policy encompasses both formal decisions and actions. He points out that a decision by itself is not an action, but merely the selection among alternatives. What happens in practice may be different from what was intended by decision-makers, and it is important to focus on the processes that follow from a decision. Put another way, we need to consider how policy is implemented as well as how it is made.

A second point about Easton's definition is that it suggests that policy may involve a web of decisions rather than one decision. There are two aspects to this. First, the actors who make decisions are rarely the same people as those responsible for implementation. A decision network, often of considerable complexity, may therefore be involved in producing action, and a web of decisions may form part of the network. The second aspect is that even at the policy-making level, policy is not usually expressed in a single decision. It tends to be defined in terms of a series of decisions which, taken together, comprise a more or less common understanding of what policy is.

Third, policies invariably change over time. Yesterday's statements of intent may not be the same as today's, either because of incremental adjustments to earlier decisions, or because of major changes of direction. Also, experience of implementing a decision may feed back into the decision-making process, thereby leading to changes in the allocation of values. This is not to say that policies are always changing, but simply that the policy process is dynamic rather than static and that we need to be aware of shifting definitions of issues.

Fourth, the corollary of the last point is the need to recognise that the study of policy has as one of its main concerns the examination of non-decisions and inaction. Although not encompassed in Easton's definition, the concept of non-decision-making has become increasingly important in recent years, and a focus on decision-making has been criticised for ignoring more routine activities leading to policy maintenance and even inertia. Indeed, it has been argued that much political activity is concerned with maintaining the status quo and resisting challenges to the existing allocation of values. Analysis of this activity is a necessary part of the examination of the dynamics of the policy process (Bachrach and Baratz, 1970).

Fifth and finally, Easton's definition raises the question of whether policy can be seen as action without decisions. While Easton wishes to stress that policy is more than a formal, legal decision it is also appropriate to consider the view that there may be policies in the absence of decisions. Can it be said that a pattern of actions over a period of time constitutes a policy, even if these actions have not been formally sanctioned by a decision? In practice it would seem that a good deal of what happens in public agencies occurs because 'it has always been done this way', and cannot be attributed to any official pronouncement. Further, writers on policy have increasingly turned their attention to the actions of lower-level actors, sometimes called street-level bureaucrats, in order to gain a better understanding of policy-making and implementation. It would seem important to balance a decisional 'top-down' perspective on policy with an action-oriented, 'bottom-up' perspective (Barrett and Fudge, 1981). Actions as well as decisions may therefore be said to be the proper focus of policy analysis. Accordingly, in this and the subsequent chapter the main focus of attention is on the policy-making process in central government, while Chapter 7 examines the implementation of centrally determined policies and the local influences on health policy-making.

The policy process

The discussion may be taken a stage further by considering a framework for analysing the policy process. Easton's work again provides a starting point, and his analysis of political activity in terms of systems theory may help to clarify the complex range of phenomena under investigation. Later on we shall note some criticisms of Easton's approach, but to begin with let us examine the central elements of his analysis.

Easton, unlike many other political scientists, does not take as his starting point the analysis of power in political systems. This, he feels, is of secondary importance compared with the question of how it is that political systems persist and change over time. Power analysis presupposes the existence of relatively stable political activity and does not consider the conditions under which this activity is able to continue. It is the latter question which interests Easton, who seeks to develop a general theory of political life (Easton, 1953; 1965a; 1965b).

Underpinning Easton's theory is the assumption that political activity can be analysed in terms of a system containing a number of processes which must remain in balance if the activity is to survive. The paradigm that he employs is the biological system whose life processes interact with each other and with the environment to produce a changing but nonetheless stable bodily state. Political systems are like biological systems, argues Easton, and exist in an environment which contains a variety of other systems, including social systems and ecological systems.

One of the key processes of political systems is inputs, which take the form of demands and supports. Demands involve actions by individuals and groups seeking authoritative allocations of values from the authorities. Supports comprise actions such as voting, obedience to the law, and the payment of taxes. These feed into the black box of decision-making, also known as the conversion process, to produce outputs. Outputs are essentially the decisions and the policies of the authorities. Outputs may be distinguished from outcomes, which are the effects that policies have on citizens. Easton's analysis does not end here, for within the systems framework there is allowance for feedback, through which the outputs of the political system

Figure 5.1 *A simplified model of a political system*

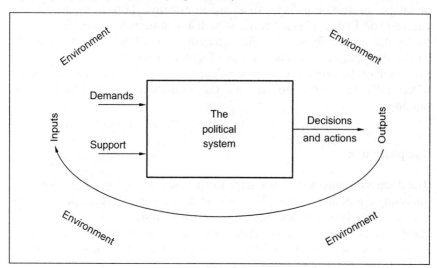

Source: Easton (1965a).

influence future inputs into the system. The whole process is represented in Figure 5.1.

The objects of support in political systems are threefold. First, there are the authorities, that is those who hold office at a particular point in time. Second, there is the regime, or the set of constitutional arrangements within which political activity takes place. Third, there is the political community, by which Easton means the readiness of the members of the political system to cooperate in solving political problems.

Easton notes that stress may result from a decline in support or from the pressure of demands. Demand stress may be produced by the sheer volume of demands being placed on the political system or by the content of demands. That is, the authorities may be faced with more demands than they are able to cope with, as well as demands which are unacceptable in terms of the prevailing system of values. Demand stress can occur even though processes of demand regulation are at work serving to reduce pressures on the authorities.

Support stress may result from neglect of demands by the authorities, or by the failure of outputs to satisfy demands. In Easton's analysis, one of the characteristics of political systems is their ability to respond and adapt to stress. Responses may take the form of authoritative allocations of values, changes in the authorities, or adaptations to the regime. Put another way, there may be changes in policies, movements in the personnel in authority, or fundamental alterations to the constitutional order, including the creation of new political structures. Political systems are able to develop in these ways without threatening the political community. Systems are therefore responsive and dynamic, and open to influences from a wider environment.

Limits of the systems model

A number of writers have found Easton's framework to be a useful tool in analysing the policy process (Jenkins, 1978; Hall, Land, Parker and Webb, 1975). Certainly the systems approach has merit in offering a way of conceptualising and simplifying the study of policy-making. Systems theory is also valuable in emphasising the interdependence of the various processes which comprise political activity, and in showing how these processes fit together to form a whole. A particular strength of the approach is Easton's detailed analysis of demands and the process of demand regulation through gatekeepers and cultural exclusion. However, the approach is not without its drawbacks, and our understanding of the policy process may be developed further by examining various points of criticism.

First, while Easton's identification of processes is valuable for analytical purposes, the neat, logical ordering of those processes in terms of demand initiation, through the conversion process to outputs, rarely occurs so simply in the real world of policy-making. We noted in Chapter 2 that policy is often made as it is implemented, and the sequential connotations contained within the systems model may not allow for the iterative and continuous nature of policy development. The model also does not give as much attention to the importance of the implementation stage of the policy process as recent work by policy analysts suggests is necessary.

Second the authorities themselves may be the source of demands. Although Easton recognises the significance of what he terms 'withinputs', consideration needs to be given to the manner in which individual and group behaviour may be shaped by political leaders. A growing body of work suggests that, far from arising autonomously in the community, political demands may be manufactured by leaders, who thereby create the conditions for their own action (Edelman, 1971). Through the manipulation of language and the creation of crises, the authorities may impose their own definitions of problems and help to frame the political agenda. Recognition of these processes is an important corrective to the naive assumptions found in some applications of systems theory. This is a theme we return to in Chapter 6.

A third criticism is that the systems framework highlights the central importance of the conversion process, the black box of decision-making, but gives it relatively little attention when compared with the detailed analysis of demands and supports. Of course, for some researchers the conversion process remains a black box because of the difficulties of penetrating the decision-making activities of governmental agencies. Traditionally, accounts of the organisation of central government in Britain have been limited to formal descriptions of the major institutions such as the Cabinet and Parliament. In recent years, however, recollections by former Cabinet Ministers of their experiences in office have provided new inside views of the black box, views which we will next discuss in exploring the policy-making machinery in the British political system.

Fourth, the insights offered by the systems model need to be complemented by more recent work highlighting the role of both policy communities (Heclo, 1978) and political institutions (March and Olsen, 1989) in the policy process. As we discuss in the following chapter, the organisations surrounding government departments comprise policy communities which coexist with issue networks. The decisions that emerge from these communities and networks determine, in Easton's terms, the authoritative allocation of values. Some communities are relatively stable and closed while others are much more fluid. Within policy communities, institutions both inside and outside government influence the agenda for discussion and how issues on the agenda are resolved (Kingdon, 1995). This has given rise to a wide variety of perspectives all of which can contribute to our understanding of policy development (see Parsons, 1995, for a comprehensive review) and many of which are referred to in the rest of this book. The point to emphasise here is that the systems model needs to be used alongside other approaches in explaining the dynamics of the policy process.

British central government

The organisation of British central government can be described simply. General elections, which must be held at least every five years, result in the election to the House of Commons of some 650 Members of Parliament (the precise number varies as constituency boundaries are redrawn). The leader of the largest single party in the Commons is asked by the monarch to form a government and the leader becomes the Prime Minister. The Prime Minister appoints from among his or her supporters around 100 people to take up ministerial appointments. The most senior of these, usually numbering 20, comprise the Cabinet. The government is thus made up of Cabinet and non-Cabinet ministers, the majority of whom will be MPs. The remaining members of the government come from the House of Lords. Occasionally people from outside Parliament are appointed to the government, but they must become MPs or be made life peers.

Ministers are responsible for the day-to-day running of the government's business through the departments of state. These departments include the Treasury, which is responsible for all matters to do with finance, and the Department of Health. Most of the work of the departments is in practice carried out by civil servants. Ministers are, however, individually responsible for the work done by civil servants in their name, and are held accountable by Parliament. Parliament also monitors the work of government departments through a system of select committees.

There is no written constitution in Britain and the relationship between the different institutions of government has evolved over the years. As one of the foremost students of the constitution has observed, the result is a 'curious compound of custom and precedent, law and convention, rigidity and malleability concealed beneath layers of opacity and mystery' (Hennessy,1995, p. 7). In seeking to unravel the mystery of the unwritten constitution, much has been written about the role of the monarchy, the legislature and the executive. To summarise this literature briefly, the historical decline in the power of the monarchy and the House of Lords gave rise to the thesis that Britain had a system of 'Cabinet government'. In his book, *The English Constitution*, published in 1867, Walter Bagehot argued that the monarchy and the Lords had become 'dignified' elements in the constitution, compared with the Commons, the Cabinet and the Prime Minister which he described as the 'efficient' elements (Bagehot, 1963). Of these latter institutions, Bagehot saw the Cabinet as preeminent.

Almost 100 years later, Richard Crossman, writing an introduction to a new edition of Bagehot's book, contended that Prime Ministerial government had replaced Cabinet government. In Crossman's view, the extension of suffrage to all adults, the creation of mass political parties and the emergence of the civil service administering a large welfare state all contributed to the Prime Minister's power (Crossman, 1963). This interpretation was confirmed by Crossman's experience as a Cabinet Minister. In addition, he noted the important part played by official committees in Whitehall, a facet of government he had not observed while in opposition; and he encountered the power of civil servants to challenge and frustrate the wishes of ministers.

It follows that in the British unitary state the most important source of power lies in the executive rather than the legislature with a small group of ministers and senior civil servants forming the core of government. This was illustrated by our account in Chapter 2 of the reforms to the NHS intiated by the Thatcher government. Relationships between the members of this group have been likened to a village in which behaviour is influenced by shared norms and values and the proximity of the inhabitants to each other. Studies of the 'Whitehall village' (Heclo and Wildavsky, 1981) have described the way in which business is done within government and the sense of community that binds together the participants. The idea that government is like a community has been taken forward by policy analysts who have used this metaphor to describe not only relationships within government but also the involvement of pressure groups in policy-making. The influence of pressure groups has contributed to the view that Britain is a 'post-parliamentary democracy' (Richardson and Jordan, 1997) and it is to the role of Parliament – specifically the House of Commons – that we now turn.

Parliament

It is important to distinguish the formal power of Parliament from its effective role. Although formally Parliament passes legislation, examines public expenditure and controls the government, effectively it carries out these functions within strictly defined limits. As long as there is a House of Commons majority to support the government, then Parliament has few significant powers within the system of central government. In Mackintosh's words, 'Parliament is one of the agencies through which the government operates and it is the place where the struggle for power continues in a restricted form between elections' (Mackintosh, 1974, p. 125).

The task of securing the government's majority in the House of Commons falls to the party whips. They ensure that MPs are present to vote, and that the government's legislative programme is passed safely. Most legislation originates from the government, and bills have to go through a number of stages before becoming law. Parliamentary debates on legislation provide an opportunity for party views to be reiterated, and occasionally the government will accept amendments put forward by opposition parties. On occasions, important legislation may be defeated or withdrawn. But the existence of a parliamentary majority coupled with strong party discipline ensures that these occasions will be rare.

Parliament provides opportunities for individual MPs to propose legislation in the form of private members' bills. The most important method of promoting a private member's bill is through the ballot of members which takes place every session. Usually, around 20 names are drawn in the ballot, but because of the pressure on parliamentary time only one-third to one-half of the MPs who are successful in the ballot stand a chance of having their bills enacted. Even in these cases, though, the MPs concerned are dependent on the government not being opposed to the legislation they propose. The Abortion Act of 1967, promoted by the Liberal MP David Steel, is an example of a private member's bill which became law.

Individual MPs are able to use Parliament in two other main ways. First, they can put down parliamentary questions, asking ministers about aspects of the work for which they are responsible. Some of these questions receive written replies, while others are answered orally, in which case there is an opportunity to ask a supplementary question. Second, MPs can raise adjournment debates, which are often on local or constituency issues. These debates provide a chance to air matters of concern to MPs and their constituents, and force ministers and departments to make a response. Also, although most of the parliamentary timetable is controlled by the government, certain days are available to the opposition to debate subjects of their choosing.

One of the key developments in Parliament in recent years has been the use of select committees. These are committees of MPs which investigate particular topics and publish reports on their findings. The aim of the committees is to provide MPs with a more effective means of controlling the executive, and to extract information about the government's policies. The establishment of the committees was in part a response to the perceived decline in the power of the Commons to control the government.

Although select committees have existed in a variety of forms ever since the establishment of the Public Accounts Committee in 1861 and the Estimates Committee in 1912, they have developed most recently in the period since 1966 when Richard Crossman, as Leader of the House of Commons, began an experiment with the setting up of select committees on agriculture and on science and technology. The experiment was taken a stage further in 1971 when the Expenditure Committee was established in place of the Estimates Committee and a number of the select committees. The Expenditure Committee worked through a range of sub-committees, including one on employment and social services. In 1979 the Expenditure Committee was replaced by 14 new committees, organised along the lines of government departments. Among these committees, it was the job of the Social Services Committee to investigate the work of the DHSS. Following the decision to split up the DHSS in 1988, the Committee continued to monitor the activities of both the Department of Health and the Department of Social Security until the end of 1990 when its responsibilities were themselves divided between two new committees on health and social security. The Health Committee subsequently scrutinised the work of the Department of Health and examined a wide range of issues to do with both the NHS and social services.

During its lifetime, the Social Services Committee undertook a number of major inquiries, including investigations into perinatal and neonatal mortality, the Griffiths Inquiry into NHS Management, and community care. Also, the Committee regularly reviewed the expenditure plans and priorities of the DHSS. The reports from the Committee in this area and the replies by the DHSS provided a continuing dialogue on the issues involved in planning and monitoring the expenditure programmes within the control of the DHSS. The MPs on the Committee were supported by a House of Commons clerk and his staff, and by specialist advisers (Nixon and Nixon, 1983). As well as taking evidence from civil servants and ministers, the Committee called witnesses from outside the DHSS, including the officers and chairmen of a number of health authorities This practice has also been followed by the Health Committee whose investigations have covered issues such as priority-setting and community care. Alongside the Health Committee, the Public Accounts Committee continues to examine the way in which government money has been spent, including spending on health services. The Public Accounts Committee has published a number of reports which have been critical of the management of the NHS, including analyses of manpower control, building defects and arrangements for premature retirement of staff.

The actual impact of select committees on policy is largely determined by the government's willingness to accept their recommendations. Although it is expected that departments will respond to committee reports, this does not mean that the committees' findings will have an immediate influence on policy. Nevertheless, it can be suggested that committees create a more informed House of Commons, force departments to account for their actions, submit ministers to a level of questioning not possible on the floor of the House, and help to put issues on the agenda for discussion. Furthermore, at a time when the role and influence of individual MPs have come into question, the committees have given MPs useful and often satisfying work to do. They also enable outsiders to gain a better understanding of what is going on in Whitehall, and the information they extract provides ammunition for pressure groups to use in particular campaigns.

The establishment of the new select committee system in 1979 is one of the factors which has led some writers to argue that the House of Commons is more powerful than often assumed. This is the view held by Norton (1981), who has drawn on evidence of a decline in the cohesion of political parties within Parliament and an increase in government defeats in division lobbies to suggest that the Commons can effectively scrutinise and influence government. As Norton points out, the key to government control of Parliament historically has been the existence of a single majority party with strong discipline being exercised by the whips, and any moves away from this system, such as the formation of minority or coalition governments, would further strengthen the position of those who wish to reassert the influence of the House of Commons. Norton himself summarises the role of Parliament in the following way:

> Parliament has never really been a law-making or policy-making body on any continuous basis. Its principal task in terms of proposals for public policy, as well as the conduct of government, has been one of scrutiny. . . The fact that government needs Parliament to give assent to measures and its request for money means that Parliament has some leverage. . .The impact of the British Parliament today, as in the past, might not be great, but it can and does have some effect on public policy. (Norton, 1997, p. 157)

The Prime Minister and Cabinet

The preeminence of the Prime Minister in the British system of government noted by Crossman and other commentators can be explained in a number of ways. First there is the Prime Minister's patronage. He or she has sole responsibility for appointing members of the government, and in addition has considerable discretion over the conferment of honours. Of course, the Prime Minister's power of patronage is not total, and is usually exercised with regard to the influence of other actors in the system. In appointing the Cabinet, for example, the Prime Minister will want to include people drawn from different parts of the majority party, possibly including former opponents. Nevertheless, it is ultimately the Prime Minister alone who decides, and who accepts responsibility for the appointments made.

Second, there is the Prime Minister's position as chairman of the Cabinet. This gives the Prime Minister control over the Cabinet agenda, and the power to appoint the members and chairmen of Cabinet committees. Much of the Cabinet's work is now done by committees whose activities were surrounded by secrecy until details of their work were published for the first time in 1992. This revealed that a subcommittee existed on health strategy and that this reported to a main committee on home and social affairs. In 1999 the home and social affairs committee was chaired by the Deputy Prime Minister and the health strategy committee by the leader of the House of Commons. In addition, both the Major and Blair governments attached priority to the integration of policy across government and initially under the Blair government it was the Prime Minister's close ally, Peter Mandelson, as Minister without Portfolio, who chaired a daily meeting on coordination and presentation of policy (Hood and James, 1997).

Third, the Prime Minister may establish informal groupings of senior ministers to act as an inner Cabinet. The inner Cabinet may serve as a sounding board for the Prime Minister, and may help to incorporate potential rivals into the centre of government decision-making. The Prime Minister will also negotiate with individual ministers in order to gain influence over specific policies. This was very much Mrs Thatcher's style of government. Under Mrs Thatcher, the Cabinet and formal Cabinet committees declined in importance, and greater use was made of *ad hoc* groups of ministers selected by the Prime Minister to deal with specific issues (Hennessy, 1986). This was confirmed by one of her most senior ministers, Nigel Lawson, who commented:

> When I was a minister I always looked forward to the Cabinet meeting immensely because it was, apart from the summer holidays, the only period of real rest that I got in what was a very heavy job. Cabinet meetings are ninety per cent of the time a dignified (rather than an) efficient part of Cabinet government. (quoted in Hennessy, 1995, p. 97)

Fourth, the Prime Minister's position is strengthened by the support of the Cabinet Office. Within the Cabinet Office the Cabinet Secretary is the key person, and the Secretary acts as the personal adviser to the Prime Minister. The Cabinet secretariat controls the distribution of minutes and papers in the Cabinet system and enables the Prime Minister to keep a close eye on what is taking place in Cabinet committees.

Fifth, since 1974, successive Prime Ministers have made use of their own Policy Unit located in 10 Downing Street. The Unit's principal purpose is to assist the Prime Minister in implementing the strategic goals of the government. One of its members during the 1980s has identified seven functions performed by the Unit. These are to serve as a think-tank, to act as an adviser, to follow up on the implementation of policy decisions, to raise important issues that might not otherwise have been passed to the Prime Minister, to lubricate relations between No. 10 and departments, to brief the Prime Minister directly on issues, and to help discover frustrated reformers and give their ideas another chance (Willetts, 1987). As well as these sources of strength, the Prime Minister's powers are underpinned by his or her position as leader of the majority party and head of the Civil Service. All of these factors give the Prime Minister a more powerful role than the traditional description, *primus inter pares,* suggests. Crossman's *Diaries* indicate that there were occasions when the Cabinet did engage in collective decision-making, but these tended to be when the Prime Minister had no definite view and was prepared to let the Cabinet decide.

What seems clear is that the Prime Minister is rarely defeated in Cabinet, and an alliance between the Prime Minister and the Chancellor of the Exchequer, or the Prime Minister and the Foreign Secretary, is virtually unstoppable. Yet before consigning the Cabinet to the dignified realm of the British constitution, the limits of prime ministerial power should be noted. For example, during the course of 1981 proposals for cuts in public expenditure put forward by the Chancellor of the Exchequer with support from the Prime Minister were defeated by the so-called 'wets' in the Conservative Cabinet (Young, 1989). Even more dramatically, Margaret Thatcher was forced to resign as Prime Minister in 1990 when she lost the confidence of her colleagues. Her successor, John Major, faced a similar challenge to his position in 1995 and chose to resign as leader of the Conservative Party in order to fight a leadership election with his critics. Major's victory in this contest reestablished his authority within the Party and as Prime Minister, although it weakened his standing in the country and contributed to the defeat of the government at the 1997 general election. In this case, the challenge to the Prime Minister arose not out of concerns about the dimunition of the role of the Cabinet, which had become more significant following the departure of Mrs Thatcher, than through deep divisions within the Conservative Party in relation to Britain's role in Europe. In both of these examples, the challenge to serving prime ministers demonstrates the existence of a number of checks and balances in the British system of government, if not in the form of codified rules of the kind found in the United States constitution, then nonetheless effective for that.

The election to office of a Labour Government in 1997 marked a return to the centralisation of power around the Prime Minister and his close advisers. Indeed, Tony Blair adopted a presidential style and strengthened the Cabinet Office and the Policy Unit in 10 Downing Street to ensure that adequate support was available. The position of the Prime Minister in British government is reinforced by the fact that on questions of government strategy or on broad economic policy departmental ministers are often reluctant to step outside their own areas of concern. Crossman bemoaned the absence of an overall strategy in the 1964–70 Labour government, and he explained it in terms of the entrenched departmentalism within Whitehall (Crossman, 1975, 1976, 1977). The Prime Minister, unencumbered by specific departmental responsibilities, is able to take the wider view, and so can set the direction of government policy as a whole. Only when the Prime Minister's leadership poses a threat to the government and its future electoral chances is the Prime Minister's dominance likely to be seriously challenged by Cabinet colleagues.

Ministers and civil servants

The traditional view that ministers decide policy and civil servants carry it out is no longer widely held. The memoirs of Crossman, Castle and other former ministers (RIPA, 1980) indicate that civil servants have considerably more influence over policy-making than allowed for in conventional text-book accounts. In the first volume of the Crossman diaries (1975) the struggle between ministers and civil servants became personalised in terms of the battle between Crossman and his permanent secretary at the Ministry of Housing, Dame Evelyn Sharp. Later volumes of the diaries suggested that it was not simply the personality of Crossman or Dame Evelyn that was important, but the very nature of civil service power. At the DHSS, for example, Crossman had to overcome the reluctance of civil servants before he succeeded in establishing the Hospital Advisory Service in 1969 after the Report of the Committee of Enquiry into Ely Hospital, Cardiff (Crossman, 1977). What the Ely example demonstrates is that a minister with clear views and a strong commitment can achieve his goals. On other issues, though, ministers may have to bargain, cajole and compromise before they get their way. This is epitomised by the 'Yes, Minister' and 'Yes, Prime Minister' television series which offer a popular portrayal of life in government departments in which civil servants more often than ministers shape the development of policy.

The Crossman diaries show that a proposal included in an election manifesto carries considerable weight with civil servants. This draws attention to the role of political parties as sources of inputs into the policy process. A newly elected government is likely to use its election manifesto as a basis for formulating a programme of legislation to put before Parliament. What is more, a government will seek to claim a mandate to implement any proposals contained in a manifesto. Manifesto proposals therefore constitute an influence on policy-making, particularly in the early years of a government. An example was the commitment made by the Labour government elected in 1997 on NHS waiting lists – a commitment which became the overriding health policy priority following the election because of the personal pledge given by the Prime Minister (as leader of the Opposition) to ensure that waiting lists came down. Yet with few exceptions, the ideas articulated by political parties are often very general and may be modified, sometimes in significant ways, as they are developed in detail by civil servants. It is therefore important not to overemphasise the influence of political parties on policy-making within central government. As Klein (1984) has demonstrated in the case of health policy, party ideology does not always predict policy, and the areas about which politicians are most concerned are often those of least significance in terms of their actual impact on the services provided to the public.

Civil servants influence policy-making in various ways. Their familiarity with the Whitehall machine, coupled with access to information and a repository of knowledge developed over a period of years, creates an expertise which is not easily challenged. Often, it is the strength of the departmental view on an issue, rather than any ideological antipathy, which politicians have to overcome (Young and Sloman, 1982). In many cases, ministers are not well-placed to challenge this view, if only because parties in opposition devote relatively little time to developing the policies they intend to carry out when in office. In addition, ministers may not always have the intelligence or skill to counter the weight of advice offered by civil servants. The debate about the relative influence of ministers and civil servants may therefore be more to do with weak ministers than conspiratorial civil servants. Ministers are not always appointed for their administrative ability or their analytical skills, and it is perhaps not surprising that they do not always carry through significant changes in policy (Hennessy, 1989).

Apart from personal factors – and these should not be underrated – there are organisational reasons why ministers sometimes do not make a major impact. One of the most important is the key role played by interdepartmental committees of civil servants, which prepare the ground for ministers and for Cabinet committees. Interdepartmental committees have been seen by Richard Crossman and Tony Benn, among others, as a key source of civil service power within Whitehall. As Crossman noted:

> in addition to the Cabinet committees which only ministers normally attend, there is a full network of official committees . . . . This means that very often the whole job is pre-cooked in the official committee to a point from which it is extremely difficult to reach any other conclusion than that already determined by the officials in advance; and if agreement is reached at the lower level of a Cabinet committee, only formal approval is needed from the full Cabinet. This is the way in which Whitehall ensures that the Cabinet system is relatively harmless. (Crossman, 1975, p. 198)

Unfortunately it is not possible to discover a great deal about the work of official committees because of the secrecy which surrounds their operation.

However, commentators from both inside and outside the system of central government have increasingly pointed to the importance of their work.

Another reason why ministers may be less than fully effective is the variety of different jobs they are expected to do: run their department; participate in Cabinet and Cabinet committee discussions; take care of their constituents as MPs; and take part in the work of the House of Commons. With so many competing demands on their time, it may be easier for ministers to accept the advice they are given and to rely on their departmental briefs than to attempt to exercise an independent policy-making role. It is worth noting, though, that there have been attempts to bolster the position of ministers through the appointment of specialist political advisers. These advisers were first appointed on a large scale in the 1960s by Labour ministers as a source of outside information and to provide an alternative form of briefing to that supplied by civil servants. Harold Wilson has identified seven functions for advisers:

> as a sieve, examining papers for politically sensitive or other important problems; as a deviller, chasing ministers' requests or instructions; as a thinker on medium and long term planning; as a policy contributor to departmental planning groups; as a party contact man, keeping in touch especially with the party's own research department; as a pressure group contact man; and as a speech writer. (Quoted in Blackstone, 1979)

Advisers have been used by both Labour and Conservative governments, and they come and go with governments. Professor Brian Abel-Smith of the London School of Economics was used as a political adviser in the DHSS by Richard Crossman in the late 1960s, and by Barbara Castle and David Ennals in the mid-1970s. The more astute advisers are able to enhance their position by building up relationships directly with civil servants, senior and junior, rather than always working with or through ministers (Young and Sloman, 1982). In this way they seek to extend their influence over policy-making. A number of former ministers, including Shirley Williams, Barbara Castle and William Rodgers, have argued that political advisers perform a useful function (RIPA, 1980; Castle, 1980) and they are likely to become increasingly significant as they are used on a more regular basis.

Relationships between departments

In discussing the role of the Cabinet, we noted that attempts to develop overall government strategies were frustrated by the strength of individual departments. The importance of 'departmental pluralism' (Richardson and Jordan, 1979, p. 26) is nowhere more apparent than in the budgeting process of central government, which until recently centred on the PESC cycle. PESC is the acronym for the Public Expenditure Survey Committee, the committee of officials which coordinated the preparation of the government's expenditure plans. PESC was one example of the interdepartmental committees of civil servants which organise much of the government's business. The Public Expenditure Survey Committee was especially important because of the impact of overall spending levels on the policies which it is possible to pursue. Ministers were not be able to launch new policy initiatives unless the expenditure involved had first been approved during the PESC process. In this process, a great deal of time was taken up with bilateral negotiations between the Treasury and individual spending departments on the departments' estimates of their expenditure plans. The Public Expenditure Survey Committee prepared a report for ministers on the basis of these negotiations, pointing out where agreements could not be reached. Cabinet and ministerial deliberations followed and if any issues remained unresolved then a Cabinet Committee known as the Star Chamber was set up to adjudicate (Likierman, 1988).

The Castle Diaries 1974–76 provide fascinating insights into the PESC negotiations, particularly as they affected health services. During the later months of 1975 and early 1976 – a time of increasing control over public expenditure – Castle and her officials were in the position of defending the NHS budget against attempts by the Chancellor of the Exchequer and the Treasury to achieve significant reductions in planned spending levels. As Castle records in her diaries, the public expenditure White Paper 'demonstrated vividly how much more successful I have been than some of my colleagues in defending my programmes' (Castle, 1980, p. 641). And as she explained to a meeting of Regional Health Authority chairmen, the outcome was:

> no absolute cut; overall growth rate for health of 1½ per cent per annum; expansion of health centre programme; yearly growth of family practitioner services of 3½ per cent; no need to cut back services; capital programme levelling out at £250 million a year; joint financing to the tune of £20 million by 1978–79; enough elbow room to move towards the better system of regional allocation under the Resource Allocation Working Party criteria, based on deprivation; the greater flexibility in switching between revenue and capital which Dick Bourton (a Deputy Secretary in the DHSS) has won from the Treasury (I paid him a public tribute on this); last, but not least, greater flexibility in carrying over spending from one year to the next (1 per cent instead of the ¼ per cent we had won from them this year). Tough, but not catastrophic. (Castle, 1980, p. 654)

The PESC negotiations were important not least in influencing the reputation of a minister. In particular, a minister who was successful in the negotiations earned the respect of his or her civil servants and achieved a reputation for toughness.

Since the period referred to in the Castle diaries, constraints on public spending have become even tighter, especially following the election of a

Conservative government in May 1979. As a result, while traditionally the vast bulk of inherited expenditure was left unquestioned, and most of the detailed negotiations within the PESC process occurred at the margins, increasingly all spending came under scrutiny. At the same time, PESC itself became more an instrument for controlling public expenditure than a means of planning future spending patterns (Heclo and Wildavsky, 1981). One of the key difficulties was the development of a corporate approach to public expenditure planning through PESC. The strength of departmentalism meant that individual departments sought to defend their own budgets and were reluctant to attack those of other departments. In theory, the Treasury and Cabinet were in a position to provide a wider view of priorities, but the Treasury was mainly concerned with the overall scale of public expenditure, while attempts within the Cabinet system to transcend departmentalism, such as the establishment of a Committee of Non-Spending Ministers in the early 1960s under the Conservatives and again in the late 1960s under Labour, did not prove effective.

The need to develop joint approaches between departments has been emphasised many times. The Central Policy Review Staff (CPRS), the government think-tank which started work in 1971 and was disbanded in 1983, had as one of its functions the examination of issues with implications for more than one department, but its resources were small compared with those of the departments. The CPRS, which worked for ministers as a whole under the supervision of the Prime Minister, carried out strategy reviews of government policy, prepared major studies on specific issues, and provided collective briefs for ministers. In a report published in 1975 the CPRS argued the case for a joint approach to social policies, stressing the importance of greater coordination between the various central government departments concerned with social policies.

From time to time government departments do publish joint circulars or joint White Papers, but most of their activity is concerned with single programmes or services, and the CPRS argued that 'a new and more coherent framework is required for the making and execution of social policies' (Central Policy Review Staff, 1975, p. 1). As at the local level, collaborative planning and policy-making is beset by such difficulties as different organisational and professional structures, a mismatch between planning systems and cycles, and competing definitions of social problems. Although the CPRS report resulted in the establishment of a coordinating committee of ministers, this had a short life and the initiative slowly fizzled out. The demise of the CPRS itself is a further indication of the difficulty of developing cross-departmental approaches within Whitehall. Despite this, the Blair government elected in 1997 made renewed efforts to break down departmental barriers, setting up a Social Exclusion Unit in the Cabinet Office to coordinate the contribution of different departments to tackling social exclusion, and emphasising the need to develop 'joined up solutions' to complex policy problems. Also, as we note in the next chapter, the Department of Health itself was reorganised by the Blair government to achieve closer integration of public health, NHS and social care responsibilities. The other significant change made by the government was to replace PESC with the Comprehensive Spending Review. Like PESC, the CSR centred on bilateral discussions between departments and the Treasury with negotiations between Ministers and the Chief Secretary to the Treasury following detailed discussions between officials. This process culminated in a report to the relevant Cabinet Committee and decisions on public spending covering a three-year period. As we noted in earlier chapters, unlike PESC the CSR sought to link expenditure plans with performance targets, and it also attempted to focus on existing budgets and not simply the margin for growth.

Outside interests

So far we have discussed the black box of decision-making itself and have focused on the institutions of government and the relationship between them. It is now necessary to examine inputs into the system from outside interests, in particular from pressure groups. In examining this issue, Richardson and Jordan suggest that the central policy-making machinery is divided into sub-systems organised around central departments. They designate these sub-systems as 'policy communities' (Richardson and Jordan, 1979, p. 44) and point to the close relationships which exist in these communities between departments and pressure groups. Indeed, the relationships may be so close that shared priorities develop between the inside and outside interests, amounting to 'clientelism' (Richardson and Jordan, 1979, p. 55). The boundaries between groups and government thereby become indistinct, with in some cases a high degree of interpenetration taking place.

The significant place occupied by pressure groups in the British political system exemplifies the growth of what Beer has called 'the collectivist theory of representation' (Beer, 1969, p. 70). This legitimises a much greater role for groups than earlier theories of representation. As Beer notes, as government sought to manage the economy it was led to bargain with organised groups of producers, in particular worker and employer associations. Governments of both parties sought the consent and cooperation of these associations, and needed their advice, acquiescence and approval. Similarly, the evolution of the welfare state provoked action by organised groups of consumers of services, such as tenants, parents and patients. The desire by governments to retain office led them to consult and bargain with these consumer groups, in an attempt to win support and votes.

Relationships between groups and governments vary, but it is the producer groups which tend to have the closest contacts and the greatest degree of influence. The extent to which some of these groups have been incorporated into the political system was illustrated by moves towards tripartism in the 1960s and 1970s, that is the three-sided talks between government, employers' organisations and trade unions which occupied a central place in the development of economic policy at that time. Likewise, a close relationship exists between the British Medical Association (BMA) and the DH. As Beer points out, producer groups and governments are brought together by the desire of groups to influence the authoritative allocation of values, and by the need of government departments for the information which groups are able to offer, the cooperation they provide in the implementation of policy, and the importance which group endorsement of policy brings.

Consumer groups tend to have somewhat less influence, partly because their cooperation is usually not as significant for policy-makers. It is mainly information and expertise they have to offer, and consumer groups have to operate through influence rather than through the use of sanctions. Traditionally, the consumers of services have been less well-organised than the producers. However, a variety of consumer groups are active in the central policy-making system, including generalist organisations like the National Council of Voluntary Organisations, and specialist associations such as Shelter, representing homeless people, Age Concern, campaigning on behalf of elderly people, and MIND, concerned with mental health. Many of these organisations are consulted on a regular basis by government, and indeed public money is spent supporting their activities. These groups also participate in the extensive network of advisory bodies which assist government departments in the development of their policies. It is important to add, though, that while some groups have close connections and good relationships with government, others have to attempt to exert pressure from a distance. Not all organisations are as well integrated into the decision-making system as the BMA, and attempts to influence policy indirectly through Parliament and the mass media are still an important part of pressure group behaviour.

Pluralism or corporatism?

The growth of pressure groups has been paralleled by work which has attempted to redefine democracy in a way which accommodates the part played by groups in the political system. Beer's (1969) analysis of the collectivist theory of representation was one of the first efforts in this direction, and Dahl's (1961) elaboration of pluralist theory was another. Pluralist theory argues that power in western industrialised societies is widely distributed among different groups. No group is without power to influence decision-making, and equally no group is dominant. Any group can ensure that its political preferences are adopted if it is sufficiently determined. The pluralist explanation of this is that the sources of power – like money, information, expertise and so on – are distributed non-cumulatively and no one source is dominant. Essentially, then, in a pluralist political system power is fragmented and diffused, and the basic picture presented by the pluralists is of a political marketplace where what a group achieves depends on its resources and its 'decibel rating'.

The importance of pluralist theory is demonstrated by the fact that. implicitly if not always explicitly, its assumptions and arguments now dominate much writing and research on politics and government in Britain. An example is Richardson and Jordan's analysis (1979) of post-parliamentary democracy, a study very much in the pluralist tradition. Yet, despite its influence, pluralism has come under increasing challenge in recent years from writers who have questioned whether the British political system is as open to group influence as the pluralists maintain. In particular, it has been suggested that pluralism has given way to a system of corporatism in which some groups are much stronger than others and are in a good position to influence the decisions of government agencies.

The political history of corporatism in Britain has been outlined most fully by Middlemas (1979). Middlemas argues that a process of corporate bias originated in British politics in the period 1916 to 1926 when trade unions and employer associations were brought into a close relationship with government for the first time. As a consequence, these groups came to share government power, and changed from mere interest groups to become part of the extended state. Effectively, argues Middlemas, unions and employers' groups became 'governing institutions' (Middlemas, 1979, p. 372) so closely were they incorporated into the governmental system. By incorporation, Middlemas means the inclusion of major pressure groups into the governing process and not their subordination to that process. The effect of incorporation is to maintain harmony and avoid conflict by allowing these groups to share power.

Middlemas' thesis finds echoes in Cawson's (1982) discussion of corporatism and welfare. Cawson argues that 'The pressure-group world is not fluid and competitive, but hierarchical, stratified and inegalitarian' (Cawson, 1982, p. 37). He maintains that groups are not all of the same kind, and that organisations such as the BMA are well-placed to bargain for favourable policy outcomes by virtue of their strategic location in society. According to this argument, corporatism is not confined to the field of economic policy-making but extends into the sphere of social policy. Indeed, for Cawson, the NHS provides one of the best examples of corporatist policy-making because government intervention in the provision of health services has necessitated close cooperation between the medical profession as the key producer group and government agencies. While some writers argue that corporatism has replaced pluralism, in Cawson's analysis corporatist policy-making coexists with pluralist or competitive policy-making. In the latter, consumer groups like MIND and Age Concern bargain with government agencies but lack the leverage available to producer groups.

In making these points, the dynamic nature of policy-making and power relationships must be acknowledged. As an example, the influence of trade unions and employer associations reached a peak in the 1970s and thereafter declined, particularly in the case of trade unions, as the Thatcher government departed from the corporatist tendencies of previous administrations and reasserted the role of government itself in policy-making. There were parallel developments in the field of health policy where again the Thatcher government unsettled established relationships between the DH and organisations like the BMA and implemented reforms such as the new contract for GPs and the internal market in the face of opposition from key producer groups (Lee-Potter, 1997). These developments marked a break with the post war consensus that had bound together the Conservative and Labour parties in many areas of public policy and reflected the commitment of the Thatcher government to tackling the sclerosis that it diagnosed had invaded the body politic. As David Owen has commented on the handling of the dispute over private practice in the NHS in the 1970s:

> we were in the last throes of the corporatist state. Leaders of the trade unions and the BMA expected to bargain directly with Ministers. It was the era of beer and sandwiches at No. 10 which ended with the Winter of Discontent in 1979 and with the defeat of the Labour Government. (Owen, 1991, p. 233)

In keeping with the Thatcher government's diagnosis, a series of reforms were introduced to the civil service involving significant reductions in the number of civil servants and the application of the new public management to the machinery of government. Among other things, this resulted in the establishment of over 120 executive agencies to take responsibility for the management of some public services at arm's length from government departments. Four executive agencies were set up under the Department of Health, namely the Medical Devices Agency, the Medicines Control Agency, the NHS Pensions Agency and the NHS Estates Agency, while the NHS Executive was created within the Department to oversee the management of the NHS. The common theme in all of these changes was the challenge thrown down to established interests whether in the executive arm of government or in its associated pressure groups. This did not bring an end to bargaining and negotiation in the health policy community but it did tip the balance back to politicians.

The process of reform did not end with the election of the Blair government in 1997. Indeed, with its commitment to the devolution of power within the United Kingdom, including the setting up of a Scottish Parliament and a Welsh Assembly, new Labour's policies were even more radical than those of its Conservative predecessors. Not least, they raised questions about the future of the United Kingdom as a unitary state and held out the prospect, as we noted in the Chapter 3, of increasing divergence in the organisation of the NHS and the development of health policy. The priority attached to devolution at a time when the European Union's influence on policy-making in Britain was increasing also implied a reduction in the role of the institutions of government in Whitehall and Westminster. This was under-lined by the establishment of regional development agencies in England and plans for elected mayors in major cities like London. With power moving up to Brussels in what became seen as an embryonic federal European state, and down to the territories and regions of the United Kingdom, the preeminence of central government appeared to be ending.

Within central government, recent research into the 'core executive' (Smith, 1999) has challenged both conventional accounts of the Westminster model and interpretations in the pluralist and corporatist traditions. As an example, Smith contends that arguments over whether Britain has a system of Prime Ministerial or Cabinet government are largely irrelevant when even powerful actors are dependent on others to achieve their goals. He also emphasises the extent of fragmentation at the centre and the difficulty of coordinating the work of different actors and institutions. Smith goes further in arguing that politicians and civil servants are themselves constrained by the structure and context in which they operate, a theme we return to in Chapter 9. The main point in his analysis of relevance to this chapter is the interdependency of the policy communities and networks in and around Whitehall and the shifting pattern of power and influence.

Conclusion

It was stated earlier that it is possible to describe the organisation of the British political system in simple terms. It is more difficult to locate precisely the key points of power and decision-making within the system. In Easton's terminology, the conversion process involves a complex range of actors and institutions, and the boundaries of the process, as we saw in the discussion of pressure groups, are by no means clear cut. So what conclusions can be drawn about the system?

In general terms, the main centres of decision-making are to be found in Whitehall rather than Westminster. Although Parliament retains formal, and in a few cases effective, powers over legislation, expenditure and adminis-tration, in Bagehot's language it is more of a dignified than an efficient element of the constitution. The efficient elements are government depart-ments, the Cabinet and the Prime Minister, with an increasingly important part being played by outside interests. Within departments power is shared between ministers and civil servants, the exact balance depending to a considerable extent on the strength and personality of the minister. It is naive to assume that civil servants exercise no influence, and it is equally erroneous to argue that they have absolute control. Much depends on the weight of the departmental view on issues, the quality of the advice rendered by political advisers, and the commitment of the minister to a particular course of action.

Civil service influence extends beyond departments into the Cabinet system. The network of official committees which support Cabinet committees is the main means by which this influence is secured. Cabinet committees occupy a key place within the central decision-making system, and, through the Prime Minister's power of appointment, assist in strengthening the Prime Minister's position.

We have noted that the strength of individual departments is a feature of central government, and this bears out the argument of researchers who emphasise the role of political institutions in the policy process (March and Olsen, 1989). Yet departmentalism, although a barrier to the development of corporate approaches, facilitates the establishment of policy communities between departments and their client pressure groups. And it is in these policy communities that a great deal of the more routine and less controversial aspects of government policy are worked out.

Our discussion of the dynamics of the policy process indicates the need for caution in drawing firm conclusions about the role and influence of the institutions of government. The changes introduced by the Thatcher government and those initiated by the Blair government have affected the machinery of government and relationships with outside interests. The impact of these changes will continue to be felt as policies on devolution are implemented and as the role of the European Union increases.

The emphasis in this chapter on the power of a small group of actors at the core of central government will then need to be reassessed. In the future, it seems likely that power will be dispersed more widely, although in the case of the NHS in England it remains to be seen whether the rhetoric of devolution outweighs the tendency to recentralise power in Whitehall. Only through the unravelling of the dialectic of the third way will this tension be resolved.

What are the implications of this discussion for the student of health policy? It should be clear that the starting point for gaining an understanding of the dynamics of health policy-making is to focus on the operation of the DH. An analysis of the workings of the Department, including its relationships with outside interests and its connections with other parts of Whitehall and Westminster, would seem to offer valuable insights into how health policies are made within central government. In turn, this analysis will form the basis of a discussion of the micro politics of health policy within the NHS.

6

Making and Changing Health Policy

The aim of this chapter is to examine the policy-making process in the Department of Health. The chapter begins by describing the structure of the Department and the way in which this has evolved. This leads into a discussion of the health policy community and the influence of different organisations and interests in policy-making. The chapter concludes by reviewing attempts to strengthen the Department's capacity for policy analysis.

The Department of Health

Originally established as the Ministry of Health in 1919, the work of the Department of Health has evolved as a result of changes to the machinery of government and the structure of the NHS. The Ministry was merged with the Ministry of Social Security to form the Department of Health and Social Security in 1968, but 20 years later the Department was divided by Margaret Thatcher when it was perceived to be too large for any Cabinet minister to run effectively. Reforms to the civil service in the 1980s resulted in a reduction in the number of civil servants and the establishment of the NHS Executive (formerly the NHS Management Executive and Management Board) within the Department to oversee the implementation of policy and the performance of the NHS. In the 1990s, the functions and manpower review and the Banks review of the wider Department of Health strengthened the role of the NHS Executive and led to changes in the Department's structure and method of working, out of which the current organisation (see Figure 6.1) has emerged.

The Secretary of State for Health sits at the head of the Department and is a member of the Cabinet. He or she is supported by a number of ministers and currently there are two Ministers of State and two Parliamentary Under Secretaries of State. On a day-to-day basis, the work of the DH is carried out

Figure 6.1 *Structure of the Department of Heath*

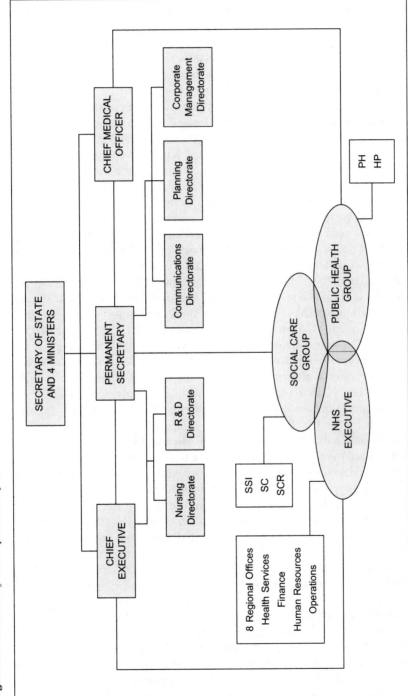

by civil servants, and in 1999 there were over 3700 civil servants working in the Department, excluding those employed in executive agencies. The most senior of these civil servants is the Permanent Secretary. He (there has not yet been a woman in this post) works closely with the Chief Medical Officer and the Chief Executive of the NHS Executive and this triumvirate forms the Department's top management team.

The Secretary of State's statutory responsibilities relate mainly to England with his counterparts in Northern Ireland, Scotland and Wales having had responsibility in the past for health and social services in those countries. The devolution of power within the United Kingdom means that this responsibility will pass to the elected parliament and assemblies being established in these countries. In Scotland, the parliament will oversee the NHS and it will have limited powers to raise revenue through taxation. These powers are not available to the Welsh assembly. It is anticipated that the NHS will be a major concern of both the Scottish parliament and the Welsh assembly with a senior politician from each body assuming a role in relation to the NHS broadly equivalent to that of the Secretary of State in England.

The Secretary of State sets the aims and objectives for the Department, decides on policy and priorities, and approves the allocation of resources to meet those objectives. Until recently the Policy Board supported the Secretary of State in relation to the objectives and performance of the NHS and its members comprised ministers, senior civil servants, and the eight regional NHS chairmen. In place of the Policy Board, the Secretary of State continues to meet regional chairmen to discuss current NHS management and policy issues. The NHS Executive is responsible for advising ministers and for formulating and ensuring implementation of policy on health care. It is chaired by the Chief Executive and comprises the eight regional directors, headquarters directors and the Chief Medical Officer. The structure of the NHS Executive is illustrated in Figure 6.2.

The NHS Executive together with the Public Health Group and the Social Care Group cover the three main business areas of the Department. The Public Health Group works closely with other government departments, the NHS, international agencies and other bodies in the development and implementation of policies to prevent disease and promote the health of the public. The Social Care Group provides a focus for work on social care issues and advises ministers on the discharge of their responsibilities in this area. The Corporate Management Directorate, the Communications Directorate and the Planning Directorate provide services for other business areas and assist in the coordination of the Department's work. The Permanent Secretary is responsible for the work of these directorates as well as the Public Health Group and the Social Care Group. He is also responsible for part of the work of both the Nursing Directorate and the Research and Development Directorate. Four executive agencies have been created under the Department as part of the move across government as a whole to place

Figure 6.2 *Structure of the NHS Executive*

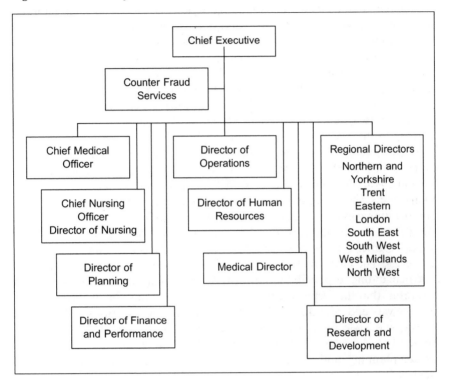

responsibility for certain functions in the hands of organisations that operate at arm's length from ministers (see Chapter 5).

As these comments indicate, the work of the Department is organised into groups, directorates and divisions. The number and function of these groups changes from time to time in line with the developing role of the Department. For most of its life, the Department of Health and Social Security was divided into four main groups in relation to its responsibilities for health and personal social services. These were the NHS Personnel Group, which dealt with pay and conditions of service, and the recruitment and training of staff; the Finance Group, which handled all issues to do with finance, including negotiations with the Treasury; the Regional Group, which maintained contact with health authorities; and the Services Development Group, which was concerned with the development of policy. In addition, the Administration and Social Security Operations Group provided help across the Department on matters such as research and computers, and the Top of the Office helped the Secretary of State to provide central leadership and advised him on choices and priorities. Each group was led by a Deputy Secretary and divisions within groups were organised around Under-Secretaries.

Just as government departments as a whole differ in that they have distinctive characteristics and working styles, so too groups, directorates and divisions within departments vary. In the case of the DHSS, the divisions and branches of the Services Development Group came to be identified to a certain extent with the client groups or services for which they had responsibility, such as the elderly or mentally ill, and acted as a lobby for those groups or services. Similarly, the Regional Group, as well as communicating government policy to health authorities, at times acted as a pressure group for the NHS within the Department. These differences meant that policy-making in the DHSS tended to be fragmented.

The fragmentation at the centre was highlighted in an enquiry into the workings of the DHSS carried out by three regional health authority chairmen in 1976. The chairmen argued that many of the tasks performed by the Department should be devolved to health authorities, and they called for a sharper management focus for the NHS within the Department. These points were reiterated in the Griffiths Inquiry into NHS Management. Sir Brian Bailey, former chairman of the South Western RHA, was a member of both enquiries. The Griffiths Report pointed out that ministers and civil servants had demanding responsibilities other than the management of the NHS, with the result that the Department's capacity for overseeing the operation of the Service was underdeveloped. The Report argued for a significant shift in the stance and style of management in the Department involving the centre setting broad strategic objectives for the NHS and ensuring through appropriate planning and monitoring mechanisms that these objectives were achieved.

It was in response to the Griffiths Report that the Secretary of State established a Supervisory Board and a Management Board within the Department to provide the focus for the NHS that Griffiths argued was lacking (see Chapter 2). There was also a realignment of roles among groups. This involved the Services Development Group continuing to carry responsibility for policy. Those divisions concerned with the management of health authorities were brought together under the NHS Management Board, and a new group was formed to take responsibility for the family practitioner services and the pharmaceutical industries. The Services Development Group was later renamed the Policy Group and in the second half of the 1980s the key distinction that emerged within the Department was that between health policy and the management of the NHS.

Following the establishment of the Department of Health in 1988, responsibility for policy came under the Health and Social Services Group (HSSG) and oversight of the NHS and implementation of policy fell to the renamed NHS Management Executive. The functions and manpower review which reported in 1993 examined the possibility of the Management Executive becoming an executive agency but ministers concluded that this option should not be pursued. This was mainly because of the intense public and political interest in the NHS and the need to ensure effective accountability in a service spending over £30 billion a year at that time. Instead, following the report of the Banks review of the organisation of the Department of Health in 1994, ministers agreed to strengthen the role of the NHS Executive (as it then became known) within the Department by placing responsibility for health policy and the NHS under the NHS Executive. This followed from the analysis undertaken by the Banks review which highlighted 'two main sets of tensions' in the separation of policy development and implementation, namely:

1. HSSG can find it difficult to identify and access the levers of influence within the NHS. . . There is a perception in parts of the HSSG that the NHS Executive is not always geared up to implement policies effectively, and that its emphasis on implementation of a few key priorities down the general management line is in conflict with the number and range of areas in which Ministers wish to be active and where they currently look to HSSG for support.
2. From the NHS Executive perspective, there is a perception of a worrying mismatch between policy aspirations and the capacity of the NHS. There is a sense that some policies are unrealistic and do not take adequate account of the practical difficulties of implementation, nor is sufficient attempt made to reconcile competing claims for resources. (Banks review, 1994, p. 12)

The Banks review also recommended that the coordination of the work of the Department should be strengthened by developing the work of the Departmental Management Board. This recommendation was also accepted and the Board (now known simply as the Departmental Board), which is chaired by the Permanent Secretary, comprises the Chief Executive of the NHS Executive, the Chief Medical Officer and their senior colleagues. Further changes followed the 1997 election when the concern of the Blair government to achieve greater integration between the NHS Executive, the Public Health Group and the Social Care Group led to the creation of three directorates, concerned with Communications, Corporate Management and Planning, to work across the whole Department. The heads of these directorates are members of the Departmental Board.

One feature of continuing importance in the DH is the strong professional contribution to policy-making. As well as the generalist administrators who make up the bulk of the Department's senior staff, there are a wide range of civil servants from professional backgrounds. These include doctors, nurses, and social workers. Writing in the 1970s, Brown noted that the tradition in the Department is one of 'multidisciplinary working in which questions are settled by agreement between the administrators and members of the appropriate professional hierarchy' (Brown, 1975, p. 58). An example from that time was policy development for elderly people which was organised around an assistant secretary working with a team consisting of a senior medical officer, a nursing officer, and a principal social work services officer (Kaye, 1977). More recently, there have been moves to establish integrated working within the Department by abolishing separate divisions in which civil servants from professional backgrounds report to their professional head. These moves were accelerated by the Banks review which came down firmly in favour of a single management hierarchy and which also advocated greater team working.

Yet at the same time as these traditional divisions have become less significant, the increasing range of responsibilities taken on by the NHS Executive and the appointment of senior NHS managers to lead the work of the NHS Executive have opened up new tensions. The Banks review noted that 'the NHS Executive faces in two directions' and added:

> As the top management of the NHS, the Executive must be 'of' the NHS, culturally close to it and credible if it is to lead and influence. That is why a distinct identity is so important. At the same time, the Executive is unequivocally a part of government, responsible for implementing the Government's policies for the NHS, holding health authorities to account on behalf of Ministers, and supporting and advising Ministers on health service matters. (*Ibid.*, p. 11)

The Janus-like character of the Department, in particular the NHS Executive, was dissected in a study of the two cultures of mandarins and managers (Day and Klein, 1997) and we shall return to explore this theme towards the end of the chapter.

The policy community

In the previous chapter we introduced Richardson and Jordan's idea of the policy community to denote the extent to which policies are increasingly developed in consultation between government departments and the organisations concerned with their work. Consultation may take place through a variety of channels: through standing advisory committees or groups; through *ad hoc* enquiries or working groups set up to advise on particular issues; and through the more or less regular pattern of negotiation and discussion in which the DH engages with outside interests like the British Medical Association. In Richardson and Jordan's terms it may be misleading to use the word 'outside' to describe these interests. Their analysis emphasises the high degree of interpenetration which exists between pressure groups and government, and they point to the similarities which develop between departments and their client groups (Richardson and Jordan, 1979).

Valuable as this analysis is, it is necessary to recognise that not all groups are equally well-integrated into the national health policy community. Consumer groups, for example, are relatively weak and Brown, commenting on this in the 1970s, has noted that 'the machinery on the health and welfare side of the DHSS tends to be dominated by those who provide services rather than those for whom the services are intended' (Brown, 1975, p. 193). Thus, although the health policy-making system appears to be pluralistic in that a wide range of interests is involved in the policy process, in practice this system may be skewed in favour of the well-organised groups who have a key role in the provision of health services. Producer groups are well able to promote and defend their interests, and this puts the DH in the position of appeasing these groups and resolving conflicts whenever they occur. As we argued in Chapter 5, corporatism may be a more accurate description than pluralism of a policy-making system in which producer groups are dominant.

One of the consequences of producer group dominance is that policy-making tends to be incremental, characterised by what Lindblom (1965) has termed 'partisan mutual adjustments'. Bargaining between the DH and pressure groups often results in small changes in the status quo, and this tends to be to the advantage of established interests. A great deal of the activity of the DH is not in fact concerned with policy-making as such. Rather, it is aimed at the continuation of existing services and policies and the maintenance of good relationships with key interests. Policy-making is a comparatively rare occurrence because:

> public resources for dealing with issues are relatively scarce. They are scarce in many terms – money and manpower obviously since public finance and public servants are finite quantities, but scarce also in terms of legislative time, media coverage, political will, public concern . . . Political systems can only cope with a limited number of issues at once and these are always subject to displacement by new emerging issues of greater appeal and force. (Solesbury, 1976, p. 382)

In Easton's terms, then, gatekeepers reduce the number of demands competing for the time and attention of policy-makers, and non-decision-making operates to rule some issues off the agenda and to prevent others from progressing to the point of action within the political system. Becker (1967) has examined the means by which situations come to be defined as social problems, and he notes that problems have two components: a set of objective conditions, and the definition of those conditions as problematic. It is not sufficient for the conditions alone to exist, because however serious the conditions are, they will not receive consideration unless an individual or group draws attention to them. What is important is the subjective definition of those conditions as problematic.

An example will help to illustrate this. In the NHS, there has always existed a geographical imbalance in the allocation of resources, yet it was not until a number of civil servants and researchers drew attention to this imbalance that the situation came to be identified as a problem. A second example would be the relative neglect of hospital services for the mentally ill, people with learning difficulties and the elderly. The condition of these services came to be defined as a problem in the late 1960s following enquiries at a number of hospitals, extensive media coverage, pressure group activity and ministerial concern. It could be argued that objectively conditions in these hospitals were worse a decade earlier when, particularly in mental illness hospitals, overcrowding was greater, and staffing levels lower. Here again, it was the definition of the conditions as problematic that placed the issue on the political agenda.

In a similar vein, Solesbury argues that issues must pass three tests if they are to survive. They have to command attention, claim legitimacy, and invoke action. It helps issues to command attention if they have particularity. Part of the reason why long-stay hospitals commanded attention is that they were associated with specific institutions, such as Ely Hospital, which came to symbolise the problems in this area of the NHS. Crises and scandals of this kind are often important in forcing an issue on to the agenda. Issues also need to become generalised. This helps them to claim legitimacy and attract the attention of existing political forces. Thus, a particular interest in Ely Hospital came to be generalised into a wider concern with social justice and humanitarian values, thereby bringing it within the dominant political culture and drawing the interest of established political groupings. An issue which has commanded attention and acquired legitimacy has passed two tests, but it must also invoke action. At this stage, issues run the risk of suppression, transformation into other issues, and token or partial responses.

Also relevant here is the notion of symbolic policy-making, a term developed by Edelman (1971) to refer to action intended to demonstrate that something is being done about a problem, rather than action which is a real attempt to tackle the problem. While there are undoubtedly difficulties in identifying the intentions and motives of policy-makers, in a number of areas it would appear that policies have significant symbolic elements. For instance, successive attempts to give greater priority to groups such as the mentally ill, people with learning difficulties and the elderly have not been accompanied by the allocation of significant amounts of additional resources, nor have ways been found of achieving a major shift towards these groups within existing budgets. In cases such as this, policies may act primarily as a way of maintaining political support and stability. Support is maintained in that the messages contained in policy statements may satisfy key political groups, thereby forestalling demands for more fundamental reforms. It is in this sense that words may succeed and policies fail (Edelman, 1977).

To return to Solesbury's discussion, what is valuable in his analysis is the examination of the hurdles which issues have to jump before they invoke action, the changing nature of issues, and the importance of subjective definitions in issue emergence. As Solesbury notes, it is too simple to see the policy process as linear or sequential as is implicit in the systems model discussed in Chapter 4. It is more complex:

moving forward on many fronts, sometimes concerned with legitimacy, sometimes with attention, the issue itself changing its definition as it goes forward, linking with other issues, splitting from yet others, sometimes becoming totally transformed into a new issue altogether. The agenda metaphor provides the best indication of the nature of the process. (Solesbury, 1976, p. 396)

The agenda metaphor is developed at much greater length by Kingdon (1995) who contends that agendas are forged through the interaction of problems, politics and participants. In some cases, issues emerge onto the agenda because conditions are defined as problems. In other cases, changes in the political environment help shape the agenda. In yet other cases, participants may be important either in raising the salience of an issue or in framing the alternatives. These different streams come together into a 'policy primeval soup' (p. 200). The outcome is affected by the activities of policy entrepreneurs and by the opportunities offered by policy windows. There is a much greater chance of policy development occurring when problems, politics and participants are linked together, although this is not essential. Kingdon's framework allows for both random responses and predictable patterns of development, his key point being the complexity and messiness of the policy process and the lack of any simple explanations.

There are similarities between Solesbury's approach and that of Hall, Land, Parker and Webb. Working within Easton's systems framework, Hall and her colleagues advance a number of propositions about what determines the priority of a social policy issue. Like Solesbury, they argue that an issue needs to command legitimacy, but they also suggest that the feasibility of a policy and the support it receives are important variables. Certain issue characteristics are also relevant, including their association with other issues, the development of issues into crises, and the origins of issues. In relation to the last characteristic, they suggest that 'prima facie the closer to government the point of origin the better the prospects' (Hall *et al.*, 1975, p. 500). This leads us into a more detailed consideration of the sources of inputs into the policy process.

The sources of policy inputs

Pressure groups

There are many sources of inputs into the health policy-making system, several of which have already been mentioned. First, there are the inputs which come from pressure groups. As we noted in Chapter 4, the collectivist theory of representation legitimates a much greater role for groups than earlier theories of representation, and increasing state involvement in managing the economy and in the welfare state has led governments to negotiate and consult with pressure groups. A distinction has already been made between producer groups, which are often in a strong position to bargain for what they want, and consumer groups, which are relatively weak. There are also groups that exist to pursue a particular cause, an example being Action on Smoking and Health (ASH) which campaigns for control of smoking and limitations on advertising by tobacco companies. Yet ASH has backing from a key producer group, the Royal College of Physicians (RCP), demonstrating the difficulty of making clear distinctions in the pressure group world surrounding the DH (Popham, 1981).

Both the British Medical Association (BMA) and the medical Royal Colleges expect to be consulted over the development of policy and Eckstein (1960) has shown how often it is negotiation rather than consultation which characterises the relationship between these groups and the government. Occasionally relationships become strained, as in the dispute over pay beds in the 1970s and the NHS reforms in the 1980s, but on many issues there is a partnership between the medical profession and the DH equivalent to those that exist in the educational and agricultural policy communities between the relevant departments and their client groups. The position of consumer groups within the health policy community is not as strong. (Ham, 1977). Consumer groups are heavily dependent on the advice, information and expertise they have to offer, and cannot threaten sanctions in the same way as producer groups. Because their cooperation is usually not vital to the implementation of policy, consumer groups are dependent on the quality of their arguments and the willingness of ministers and civil servants to listen to what they have to say. In most cases, too, they have to supplement the pressure they exert on the DH by operating through Parliament and mass media.

The pressure exerted by producer and consumer groups may be welcomed by Ministers as it may help them in their negotiations with Cabinet colleagues. This explains why some groups receive financial support from government. In her diaries, Barbara Castle indicates that in her time as Secretary of State she encouraged the National Association of Health Authorities 'to become a pressure group for the NHS' (Castle, 1980, p. 459). She also notes that during the dispute with the medical profession over pay beds, Ministers stimulated trade union activity to persuade the BMA to accept limitations on private practice within the NHS. Similarly, civil servants with responsibility for policy for particular client groups, such as the mentally ill, may welcome pressure from organisations like MIND as it may strengthen their hand in the competition for resources and priority within the DH. It is important to remember, then, that demands may not always arise autonomously in the community, and that pressure may some-times be welcomed and encouraged by policy-makers.

Pressure groups make demands on a wide range of issues. These demands may require a change in legislation, a decision by a civil servant, or intervention by ministers. Occasionally, they may involve the Prime Minister, the Cabinet and other government departments. The effectiveness of groups in pressing their demands will depend on a variety of factors: the information they possess, their contacts with policy-makers, their expertise, and the sanctions they have at their disposal. In responding to groups, policy-makers will weigh their own preferences against those of the groups. They will also be alert to the need to secure the compliance of key interests, and to the electoral consequences of their decisions. The exact process of decision-making is difficult to define because, as Solesbury notes, it is at this stage that 'one passes into the relatively closed world of the executive departments of state, and to a lesser extent interdepartmental and Cabinet committees, where the consideration given to issues and possible responses by politicians and officials is largely shielded from the public gaze' (Solesbury, 1976, p. 392).

Despite the difficulties of penetrating the intricacies of decision-making within central government, it can be suggested that the national health policy community is itself fragmented into a series of sub-communities concerned with specific aspects of policy. These sub-communities are organised around issues such as alcoholism, abortion, policies for elderly people, and so on. As we noted earlier in the chapter. different parts of the DH have different characteristics, and in one sense the Department itself can be seen to be made up of pressure groups for particular functions, services and client groups. Outside pressure groups are drawn towards those parts of the Department which have responsibility for the policies which the groups are interested in, and sub-communities are formed from the relationships which develop between these groups and civil servants.

In an attempt to analyse these relationships, one study of policies for elderly people suggested that these policies were worked out in an 'iron triangle' rather than an 'issue network' (Haywood and Hunter, 1982). The terminology is that of Heclo, who has argued, in the context of American federal government, that decision-making has moved away from iron triangles involving a small number of participants in a stable relationship with one another, to issue networks comprising a large number of participants in a less stable relationship (Heclo, 1978). In their examination of policies for elderly people, Haywood and Hunter found that the process was well-represented by the iron triangle image. The key participants were Departmental officials, leading medical and nursing professionals, and two key producer groups: the Royal College of Nursing and the British Geriatrics Society. Although the consultative process was later widened to encompass a range of other groups the crucial decisions at an early stage were arrived at by this small set of interests. However, Haywood and Hunter warn that on other issues, such as pay beds and health service organisation, issue networks may be a more appropriate metaphor.

Parliament and the mass media

Not all the demands made by pressure groups will invoke action and groups which are unsuccessful in their attempt to influence civil servants and ministers will often turn their attention to Parliament and the mass media. Here, then, are two further sources of inputs into the health policy-making system, and not just as vehicles for pressure group demands, but as originators of demands themselves. In recent years the mass media have played an active role in publicising the low standards of care that exist in the 'Cinderella' services. Ever since the appearance of newspaper reports of cruelty to patients in the mid-1960s, the media have been prominent in the campaign to improve conditions for groups such as the mentally ill and people with learning difficulties. Television programmes on Rampton Special Hospital and on hospital services for disabled people have maintained public attention on this area of the NHS to the extent that journalists and television producers have taken on the appearance of pressure groups for under-privileged sections of the community.

The role of Parliament was discussed in Chapter 5. It will be recalled that parliamentary inputs to health policy-making take the form of MPs' questions, issues raised during debates, private members' bills, and reports from select committees. Some indication of the volume of Parliamentary business is given by the fact that in 1998–99 there were over 6000 parliamentary questions, and approximately 34 000 letters were received, of which 16 000 were from MPs. The significance of these mechanisms is that they are important centralising influences in the NHS. The accountability to Parliament of the Secretary of State for Health requires a considerable amount of detailed information about health services to be fed up to the DH by NHS bodies. Equally, demands raised in Parliament may have an influence on health policy-making and on the local operation of health services. An obvious example would be legislation resulting from a private members' bill, such as the Abortion Act. On other occasions, government-sponsored legislation may be amended in the course of its passage through Parliament. The section of the NHS Reorganisation Act 1973 relating to Community Health Councils was a case in point. Not having strong views of its own, the government was prepared to listen to and take account of suggestions made by MPs and peers.

Increasingly, too, the House of Commons Health Committee and the Public Accounts Committee have provided an informed contribution to the policy-making process. As we noted in Chapter 5, the Health Committee has produced a variety of reports on health service issues. The MPs on the Committee are supported by a small group of full-time staff and specialist advisers appointed for particular inquiries. Select committees tend to have greatest impact when they present unanimous reports and in this respect the choice of topics for investigation is important. In its work, the Health

Committee has chosen to examine issues which in the main are non-controversial in party political terms and this has helped the Committee to present a united front. The work of select committees rarely leads directly to changes in policy but they have strengthened parliamentary scrutiny of government departments and over a period of time their reports may influence the work of these departments. As a study of the former Social Services Committee noted of the Committee's investigations into the expenditure plans of the DHSS, 'their cumulative effect has been to make the Department improve its own procedures for reviewing and coordinating its policies, as well as preparing and presenting expenditure plans' (Nixon and Nixon, 1983, p. 352).

The Public Accounts Committee scrutinises government spending as a whole and in recent years has examined a number of different aspects of the NHS, including the use of joint finance, the disposal of surplus land and buildings, the profits of the drug industry, and financial control and accountability. A report published in 1981 which criticised the lack of control exercised by the DHSS over the management of the NHS was one of the factors which led to the introduction of the review process in the NHS in 1982. Nairne has referred to the Public Accounts Committee as 'the premier committee of Parliament' (Nairne, 1983, p. 254) and has described the pressures placed by the Committee on the Permanent Secretary in his capacity as Accounting Officer. This has been confirmed by Stowe, another former Permanent Secretary, who has described his relationship with the Committee as:

> a powerful reinforcement of the Permanent Secretary's authority and an even more powerful incentive for him or her to take very seriously his obligation to ensure that publicly financed programmes of expenditure are managed with integrity and efficiency. (Stowe, 1989, p. 57)

As Stowe notes, the power of the Committee derives in large part from the support it receives from the Comptroller and Auditor General and the National Audit Office. Staff of the National Audit Office have continuous access to the Department's files and the reports they produce provide the basis for investigations by the Committee. Stowe has observed that the relationship between the Department and the National Audit Office 'is anything but cosy: a mutual admiration society it is not. Some of the most fractious dogfights in my experience occurred in this quarter' (*ibid.*). Certainly, ministers and civil servants have faced some rigorous questioning from the MPs on the Committee and the Committee has had a demonstrable impact on such issues as premature retirement among NHS staff, manpower control within the Service and policy on maternity services. A study of Parliament and health policy in the period 1970–75 noted, 'it is very difficult on the gathered evidence to sustain the argument that Parliament had any real influence upon health policy-making in the reviewed period' (Ingle and

Tether, 1981, p. 148). The work of the Public Accounts Committee and the Health Committee requires this judgement to be modified as quite clearly these Committees have exerted some influence in recent years.

NHS bodies

NHS bodies (the collective term for health authorities and trusts) represent a fourth source of inputs into the DH policy-making system. Indeed, as we shall discuss in Chapter 7, these bodies do not simply carry out nationally determined policies, but have important policy-making responsibilities in their own right. In many cases, policies are developed jointly by civil servants and NHS managers, an example being the performance indicators for the NHS published in 1983 which were the result of work done by staff from the Department and the Northern RHA. To carry the initiative forward, a joint NHS/ DHSS Group was set up to advise on the future development, publication and use of performance indicators. In addition, an administrator from a district health authority was seconded to the Department to oversee the initiative. There are many other examples of policy proposals developed jointly by the centre and the periphery. The DH is dependent on NHS bodies for information about the local development of services and for actually providing the services, while these bodies are dependent on the DH for the resources required to carry out their functions. This mutual dependence helps to explain why it is that national policies are often shaped and influenced by NHS bodies.

The establishment of the NHS Management Board and its successors the NHS Management Executive and the NHS Executive within the Department have served to strengthen the links between the centre and the NHS. Senior health service managers have played an important part in the work of both bodies. This was first evident in the appointment of Duncan Nichol, a regional general manager, as Chief Executive of the NHS in 1988 followed by Alan Langlands in 1994. Other staff have been seconded to work in the Department, and a number of civil servants have spent time in the NHS. These exchanges have helped in building understanding and mutual respect. Ministers as well as civil servants draw on advice from within the NHS in developing their policies and at the highest level this finds expression in regular meetings between the Secretary of State and regional chairmen. Norman Fowler, Secretary of State in the mid-1980s, explained that regional chairmen 'operate as a health cabinet as far as I am concerned' (Social Services Committee, 1984, p. 165), and this continues to be the case. Meetings with regional chairmen are a two way affair in which ministers can explain their thinking and priorities and regional chairmen can report on developments within the NHS.

A further source of advice is the NHS Confederation. This has gone through a number of guises and it exists to represent the views of NHS bodies to government. Membership of the NHS Confederation comprises a high proportion of health authorities and NHS trusts and the staff and officers of the Confederation meet regularly with Ministers and civil servants to discuss issues in health policy and the NHS. As we noted earlier, Barbara Castle encouraged the forerunner of the NHS Confederation to be a pressure group for the NHS and it publishes a number of reports on current developments and lobbies actively to ensure that the opinions of NHS bodies are heard. Alongside the Confederation, the views of primary care groups are articulated by organisations like the NHS Primary Care Group Alliance and these organisations and their predecessors have been particularly vocal on behalf of GPs and other staff working in primary care.

The consultative machinery

A fifth input to policy-making comes from the consultative machinery attached to the DH. This machinery is made up of standing advisory groups, like the Standing Medical Advisory Committee, and *ad hoc* working groups and inquiries. The latter include royal commissions which tend to be used relatively sparingly and inquiries which are set up much more frequently to advise on specific topics. In recent times these inquiries have examined issues such as inequalities in health, NHS management and community care. The reports that emanate from royal commissions and inquiries provide an almost continuous flow of demands into the DH. As with other inputs into the political system, demands coming from these sources have to compete for the time and attention of policy-makers. Some may be rejected out of hand, others may be subjected to further discussions, while others may be adopted immediately.

It is not unusual for the DH response to advisory bodies to be ambiguous or unclear. This applied to the Court Report on Child Health Services, where the Department accepted the report's demand for an integrated child health service, but rejected many of the more specific proposals put forward. Similarly, the government agreed in principle with the model of care for people with learning difficulties set out in the Report of the Jay Committee, but called for further consideration of various aspects of the Report. In this case, the opposition of powerful, established interests in the nursing profession to the Jay Committee's recommendations was one of the factors the Department had to consider.

As well as advice provided by standing or *ad hoc* groups such as the Jay Committee, there are the regular rounds of formal consultation with NHS bodies and pressure groups which have already been referred to. Formal consultation typically occurs when a consultative document on a particular issue is published. The extent to which these documents are really open to influence varies: in many cases there may be little scope for groups to influence what is decided, but on some occasions a well-organised group can have a significant impact. Whether groups are able to exercise influence may depend on the stage during the consultative process that they become involved. Haywood and Hunter (1982) point out that formal consultation is often preceded by informal consultation on draft documents. In some cases informal consultation may itself be foreshadowed by discussions among a small number of key participants, as in the iron triangle which develops policies for elderly people. As a rule of thumb, the earlier a group becomes involved, the more likely it is to influence what is decided.

Ministers and civil servants

Sixth, and most important, there are 'withinputs': demands which come from ministers and civil servants within the DH. A new Secretary of State is likely to have a number of issues he or she wants to pursue while in office. Many will have been developed in Opposition, and may have been included in an election manifesto. Both Banting (1979) and Kingdon (1995) suggest that politicians are particularly important in making certain issues salient, and in defining the agenda for discussion. In the case of health policy, Webster has noted on the basis of his historical analysis of the NHS many examples of politicians influencing the agenda (Webster, 1996). Examples cited by Webster include Kenneth Robinson's involvement with the Doctors' Charter in the 1960s, Richard Crossman's emphasis on improving conditions in long-stay hospitals, and Keith Joseph's reorganisation of the NHS in the 1970s. Another area in which politicians made a difference was private health care which for many years was not a salient issue. Only in 1974, when Barbara Castle attempted to reduce the number of pay beds in NHS hospitals and limit the growth of private hospitals, did the issue become prominent. Private medicine remained a salient issue when the Conservative government elected in 1979 reversed Castle's policy and sought to encourage the growth of the private health care sector.

Having made this point, it should also be noted that ministers have to work with and through civil servants to take forward policy. In the case of pay beds referred to above, Barbara Castle notes in her diary that the permanent secretary at the time, Sir Philip Rogers had submitted a paper stating that DHSS officials 'feel they would be failing in their duty if they did not let me know how opposed they all were to the phasing of private practice out of NHS hospitals' (Castle, 1980, p. 170). Castle's account is confirmed by the memoirs of one of her junior ministers at the time:

> In the summer of 1974 Sir Philip Rogers came to see Barbara Castle and myself to discuss privately our controversial manifesto commitment to phase pay beds out of NHS hospitals. Sir Philip deployed a strong case against our taking any action. He warned us that the mood of the medical profession was very brittle and said that the considered judgement of himself, the Chief Medical Officer and all the top

officials was that, in the best interests of the NHS, we should avoid a confrontation with the doctors on this issue. Rather movingly, he insisted that if the Secretary of State, having heard him out, came to a different conclusion then that was the last that she would hear of it and everyone in the Department would carry out her policy faithfully and to the best of their abilities. . .

Sir Philip kept his promise and from then on defended our decisions and refused to let the British Medical Association get away with the attempt to present officials as not being fully behind our policy. It was a fine example of the best of the civil service tradition of serving governments irrespective of party. (Owen, 1991, p. 232)

Of course, civil servants are not a homogeneous group, and Castle herself notes that 'the department is split into two different worlds: the conventional, change-nothing world of the top Establishment; the challenging irreverent world of the press office and some of the younger officials' (Castle, 1980, p. 209). And even where conservatism does not exist, it may result more from the need to operate in an administrative system in which long-term viewpoints are important than from the personal attributes of individuals. The point remains, though, that ministerial aspirations are likely to be modified by civil service advice.

Of particular interest in this context is the role of doctors in government. As we noted at the beginning of the chapter, there is strong medical involvement in decision-making in the DH, and a former Chief Medical Officer, Sir George Godber, has observed that 'the doctor in Government has to be facing two ways: he is a Civil Servant and his Minister must be able to rely on his complete loyalty: but he is also a member of his profession, which must be able to trust him too' (Godber, 1981, p. 2). These dual loyalties create the possibility that conflicts may arise in which professional ties will emerge the stronger. Godber notes that such a possibility arose during Crossman's tenure as Secretary of State but did not reach the point where the Chief Medical Officer would have resigned. On another occasion Godber states that 'The Permanent Secretary and I once declined to accept our Civil Service increases so long as the doctors' incomes were frozen' (Godber, 1981, p. 3). Clearly, then, civil servants have their own loyalties and views, and these views have an influence on policy-making. Further evidence of this point comes from Pater's study of the creation of the NHS. Pater argues that the credit for the establishment of the NHS should be widely shared, but he contends:

There is no doubt, however, that the main credit for the emergence of a viable and, indeed, successful service must rest with two . . . officers of the ministry: Sir William Jameson, chief medical officer from 1940 to 1950, and Sir John Hawton, deputy secretary from 1947 to 1951 and permanent secretary thereafter until his retirement through ill-health in 1960. (Pater, 1981, p. 178)

In different ways both Godber and Pater, writing as former civil servants, confirm the thesis to be found in the memoirs of ex-ministers, that the civil service has a significant impact on the development of policy.

This need not mean that civil servants pursue their own policy preferences against the wishes of ministers. Nairne acknowledges that civil servants are influential, but maintains that the influence of officials derives from a partnership between ministers and civil servants rather than conflict. In Nairne's view, it is misleading to analyse what happens within government departments in terms of whether ministers or civil servants have power because the reality is that senior civil servants have to share responsibility with ministers for formulating policy (Nairne, 1983; Young and Sloman, 1982). One of the implications of partnership is that there will be occasions when civil servants themselves put forward initiatives to ministers. These initiatives will in many cases stem from a review of existing policies and will take the form of suggestions for improving those policies. *The Crossman Diaries* provide an example, this time in relation to resource allocation. On 15 July 1969 Crossman records:

> after lunch I had a fascinating seminar on hospital revenue. Dick Bourton [who was then Under Secretary for Finance and Accountant General at the DHSS] had put up an absolutely first-rate paper on how the hospital budgets are fixed. A terrific lot of money goes into the teaching hospitals, most of which are in the South, and this shifts the balance even more in favour of the London hospitals, with great unfairness to Sheffield, Newcastle and Birmingham, which are really greatly under-financed. The trouble is that the historical costs are gigantic, with about 85 per cent already committed, and I should be very surprised if we can get even 5 per cent reallocated in any one year, especially a year of appalling constrictions such as this. Nevertheless, it was a really good discussion. (Crossman, 1977, p. 569)

Another example of a policy where internal factors were important is the Hospital Plan of 1962. This was prepared by hospital boards and committees under the guidance of the Ministry of Health. Although outside interests were pressing for increased spending on hospital buildings, the origins of the Plan owed a great deal to the Minister at the time, Enoch Powell, his Permanent Secretary, Sir Bruce Fraser, and the Deputy Chief Medical Officer, Sir George Godber. These three men effectively transformed a vague idea about the need for an expanded building programme into a detailed plan. The coincidence of interests between the Minister and senior civil servants helped to account for the promotion of this development in policy. What is also relevant is that here was a policy which had to be agreed between the Ministry of Health and the Treasury because of the major expenditure implications. Fraser, who had previously been a Treasury official, played a key role in these negotiations (Allen, 1979).

A third example of the influence of civil servants over policy-making is provided by Klein (1983) in his analysis of the establishment of the NHS. Drawing on official records, Klein demonstrates how in 1939 civil servants identified the main options available for the future organisation of hospital services unprompted by politicians. Although ministers later played a significant role in the creation of the NHS, in the initial stages it was civil servants who were most influential. This is supported not only by Pater's study (see above) but also by Webster's official history of the NHS (Webster, 1988 and 1996), although Webster emphasises that policy was shaped by politicians as well as pressure groups and officials.

An examination of the processes of policy-making and the various inputs into those processes creates, rightly, the impression of a complex policy system in which those responsible for making policy are subject to numerous competing demands. In the last part of the discussion we have drawn attention to examples of policy change, but it is worth remembering the earlier point that change is the exception rather than the rule. A considerable part of the activity of the DH is devoted to the maintenance of existing policies and to the continuation of established routines. Although change is possible, it is difficult to achieve because of the operation of demand regulation mechanisms which limit the number of issues on the agenda at any one time. And even in relation to these issues, incremental changes to the status quo are more probable than major shifts in direction. This has been clearly demonstrated in a study of government policy on smoking, where it has been argued that decisions were:

> the outcome of a process in which groups have played a major role . . . For many years tobacco interests had no difficulty in keeping the subject off the political agenda; their power took a non-decision-making form. Forerunners of ASH, such as the National Society of Non-Smokers, encountered indifferent or hostile attitudes from Government. . . . It took the prestige and evidence of elite medical groups, such as the BMA and the RCP, to break the agenda barrier. Even then Government response was cautious because possible adverse electoral consequences were feared by some Ministers if too rigorous a policy of discouragement was pursued. (Popham, 1981, p. 345)

Industrial and commercial interests

The example of smoking draws attention to the role of industrial and commercial interests in the health policy community. At least three sets of interests need to be considered. First, there are those interests which are involved in the provision of private-sector health care services. Private providers include both the provident associations such as BUPA and the private hospital groups. A second set of interests consists of those companies supplying goods, equipment and services to the NHS. These include firms seeking to obtain contracts for the provision of services such as catering and laundry; the manufacturers of medical equipment and supplies; and the drugs industry. The last of these is particularly significant in view of the fact that the drugs bill makes up over 10 per cent of total NHS expenditure. Although the industry contributes significantly to employment and exports there has been concern at the level of profits earned. Regulation occurs through the Pharmaceutical Price Regulation Scheme, a voluntary scheme in which the DH attempts to control prices and profits in the industry. Despite this, the House of Commons Public Accounts Committee has criticised the Department for not doing more to limit profits, and in response to the Committee's criticism action was taken to introduce tighter controls.

A third set of interests is represented by companies producing goods which may be harmful to health. The tobacco, alcohol and food-processing industries are included in this category. The influence of the food industry has been examined by Cannon (1984) in an analysis of the response to a report on nutritional guidelines for health produced by the National Advisory Committee on Nutrition Education. The report, which recommended reduced consumption of sugar, salt and fat, and increased intake of dietary fibre, was opposed by the food industry. Cannon demonstrates how government is divided between ministers principally concerned with issues of public health and ministers concerned with economic and employment issues. Changes in eating habits which pose a threat to jobs and profits in the food industry are likely to be resisted not only by the industry but also by politicians and civil servants involved in spheres such as trade, industry and agriculture.

Similar issues arise in the case of tobacco. In a thorough analysis, Taylor (1984) has investigated why governments have done so little to regulate the tobacco industry in the face of overwhelming medical evidence about the harmful effects of cigarette smoking. As Taylor points out, the tobacco industry is composed of a relatively small number of large and wealthy multinational companies whose power derives not so much from their activity as pressure groups – although this may be important – as from their position in the economy. The industry is significant as an employer and as a source of tax revenues, and while DH ministers may want to control the industry on health grounds, ministers in the Treasury are inclined to oppose regulations on economic grounds. As Taylor comments:

> In principle, as guardians of the public health, governments ought to be the tobacco industry's fierce opponents, but in practice they are often its firm ally. Cigarettes provide governments with one of their biggest and most reliable sources of revenue; they create tens of thousands of jobs in hard economic times; they present a healthy surplus on the balance of payments; they help development in Third World Countries where tobacco is grown. In purely economic terms, the political benefits of cigarettes far outweigh their social cost. (Taylor, 1984, p. xix)

For this reason, the introduction of health warnings and changes in advertising practices have been brought about largely on a voluntary basis.

The development of alcohol policy exhibits many of the same features. As Baggott (1986) has shown, successive governments have been slow to develop policies to control the misuse of alcohol. He attributes this to the power of commercial interests, the relatively weak and diffuse nature of the groups pressing for reforms, the hostility of voters and public opinion, and opposition by government departments who stand to benefit from a strong alcohol industry. The examples of food, tobacco and alcohol lend support to Lindblom's (1977) thesis about the power of business corporations in contemporary politics, and it is this power which helps to account for the predominance of policy maintenance and incremental changes.

The role of ideas

The policy process is not, however, entirely a matter of responding to political demands. An increasingly important part of the process is the attempt to examine a wider range of options, and to subject existing policies to a more thorough analysis. There are two aspects to this. First, there is the contribution which academics and researchers make to policy-making. As Banting (1979) points out echoing the work of Heclo (1974), policy-making is both an intellectual activity and a political process. Thus, as well as examining the impact of pressure groups, politicians and other key actors, it is necessary to look at the role of ideas and information in shaping policy. One of the areas of health policy where ideas have had an influence is the organisation of the NHS. The administrative structure introduced in 1974, for example, derived from theories of management and organisational behaviour developed by organisational sociologists at Brunel University and management consultants at McKinsey & Co. Ltd.

A second area where ideas had an impact was in the thinking behind the Black Report on inequalities and health. The Report was the outcome of the deliberations of an expert working group whose most influential member was Peter Townsend, then Professor of Sociology at Essex University. Townsend's previous work on the nature and causes of poverty and deprivation clearly contributed much to the analysis and recommendations of the Black Report. What is interesting is that Townsend's work is very much in the LSE social administration tradition which Banting found had had a strong influence in other areas of social policy (Banting, 1979). It is apparent, though, that this tradition, of which Brian Abel-Smith, a political adviser to a number of Secretaries of State, was also a part, has had a greater impact on Labour governments than Conservative governments. Political advisors are often a channel through which ideas find their way into the policy process as studies of the history of the NHS have noted (Webster 1996).

A third example of ideas contributing to policy formulation was the influence of the American economist, Alain Enthoven, during the Ministerial Review of the NHS. In 1985 Enthoven published a monograph entitled *Reflections on the Management of the NHS* (Enthoven, 1985) in which he proposed the establishment of an internal market in health care. These ideas were picked up and developed during the Ministerial Review and had an appreciable influence on the White Paper, *Working for Patients*. The government's debt to Enthoven was acknowledged by the Secretary of State at the time of the Review, Kenneth Clarke. In an interview about the NHS reforms, Clarke referred to Enthoven's advocacy of internal markets, arguing 'I liked it because it tried to inject into a state owned system some of the qualities of competition, choice, and measurement of quality that you get in a well run private enterprise' (Roberts, 1990, p. 1385).

Academics and researchers apart, there have been a number of attempts within the DH to develop a more 'rational' approach to policy-making. In varying degrees, these mechanisms have sought to introduce a greater measure of analysis into the policy process, and in the penultimate part of this chapter we review the recent experience of policy analysis in the Department.

Policy analysis in the Department

In 1970 the Conservative government published a White Paper setting out proposals for increasing the policy analysis capabilities of central government. Among the innovations to follow from the White Paper were the Central Policy Review Staff, established to provide advice on government policies independent of that offered by existing departments, and Programme Analysis and Review, involving an in-depth study of specific topics within departments. Both innovations affected central government as a whole. At around the same time, and reflecting the spirit of the White Paper, a number of specific developments were taking place in the DHSS designed to improve the Department's capacity for reviewing its policies and priorities. Two developments in particular merit consideration: the introduction of programme budgeting, and the creation of a planning system for the Department.

Programme budgeting was developed in the United States in the 1960s, and its use was first considered within the DHSS in 1971. Its aim is to provide a framework for linking policies with resources, thus enabling priority decisions to be made within an overall strategy. The programme budget originally developed within the DHSS covered both health and personal social services and grouped these services under seven main headings: primary care; general and acute hospital and maternity services; services mainly for the elderly and the physically handicapped; services for the mentally handicapped; services for the mentally ill; services for children; and other services, for example social work. Expenditure on each of these services can be compared through the programme budget, enabling a comprehensive analysis to be undertaken (Banks, 1979).

Alongside the programme budget was developed the DHSS planning system. This was started on an experimental basis in 1973. The intentions behind the system were to link policy development with resource availability, to provide the Department with information on objectives which could be used in the PESC negotiations (see Chapter 5), and to form the basis of national guidance to health authorities and local authorities. The system was based on planning statements prepared by branches within the DHSS which were then grouped under a number of main headings such as primary care, the mentally handicapped, children and manpower. A central planning unit within the DHSS prepared a consolidated document on the basis of these grouped statements. This document was submitted to the Planning Committee, located in the Top of the Office and chaired by a Deputy Secretary, which advised ministers on overall strategy. The results of the planning system eventually found their way into the consultative document on *Priorities*, providing guidance to field authorities on the local development of services (Razell, 1980).

Within central government as a whole, the spirit of the 1970 White Paper gave way to a particular concern to increase management efficiency and cut down on bureaucracy after the election of the Thatcher government in 1979. Programme Analysis and Review and the Central Policy Review Staff were terminated, to be replaced by Rayner Scrutinies, reductions in manpower, and an initiative on financial management (Cmnd 9058, 1983). In the DHSS, the planning system was wound down – a victim, like its NHS counterpart, of exaggerated expectations. The programme budget, split into separate programmes for hospital and community health services and personal social services, continued to be used, but more as a tool for monitoring past trends in expenditure than as a mechanism for projecting future growth rates. Not surprisingly the latter became less important in a period of limited growth. Consistent with the spirit of the times, the number of civil servants in the Department was reduced by 20 per cent between 1979 and 1984 (Social Services Committee, 1984, p. 163) and Nairne has described how the Rayner regime and the drive for efficiency and effectiveness in the civil service forced the pace of Departmental management (Nairne, 1983). Reflecting on the change in approach, James has argued 'If currently the emphasis is on tackling specific topics and on efficiency rather than grand strategy, this will prove to be a necessary adjustment to balance earlier concentration on broader objectives' (James, 1983, p. 60).

Yet, alongside the emphasis on efficiency, there was a continuing concern to improve the Department's capacity for strategic policy-making. An important influence in this respect was the House of Commons Social Services Committee whose reports on the public expenditure programmes covered by the DHSS stimulated ministers and civil servants to review the effectiveness of the Department's policy-making procedures. The Committee's first report in this field, published in 1980, could hardly have been more critical. The Committee commented:

On the basis of the evidence we have heard, we are struck by the apparent lack of strategic policy-making at the DHSS: the failure to examine the overall impact of changes in expenditure levels and changes in social environment across the various services and programmes for which the Department is responsible. We were not able to elicit any specific information about what assumptions the Department is making about the likely effects on the NHS of the planned cut-back in the personal social services. Neither does the Department appear to know what the likely impact of rising unemployment will be on the NHS or the personal social services, despite the availability of at least one relevant study . . . the Committee wishes to record its disappointment – and dismay – at the continuing failure of the DHSS to adopt a coherent policy strategy across the administrative boundaries of individual services and programmes. We do not underestimate the difficulty of this task and acknowledge that a considerable investment of effort, and perhaps research, will be needed. We recommend that the DHSS should give high priority to developing its capacity for devising coherent policy strategies for all areas for which the Secretary of State is responsible. (Social Services Committee, 1980, p. viii)

The Department's reply was robust. After pointing out that 'In a number of cases (for instance on policy analysis and research, monitoring and the information base) the Committee appear to have expressed views on matters on which (perhaps because of shortage of time) they sought little or no detailed evidence' (DHSS, 1980f, p. 1), the Department gave details of a number of committees and groups which existed to undertake strategic policy analysis. These included the Health and Personal Social Services Strategy Committee, chaired by the Permanent Secretary and meeting quarterly to review overall policy developments; and the Cross-Sector Policy Review Group, established in 1979 to look at issues of cross-sector policy and wider social policy. The DHSS added in its reply that ministers were considering how to strengthen arrangements for policy-thinking across administrative boundaries.

By the time of the Social Services Committee's second investigation into public expenditure in 1981, the Department was able to point to the Policy Strategy Unit, set up to replace the Policy and Planning Unit, as a further example of a group concerned with policy in the round. Working under the leadership of an Assistant Secretary, the Policy Strategy Unit prepared periodic reviews of policy initiatives, identified gaps in policy development, and carried out specific studies usually of a short-term nature. Issues examined by the Unit included ophthalmic services, prescription charges, strategy for the elderly, unemployment and health and the role of voluntary bodies in the field of alcohol misuse (Social Services Committee, 1981, p. 15). In some ways, the Policy Strategy Unit was similar to the Central Policy Review Staff, except that it worked only within the DHSS. In the end, the Unit met the same fate as the CPRS, being superseded in 1984. One of those closely involved in this area of work has argued that the Unit's 'coordinating role has proved the most durable element, and . . . its policy analyses have had only limited impact' (James, 1983, p. 60).

Here, then, are some examples of groups within the DHSS attempting to improve the Department's policy analysis capability. While we have focused on particular units and committees established specifically to contribute to strategic policy-making, it is useful to bear in mind the point made by Birch (1983), himself a senior official, to the effect that civil servants in the course of their day-to-day work are engaged continuously in policy analysis activities. The absence of special policy-planning units should not therefore be taken to indicate that policy analysis is not undertaken. Yet the particular significance of innovations like the programme budget and the Policy Strategy Unit lies in their attempt to bring greater coherence to the Department's work, to enhance the basis on which policy choices are made, and to provide a counter balance to the clamour of political interests. To use a phrase from a slightly different context, these developments seek to challenge the system of 'planning by decibels' (DHSS, 1975b). In practice, of course, political factors cannot be discounted, and the machinery we have described will not necessarily overturn the incremental bargaining processes which are so much in evidence. What it may do, however, is challenge the conservatism inherent in incrementalism, and provide a wider basis for decisions than would otherwise be available.

Back to management

We have noted already the increasing interest in management efficiency during the 1980s. As the decade progressed, the concern to strengthen the Department's capacity for managing the NHS gained momentum. The most visible manifestation of this was the establishment of the NHS Management Board following the Griffiths Report of 1983. As Griffiths argued, there was a need for the Secretary of State to be supported at the centre by:

> a small, strong, professional management group, able to devote considerable time to running the NHS. This is in no way intended to derogate from your strategic role of Chairman and Chief Executive, but in fact to allow that role to be given expression through a General Manager seen to be vested with your authority and to be acting on your behalf and as your right hand man, in ensuring that the statutorily appointed authorities manage the NHS effectively. (Griffiths Report, 1983, p. 15)

Griffiths went on to propose that the Board should develop a coherent management process in which isolated initiatives would disappear and the Department would no longer concern itself with detailed management issues. Instead, it would set the overall direction of the NHS and hold authorities accountable for their performance. This would enable the Department to 'rigorously prune many of its existing activities' (*ibid.*). To signal a clear break with the past, Griffiths proposed that the chairman of the Board should come from outside the NHS and the civil service.

These recommendations were accepted and Victor Paige was appointed as the Board's first chairman. Almost immediately, difficulties emerged. In the words of the then Permanent Secretary, Sir Kenneth Stowe, 'it was nearly a disaster' (Stowe, 1989, p. 52). One of the reasons for this was the limit imposed on the Board's activities by politicians. As Paige has written:

> because of Ministers' accountability to Parliament, the high political pressures and sensitivity associated with virtually every central management decision within present policies, then the reality is that ministers take all the important decisions, political, strategic and managerial. (Paige, 1987, p. 7)

This meant that it was impossible to devolve executive authority to the Board. Unable to operate within political constraints, Paige resigned in 1986. Reflecting on what happened, Stowe has maintained that government will never be able to operate like a commercial business. He continued:

> Inevitably tensions will arise between, on the one hand, Ministers (and those officials supporting them) who must always be accountable to Parliament, and on the other, officials (irrespective of their nomenclature) who have been charged by those same ministers with the task of achieving an efficient delivery of services within prescribed policies and predetermined resources. (Stowe, 1989, p. 54)

In an attempt to tackle these tensions more effectively, membership of the Board was changed after Paige's resignation, with the Minister of State for Health taking the chair, and Len Peach (from IBM) being appointed as Chief Executive. This was deliberately seen as an interim arrangement and it was superseded in 1988 when the NHS Management Executive was created. The NHS Management Executive was chaired by a Chief Executive drawn from the NHS and it operated under the strategic direction of the Policy Board.

Apart from political factors, there was another key influence on the work of the NHS Management Board, namely the power of established civil service interests. The recommendations of the Griffiths Report, if fully implemented, would have considerably reduced the role of the Department in relation to the NHS. In fact, the Griffiths prescription was not initially carried through as intended. The work of the Board focused on management issues and its remit was limited to hospital and community health services. Responsibility for policy was vested in the Policy Group while family practitioner services remained the responsibility of a separate group. The effect was to channel the activities of the Board into areas such as the introduction of general management and the implementation of resource management. The Policy Group continued to oversee matters of policy and emerged as a countervailing force to the Board (Ham, 1988). In this sense, civil servants in the Policy Group were successful in fending off the challenge posed by Griffiths and in preserving a major role for themselves in the Department.

There was a change of approach in 1989 under the newly-appointed NHS Management Executive (ME). To begin with, the management of family practitioner services was brought within the scope of the ME, and it was made clear that ministers were committed to establishing the ME as the apex of the NHS. Furthermore, the ME had the good fortune to be born into a world in which ministers needed effective support in implementing the NHS reforms. With the Department's agenda dominated by the introduction of far reaching organisational, financial and management changes, the ME was well placed to act on behalf of ministers in making the reforms work. In carrying out this role, it had the advantage of being staffed by experienced health service managers as well as people from business backgrounds and civil servants.

The ME put considerable effort into creating a separate identity for itself within the Department and in working closely with NHS bodies. This was reflected in its operating style which often involved NHS managers joining civil servants in working parties and project groups to produce reports and guidance on specific aspects of the reforms. As a consequence, the ME was perceived less as part of the Department and more as a 'head office' for the NHS. Although in formal terms it remained firmly within the Department and accountable to the Policy Board, the ME began to take on the appearance of an agency at arm's length from political control and able to operate semi-autonomously. This impression was reinforced by the relocation of the ME to offices in Leeds in 1992.

Both the ME and the rest of the Department were reorganised during 1991. In the case of the ME, a review of its role and functions noted:

> The present organisation of the ME is not geared to managing the NHS. With the exception of the Deputy Chief Executive's Directorate, its structure has not greatly changed since 1983. (NHSME, 1991, p. 3)

To equip the ME for its new responsibilities, the Review recommended the establishment of six directorates under the overall leadership of the Chief Executive. These covered research and development, health care, performance management, finance and corporate information, personnel and corporate affairs. Following discussion and representations from the nursing profession, a nursing directorate was added to these six. The Review emphasised that the ME's management style would be characterised by eight key features: corporate and integrated, personal accountability, credible leadership, lean, operating through task forces, attention to the medium and long term, rigorous on outputs and outcomes, and enabling. One of the implications was that:

> there will no longer be parallel hierarchies of professionals and non-professionals. Individual posts will be filled by the right person for the job, irrespective of professional background. (*Ibid.*, p. 5)

The reorganisation of the rest of the Department was less radical. The proposals in this area stemmed from parallel reviews of the Medical Divisions undertaken by a scrutiny team led by Dr Richard Alderslade and of the senior management structure of the Department by Sir John Herbecq.

In response to the Alderslade/Herbecq reviews, the Permanent Secretary and Chief Medical Officer agreed to organise the policy work of the Health and Social Services Group under two Deputy Secretaries. Three pairs of Divisions, medical and administrative, reported to the Deputy Secretaries, each pair having the same broad area of responsibility to facilitate joint working. Although the scrutiny of the Medical Divisions had strongly advocated fully integrated working between professionals and non-professionals in order to overcome duplication of effort and difficulties of coordinating work, it was decided not to follow the example of the ME Review and create a single management hierarchy. Rather, the emphasis was placed on integrated agenda setting by paired divisions, linked management boards and multidisciplinary working. This meant the retention of separate administrative and medical lines of accountability coupled with the development of stronger horizontal links.

It was not until the Banks review of 1994 that the nettle of integrated working in the wider Department was finally grasped. Implementation of the Banks review enabled the work of the Department to be streamlined with further reductions in the number of civil servants and a shift in the balance of work and power to the NHS Executive. Although, as we noted at the beginning of this chapter, the option of the NHS Executive becoming an executive agency had been considered but rejected at the time of the functions and manpower review, the decision to place responsibility for policy in the hands of the NHS Executive meant that the wider Department focused mainly on public health and social care. Leaving aside the executive agencies attached to the Department, more civil servants were employed in the NHS Executive and its regional offices than in the wider Department, and the balance of senior appointments (at Deputy Secretary level) was also weighted towards the NHS Executive.

The organisation of the NHS Executive itself underwent further change following the functions and manpower review and the Banks review, and it was as a result of this that the current structure (see Figure 6.2) emerged. The most significant change involved the coming together of finance and performance management into a single directorate. This resulted from the establishment of regional offices in place of RHAs and consequently a shift in the focus of performance management from the review of RHA performance by the NHS Executive to the review of health authority and trust performance by regional offices of the NHS Executive. These issues are explored further in the next chapter.

As a consequence of the Banks review, the recommendations of the Griffiths Report were finally implemented over a decade after its publication, although it should be emphasised that the Permanent Secretary remained the head of the Department and retained oversight of all its responsibilities. This was reflected in the wording of the Statement of Responsibilities and Accountabilities prepared after the Banks review which noted that the Permanent Secretary had the task of 'advising the Secretary of State on the discharge of all the duties of his or her office' while the Chief Executive of the NHS Executive was 'the Secretary of State's principal policy adviser on all matters relating to the NHS' (Department of Health, 1997, paras 1.7 and 1.8).

One of the casualties in the jockeying for power between the mandarins and the managers, to borrow the language of Day and Klein (1997), was the Medical Division. Integrated working meant the abolition of separate hierarchies and also resulted in a significant reduction in the number of doctors working directly to the Chief Medical Officer. This attracted comment during the official inquiry into bovine spongiform encephalopathy which was set up to investigate the government's handling of the outbreak of what was popularly known as mad cow disease. The inquiry heard that whereas in the 1980s there were four deputy chief medical officers and 14 senior principal medical officers reporting to the Chief Medical Officer, by the 1990s there was only one deputy chief medical officer. Not only this but also the incumbent Chief Medical Officer was reported as saying that his office consisted of a secretary and a mobile phone (Bower, 1998). Even allowing for an element of exaggeration, there had clearly been a fundamental shift from earlier periods, a fact attested to by two former chief medical officers who were publicly critical of the erosion of the support available to the Chief Medical Officer and his influence in government (Warden, 1998; Godber, 1998). The appointment of a new Chief Medical Officer in 1998 led to a review of these arrangements and a decision to give the Chief Medical Officer line management responsibility for the Public Health Group and other medical staff in the Department. This did not affect the commitment to integrated working within the Department.

There were no such concerns about the role of managers in the Department. The selection of Duncan Nichol followed by Alan Langlands as Chief Executive of the NHS Executive, and their appointment of colleagues from the NHS to senior positions within the NHS Executive, meant that the voice of the NHS in the Department was heard more strongly than before. The rise of the NHS Executive brought to a fore differences in the cultures of managers and civil servants, although over time a synthesis began to emerge (Day and Klein, 1997). In this synthesis it was difficult to determine whether the influence of managers was greater than that of civil servants or vice versa. Certainly at the regional level, the creation of regional offices of the NHS Executive in place of regional health authorities had the effect of increasing the influence of the civil service within the NHS and this was reinforced by the production of voluminous guidance on the implementation of *The New*

NHS White Paper by the NHS Executive headquarters during 1998 and 1999. Against this, there was some attempt to relate the number and range of priorities for the NHS to the capacity of the Service to deliver through the annual guidance on policies and priorities. In so far as there was a tendency for the demands placed on the NHS to increase, this was due as much to the promiscuity of politicians as to the enthusiasm of civil servants.

To close the circle, the end of the 1990s also witnessed a renewed interest within the Department in policy analysis. This arose less through the role of the Policy Board, which, like its predecessor, the Supervisory Board, led a shadowy existence, and was ultimately wound down, than the establishment of the Policy Management Unit to work under the Departmental Management Board following the Banks review. The remit of the Unit encompassed coordination of work across the Department as well as:

- identifying major issues affecting the Department in the medium to longer term which need tackling (drawing on existing intelligence sources or initiating mechanisms of its own); and
- taking the lead in any piece of work looking fundamentally at the nature of health or social care services. (Department of Health, 1997, para. 7.6)

Following the further changes to the Department's structure introduced after the 1997 general election (see above), the work carried out by the Unit was reallocated between the new directorates responsible for corporate management and planning. The significance of these changes was to indicate the importance attached by the new government to 'joined up' working and the perceived need to balance the stronger focus on the NHS with an enhanced capacity for planning and cross-sector working. The appointment of a Director of Operations in the NHS Executive at the same time reflected recognition of the need to provide leadership in the implementation of the government's policies.

Conclusion

As this chapter has illustrated, the DH is not a monolith. The existence of a variety of professions, divisions and groups gives rise to a high degree of pluralism within the Department and this is complicated by the interplay with outside interests. The landscape of the Department is continuously being reshaped in response to changing needs and fashions and the struggle for power between different interests. In the 1980s and 1990s the main distinction was between those responsible for policy and those overseeing the NHS and the implementation of policy. This was eventually resolved when the NHS Executive took charge of both functions. The role and influence of the NHS Executive within the Department has progressively been extended and it currently occupies a pivotal position between ministers and the wider Department on the one hand and the NHS on the other.

Yet if the increasing prominence of the NHS Executive has raised the profile of managers within the Department, the mandarins retain a central role as advisers to ministers and fixers within the Whitehall village. The settlement reached after the Banks review meant that the Permanent Secretary remained unequivocally head of the Department with the Chief Executive of the NHS Executive acting as the Secretary of State's principal adviser on NHS issues. The main losers in the recent changes to the organisation of the Department have been doctors with the integration of doctors into a single management hierarchy and the Chief Medical Officer left with a rump of staff reporting directly to him at least until recently. The reduction in the number of civil servants in the 1980s and 1990s is testimony to the power of politicians to bring about changes in the machinery of government and also illustrates that the interests of politicians and civil servants may not always coincide.

The health policy community that surrounds the Department contains a large number of organisations and interests. Pressure groups are drawn towards those parts of the Department that deal with issues of concern to them and sub-communities emerge around these issues. In these policy communities, producer groups have greater influence than consumer groups and are often involved in negotiation with ministers and civil servants rather than consultation. Other inputs to the policy process come from Parliament and the mass media, NHS bodies, standing advisory groups and *ad hoc* inquiries, industrial and commercial interests, and academics and researchers. Ministers and civil servants themselves are particularly important in policy formulation. One of the consequences of the diversity of interests in the policy community is that policy maintenance is more common than policy initiation, although as we saw in earlier chapters, the history of the NHS is characterised by long periods of incremental change and only occasional intervals of radical reform.

There have been a number of attempts to introduce greater rationality into the policy-making process. Nevertheless, bargaining, negotiation and accommodation between different interests are the principal forces that shape the development of policy. Also important is the way in which policy is adapted and amended as it is implemented, and it is to a consideration of policy implementation that we now turn.

7

Implementing Health Policy

The aim of this chapter is to examine the implementation of health policy and the micro politics of the NHS. The chapter begins with a description of the management of the NHS and the role of regional offices, health authorities, and trusts. This leads into a discussion of the relationship between the Department of Health and NHS bodies and of policy-making within the NHS. The influence of the medical profession is reviewed and the chapter concludes by summarising the various factors relevant to an understanding of health policy implementation

The management of the NHS

The Secretary of State for Health has overall responsibility for health services, and he or she is also responsible for overseeing personal social services. Different arrangements exist for the administration of these services outside Whitehall, and it is interesting to compare these arrangements. Personal social services come under the control of local authorities, who have considerable autonomy from central government. Local elections give local authorities an independent power base, while the existence of council tax as a source of revenue provides the means by which authorities can determine spending levels. In practice, central government involvement in local affairs has increased in recent years, but local authorities retain some freedom to decide on the range and mixture of services to be provided in their areas. As would be expected, local autonomy also means local variation, and there are wide differences in spending levels and types of services provided.

The Secretary of State discharges his or her responsibility for providing health services through NHS bodies whose boards are appointed to oversee the commissioning and provision of services at a local level. These bodies comprise health authorities, NHS trusts, primary care trusts and special health authorities. While the main function of these bodies is to ensure that health services are delivered in a way that is consistent with national policies and priorities, they have policy-making responsibilities in their own right and do not simply carry out the Secretary of State's wishes. On the other hand, unlike local authorities they lack the legitimacy derived from elections and have no significant independent sources of revenue. To explore these issues in more detail, we now examine the operation of NHS bodies and their functions and responsibilities.

NHS Executive regional offices

We noted in Chapter 6 the role of the NHS Executive within the Department of Health and its involvement in both policy-making and implementation. The NHS Executive comprises a headquarters based mainly in Leeds, and eight regional offices (see Figure 7.1). The latter were established in 1996 in place of regional health authorities and regional outposts of the NHS Executive. Unlike regional health authorities, regional offices form part of the civil service and they provide a presence in the field for the NHS Executive. As such, regional offices are a component of the central management of the NHS rather than an intermediate tier between the Department of Health and the NHS. There are no regional offices in the rest of the United Kingdom.

Each regional office has a regional chairman appointed by the Secretary of State and this individual works in a part-time non-executive capacity as a channel of communication between chairmen of health authorities and NHS trusts and the Secretary of State and as the latter's adviser, including on the appointment and reappointment of chairmen and non-executive directors of NHS boards. Regional offices are headed by a regional director who works with a team of senior colleagues in functions such as finance, public health, performance management and research and development. The staff of regional offices monitor the performance of health authorities and NHS trusts and carry out a range of other functions including advising on prioritisation for capital resources, liaising with universities in relation to medical and dental education, setting the local research agenda, establishing community health councils, and workforce planning and commissioning of education and training.

The need for a regional agency in the NHS has been recognised ever since the establishment of the Service in 1948. In the first phase of the NHS, regional hospital boards played a crucial role in turning a disparate collection of hospitals into a planned and coordinated service. In 1974 their functions were extended and their name changed to regional health authorities. After 1992 regional health authorities coexisted with regional outposts of the NHS Management Executive, set up to oversee the performance of NHS trusts. The functions of regional health authorities and regional outposts were combined when regional offices were established. The latter

Figure 7.1 *NHS Executive regional office boundaries from 1 April 1999*

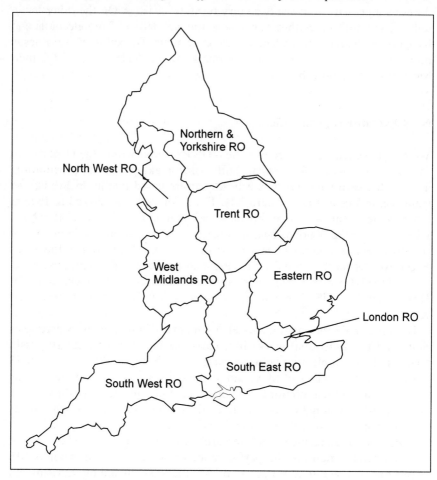

Source: Department of Health website.

emerged from the proposals of the functions and manpower review which as part of its work considered whether a regional agency was still required within the NHS. The decision to retain a regional presence reflects the difficulty of managing the performance of a large number of health authorities and trusts from the centre and also the value of having a buffer between the Department of Health headquarters and the NHS. Although the boards of regional health authorities disappeared in 1996, the appointment of regional chairmen indicates the importance attached by Ministers to having a non-executive link in the regions and a channel of communication separate from the management hierarchy.

The establishment of regional offices was associated with a reduction in the number of staff working at a regional level. This was partly the result of eight regional offices replacing what until 1994 had been 14 regional health authorities, and partly the consequence of tight controls being exercised over the staffing of regional offices. Whereas regional health authorities and regional hospital boards had each been significant bodies in their own right with a visible role in the NHS, regional offices as arms of the civil service and with far fewer staff work much more in the background. Not only this, but also regional directors are accountable directly to the Chief Executive of the NHS Executive and sit alongside him as members of the NHS Executive Board. Although the functions and manpower review argued that the purpose of these changes was to achieve greater decentralisation within the NHS by eliminating unnecessary interference in the affairs of health authorities and NHS trusts, the effect was to strengthen the grip of the centre over local management by moving towards the single chain of command for the NHS proposed in *Working for Patients*. In this respect, they built on the system of accountability reviews introduced in the 1980s and developed subsequently into the use of corporate contracts as a means of setting targets and monitoring performance within the NHS (see below). The power of regional directors in relation to NHS bodies was commented on in the Fallon Inquiry into Ashworth Special Hospital which noted that the regional director responsible 'wielded significant power once it became clear that things were going seriously wrong at Ashworth' (Fallon Inquiry, 1999, p. 335).

Health authorities

The abolition of regional health authorities means that district health authorities, now referred to simply as health authorities, are the statutory bodies mainly responsible for planning the development of services and leading the implementation of national health policy at a local level. Health authorities were established in their present form in England and Wales in 1996 as a result of the merger of district health authorities and family health services authorities. The equivalent bodies in Scotland and Northern Ireland are known as health boards and health and social services boards respectively. All of these bodies oversee the full range of health services, and in Northern Ireland the health and social services boards have, as their name implies, social care as an additional responsibility.

In 1999 there were 100 health authorities in England serving a population of around 500 000 on average. Each authority comprises a chairman and non-executive members appointed by the Secretary of State and up to five executive members. The latter are appointed by the chairman and non-executives and include the authority's chief executive, finance director and director of public health. Health authorities work as corporate bodies and are collectively responsible for their actions. This responsibility is discharged through the regional offices of the NHS Executive. The chief executive is the designated accountable officer and in this role he or she is accountable to Parliament for the finances and expenditure of the authority. The chairman is accountable to the Secretary of State and the performance of health authority chairmen is reviewed by the regional chairman. Regional directors may be involved in this process and also in assessing the performance of health authority chief executives, even though formally the latter are accountable to their own chairmen and non-executives.

The increasing influence of regional directors *vis-à-vis* the chief executives of both health authorities and trusts was noted in the Fallon Inquiry into Ashworth Special Hospital. The report of the Inquiry observed the direct involvement of the regional director responsible in decisions about the role of chief executives at the Hospital, notwithstanding the theory that 'Regional Directors do not have any powers to hire and fire Health Authority or NHS Trust Chief Executives or any other of their employees' (Fallon Inquiry, p. 335). As these comments indicate, the management line in the NHS has been strengthened not only, as we noted above, between the centre and regional offices but also between the centre (including its regional offices) and health authorities and trusts.

The functions performed by health authorities have emerged out of the functions and manpower review and the White Paper on *The New NHS*. As we noted in Chapter 3, the core responsibility of health authorities is to give leadership at a local level by assessing the health needs of the local population and developing a strategy for meeting these needs through health improvement programmes. In carrying out this responsibility, health authorities are required to work in partnership with NHS bodies, local authorities, community and voluntary organisations and other bodies. The health improvement programme is the means for delivering national targets for both health and health services and it is intended that the programme should reflect the priorities set out for public health as well as the NHS. A key function of health authorities in the light of *The New NHS* White Paper is to support the development of primary care groups, allocate resources to them and hold groups to account. Initially, primary care groups will operate as sub-committees of health authorities, although over time it is expected that they will assume more responsibility for the commissioning and provision of services with many choosing to become primary care trusts (see below).

The devolution of responsibility for commissioning to primary care groups is intended to free up health authorities to take a more active part in improving the health of their populations. In this role, they will lead the implementation of the national health strategy, building on experience since publication of *The Health of the Nation* (Secretary of State for Health, 1992), and working closely with other agencies to address the circumstances which give rise to premature mortality and ill-health. The duty of partnership placed on NHS bodies by the *Health Bill* published in 1999 symbolises the Blair Government's commitment to encourage collaborative working and is underlined by the designation of some parts of the country as health action zones. These zones have been established in areas where there are particular health problems and they provide a basis for health authorities to engage with other partners to improve the health of the population through action not only in the NHS but also in other sectors. Additional resources have been allocated to pump prime the work of health action zones and their experience is being evaluated to identify the lessons for the NHS as a whole.

Regional offices assess the performance of health authorities against the objectives set out in the health improvement programme and the annual commissioning plan, known as the service and financial framework. These objectives in turn derive from guidance on planning and priorities published each year by the NHS Executive. The accountability review process introduced in the 1980s formalised what had previously been *ad hoc* arrangements for performance management in the NHS and the current system centres on progress in implementing the health improvement programme and the service and financial framework. These documents identify the priorities and targets to which health authorities are working and progress is reviewed regularly with the regional office. The review process is supported by links between regional chairmen and health authority chairmen, regional directors and chief executives, and staff from the same functions.

Extensive as these links are, there is no certainty that national policies will be implemented locally. The existence of health authorities made of up of appointed chairmen and non-executives as well as senior managers creates the possibility that national policies will be modified during the course of implementation as the members of authorities put their own interpretation on these policies and adapt them in the light of local knowledge and circumstances. Not only this, but also health authorities themselves are not always in a position to carry through the intentions of Ministers even when they agree with the direction that has been set. As Malone-Lee has commented on the basis of his experience in the NHS:

> It is unusual for a health authority or its senior officers to be in a position to take a decision on an important matter and to have effective executive control over its implementation. The organisation is diffuse, loyalties centrifugal. To be effective most important decisions require at least the acquiescence of a large number of individuals or interest groups whose first loyalty is not to the health authority or its senior officers. (Malone-Lee, 1981, p. 1448)

This highlights the fact that there may be an implementation problem within health authorities, particularly when policy is directed at changing the actions of professional groups. We return to explore this issue more fully later in the chapter

NHS trusts

NHS trusts were established in 1991 under the changes set out in the White Paper, *Working for Patients*. Each trust is run by a board of directors comprising a chairman and up to five non-executive directors appointed by the Secretary of State, and an equal number of executive directors. The latter are appointed by the chairman and non-executives and usually include the chief executive, finance director, medical director and nursing director. Like health authorities, NHS trusts work as corporate bodies and are collectively responsible for their actions. The trust's chief executive is the designated accountable officer and is accountable to Parliament through the Chief Executive of the NHS Executive for the proper stewardship of the trust's resources. The chairman personally and the trust board corporately are accountable to the Secretary of State through the regional office of the NHS Executive. NHS trusts were set up as self-governing organisations and the intention is that within the framework of the NHS they should have considerable freedom to run their own affairs.

The main function of trusts is to manage the services for which they are responsible. The configuration of these services varies with some trusts running acute hospitals, others managing community and mental health services and yet others combining these responsibilities. There are also trusts responsible for ambulance services. The income of trusts derives from the contracts or service agreements negotiated with health authorities and primary care groups, and trusts are expected to deliver care to the specifications contained within those agreements. Under *The New NHS* White Paper, they also have a duty to put and keep in place arrangements for monitoring and improving the quality of care. This duty is a core element in the drive to improve standards and to promote clinical governance within the NHS. The accountability of trusts upwards to the Secretary of State is expressed in the form of an annual business plan which is approved by the regional office of the NHS Executive. Performance monitoring beyond the business plan was intended to be limited to key priority issues for the NHS, although in practice the extent of monitoring has progressively increased.

What this means is that the freedoms available to NHS trusts as self-governing organisations have been eroded. While the aim of *Working for Patients* was that trusts should be able to borrow money, hire and fire staff, and run their own affairs, in reality the main change brought about by trust status was to release providers from the direct management control of health authorities and to give trust boards and managers greater scope to take decisions about the running of services without the need to seek approval further up the line. Yet even this flexibility will be constrained by the proposals in *The New NHS* White Paper which require trusts to work in partnership with health authorities and other bodies and to ensure that their decisions on new medical staff appointments and capital investment are consistent with the health improvement programme. Nevertheless, the establishment of NHS trusts adds a further layer of complexity to the management of the NHS, and, in the context of the theme of this chapter, may make it more difficult to implement national policies. Certainly, trust boards in many areas have used what freedoms they have to develop their services and the ending of direct management control of hospital and community health services by health authorities places even more emphasis on service changes being negotiated rather than imposed.

Primary care trusts

The devolution of management responsibility within the NHS was taken a stage further by the Blair government with proposals to establish primary care trusts beginning in 2000. These trusts will evolve from the primary care groups set up in April 1999 and they will combine responsibility for commissioning and service provision. Unlike primary care groups, which operate as sub-committees of health authorities, primary care trusts are freestanding bodies with a chairman and lay members appointed by the Secretary of State. The remaining members include the chief executive, finance director and three professional members drawn from the trust executive.

The boards of trusts are accountable to health authorities and it is envisaged that many of these trusts will manage community health services that were previously the responsibility of NHS trusts. The implication is that the formation of primary care trusts will necessitate changes to the number and size of NHS trusts, in particular those running community health services. *The New NHS* White Paper indicated that primary care trusts would not manage specialised mental health and learning difficulty services, although in Scotland they have been given this responsibility. A different approach is being pursued in Wales where there are no primary care trusts and where local health groups perform the functions of primary care groups. At the time of writing, the role of primary care trusts in Northern Ireland was unresolved.

Primary care trusts build on the experience of fundholding and GP commissioning and provide a means of involving all GPs in the commissioning of services and their provision. To this extent, they mirror changes to the management of hospital and community health services instituted in the 1980s, centring on moves to integrate clinicians more closely in the management of services (see below). The challenge for primary care trusts is to seek to involve doctors in management in a context in which GPs consider their first loyalty to be to patients. For many family doctors, participation in the management of budgets and services is not a high priority, and as we discuss later the independent contractor status of GPs epitomises the value attached to professional autonomy. The aspiration to manage primary care and to achieve closer integration with community health services that lies behind the setting up of primary care trusts is an attempt to move general practice into the mainstream of the NHS and to ensure greater consistency in standards and services across the country. As such, primary care trusts represent a challenge to the continuing independence of the medical profession (see below) and are designed to facilitate the implementation of national policies, particularly those concerned with the quality of service delivery.

Special health authorities

A number of services are organised and delivered through special health authorities. In 1999 there were 13 of these, examples being the National Blood Authority, the Health Education Authority, and the NHS Litigation Authority. Each authority is run by a board whose chairman and non-executive members are appointed by the Secretary of State, to whom the board is accountable.

The role of the DH

It is apparent, then, that a large number of bodies are involved in the management of health services. The intentions of the DH have to be filtered down through health authorities and trusts before they have an impact on service provision. These bodies do not simply carry out the Department's wishes. As we have suggested, NHS bodies are the Secretary of State's agents, but the agency role does not involve merely implementing instructions received from above. These bodies are semi-autonomous organisations who themselves engage in policy-making, and as such exercise a key influence over the implementation of central policies.

Having stressed the point that NHS bodies are not simply a means of translating central policy into local action, it is important to note that the health service is a national service for which the Secretary of State is accountable to Parliament. The basis of parliamentary accountability lies in the voting by Parliament of funds for the NHS, and the statutory responsibility of the Secretary of State for the way in which these funds are spent. The existence of parliamentary accountability is a centralising influence, and requires that the Secretary of State is kept informed of local developments. As we noted in earlier chapters, MPs are able to ask questions and raise issues in debates about the operation of the NHS, and the Secretary of State is expected to be in a position to respond to these questions. Also, the investigations carried out in the NHS by the Public Accounts Committee and the Health Committee require that ministers and civil servants have available relevant facts about the local organisation of health services. NHS bodies therefore have to provide the DH with detailed information about specific aspects of service provision, as well as routine statistical returns, to enable the Secretary of State to answer MPs' enquiries.

The influence of the DH is most apparent in the case of the budget for the NHS and its allocation to health authorities. These matters are determined centrally and there are no significant independent sources of revenue available within the NHS. Not only that, but also health authorities have a statutory duty to balance their budgets and this acts as an overiding constraint on their freedom of manoeuvre. DH gives guidance on the use of resources in a number of forms. First, circulars are issued on a range of topics setting out national policy which NHS bodies are expected to follow. Some of these circulars are prescriptive and identify procedures that have to be implemented but much of the guidance issued in this form is advisory, allowing scope for local interpretation. Circulars are often discussed in draft form with NHS staff and this enables local influence to be brought to bear on national guidance. In theory, this increases the likelihood of local compliance, although research indicates that circulars are of doubtful effectiveness as a means of central control (Ham, 1981).

Second, the DH publishes White Papers and consultative documents proposing developments in specific areas of service provision. This form of guidance is often used to make a major statement of government policy and is intended to reach a wider audience than health circulars. Consultative documents usually prepare the ground for White Papers, and enable NHS bodies and other interests to influence the more definitive statements incorporated in White Papers. White Papers set out general directions in which the government wishes policy to develop, and may represent a departure from previous intentions. They may also prepare the ground for legislation. Examples include the White Papers *Working for Patients* and *The New NHS* which contained the proposals of the Thatcher Government and the Blair Government respectively for the reform of the NHS. A different example was the White Paper on the future of primary care which formed the basis of the 1997 Primary Care Act.

Third, the DH issues regular guidance on priorities for service development. This process started in 1976 with the consultative document on *Priorities* (DHSS, 1976b), and was followed by publication of *The Way Forward* in 1977 (DHSS, 1977b) and *Care in Action* in 1981 (DHSS, 1981c). Circulars have elaborated on these guidelines. The aim of these documents has been to inform NHS bodies of priorities for the development of health and personal social services. National guidance on priorities has varied in the degree to which it has prescribed what should be done, the advisory nature of *Care in Action* in 1981 – 'We want to give you as much freedom as possible to decide how to pursue these policies and priorities in your own localities. Local initiatives, local decisions, and local responsibility are what we want to encourage' – giving way to a more prescriptive approach in recent years. This is connected with the increased use of earmarking NHS resources for particular purposes.

DH guidance on priorities is part of the more general attempt by central government to influence local patterns of service provision through the NHS Planning System, introduced in the 1970s. The nature of DHSS planning guidelines changed between 1976 and 1981, moving away from relatively specific, quantitative targets towards broad, qualitative indications of central government's priorities. The introduction of the accountability review process in 1982 signalled a shift back towards greater central involvement in planning. A key point to note, then, is the way that centre-periphery relationships in the NHS change over time (Ham, 1981; Hunter, 1983). Yet even strong central guidance based on national standards of service provision may not result in local conformity with central priorities. The fact that NHS bodies actually provide services and have day-to-day management and planning responsibilities means that the DH has to work through and with these bodies to achieve its goals (Haywood and Alaszewski, 1980).

The NHS Planning System was intended to reveal cases where health authorities were deviating from national guidelines, and until 1984 it was the Regional Group within the DHSS which was responsible for receiving RHAs' plans. Within the Regional Group, the regional liaison (RL) divisions had the task of discussing plans with RHAs. One of the civil servants involved in this process has indicated that when there was a disparity between the plan of a region and national policies, 'the RL division goes back to the authority and says, "look, you've got this completely wrong". But there won't be many of those instances where the problems are sufficiently clear' (Clode, 1977, p. 1315). There may also be discussions between ministers and regional chairmen. This was indicated by a former Permanent Secretary, Sir Patrick Nairne, in evidence to the Public Accounts Committee. When asked what the DHSS would do about a recalcitrant region, Nairne stated, 'In my experience the Secretary of State has sometimes had to directly approach a regional chairman and say, "I have been looking at your plans and I really do not feel happy that you are making enough progress: for example, in the direction of the mentally handicapped"' (Public Accounts Committee, 1981, p. 86).

After hearing this evidence, and after considering the range of mechanisms available to the DHSS, the Public Accounts Committee concluded that the Department should be in a position to control more effectively what was happening in the NHS. This view was shared by the Social Services Committee. Both committees argued that the Department should pay more attention to issues such as manpower control, hospital building and variations in costs. Partly in response to the Public Accounts Committee's report, and partly as a result of changes among ministers and senior officials in the

DHSS, the accountability review process was established. Sir Kenneth Stowe, former Permanent Secretary at the DHSS, has recounted how the review process emerged from:

> discussions I had with the Comptroller and Auditor General (Sir Gordon Downey), the Principal Finance Officer (Geoffrey Hulme), the Under Secretary in charge of the Regional Liaison Division (Bryan Rayner), the two Junior Ministers (Sir Gerard Vaughan and Sir Geoffrey Finsberg) and the new Secretary of State, Norman Fowler. The idea was simple: the Department would each year review with each RHA chairman and his principal officers the progress achieved by the RHA towards objectives agreed with ministers for the past year, and reach agreement on performance targets for the year ahead. The RHA chairmen supported it and the policy was announced by the Secretary of State in January 1982. (Stowe, 1989, p. 45)

The review process set up in the 1980s superseded the NHS Planning System and involved a scrutiny of plans and performance leading to annual regional and district review meetings. The purpose of the meetings was to review the long-term plans, objectives, efficiency and effectiveness of the region, and to provide a means of holding the RHA to account. Discussion focused on an agenda of issues agreed in advance. These issues were drawn from a number of sources including regional plans and ministerial priorities. At the end of the review meeting, an action plan for the region was agreed. The fact that the reviews took place on an annual basis was important as it enabled the DH to assess progress made in achieving agreed objectives. Following the regional review, the RHA held a series of review meetings with each of its health authorities. The procedure was similar to that followed at regional reviews and an action plan was agreed at the end of the meeting. The review process was described by the Griffiths Inquiry into NHS Management as 'a good, recent development which provides a powerful management tool' (Griffiths Report, 1983, p. 12).

The system of accountability reviews has developed and been adapted in line with the changing structure of the NHS. The abolition of RHAs in 1996 has reduced the scope for regional variations from national policies and means that the main role of regional offices is to oversee the implementation of these policies. The principal focus of the review process has therefore shifted to health authorities, specifically the performance of health authorities in relation to implementation of the health improvement programme and service and financial framework. It is these documents that are at the heart of current performance management arrangements and form the basis of regular reviews between each health authority and its regional office. As earlier comments have indicated, performance management within the NHS has been strengthened over time and health authorities that deviate significantly from the policies set out nationally are expected to explain the reasons to regional offices and take remedial action. Indeed, in some cases the chairmen and chief executives of health authorities may be called to see ministers to explain variations from national targets. An example of this which arose in 1999 was the requirement placed on the chairmen of 13 health authorities that failed to meet the government's objectives for cervical cancer screening to meet the Secretary of State to account for their actions. Increasing centralisation is also evident in the earmarking of resources for specific purposes. Earmarking has always been used to direct funds to areas of high national priority, as in the case of long-stay hospitals in the 1970s and waiting lists in the 1990s, but it has been deployed much more extensively under the Blair government to target monies at services and initiatives seen as important by ministers.

Despite the strengthening of performance management, policies which appear to have high priority may still not be implemented. This has been demonstrated in a recent study of the impact of *The Health of the Nation* during the 1990s which found a significant gap between the objectives of the national health strategy and its implementation (DH, 1998b). As the study noted, one of the reasons for this was the large number of policies and priorities being pursued by the government at the time. In a situation of priority overload and initiative conflict, some policies did not receive particular attention and management effort was directed to other areas. Specifically, *The Health of the Nation* was seen as a low priority in the corporate contract and in the NHS Executive headquarters and the signals this sent out meant that neither regional offices nor health authorities saw it as a priority issue. It was therefore not surprising that the strategy failed to make a major impact, indicating that the ability of those at the centre of the NHS to influence decisions at a local level depended at least in part on the commitment put behind national initiatives. In areas of major significance to the government, like the reduction of waiting lists and the improvement of screening services, there was usually much greater compliance with national policies became performance management was considerably stronger, but in other areas NHS performance was more variable. By implication, the study of the implementation of *The Health of the Nation* also suggested that the number of issues where the centre could make a major difference was limited, especially when the policy agenda was so large.

The final instrument of control, and potentially the most significant of all, is the Secretary of State's power of direction. This power enables the Secretary of State to direct NHS bodies to comply with his wishes in relation to any aspect of their work. Also, the Health Services Act 1980 gave the Secretary of State specific powers to direct authorities to keep expenditure within income. In addition, the Secretary of State is able to suspend health authorities and NHS trusts, and to set up inquiries into their work. In practice, these powers are used sparingly. As Brown explains, they are used:

only when a Minister decides to use them – in other words when he feels that the political or administrative need to wield the big stick outweighs the political and administrative cost that will be incurred. The more drastic powers are about as usable in practice as nuclear weapons. None can be used as an instrument of day-to-day control. (Brown, 1979, pp. 10–11)

There is some overstatement here, as the suspension of the Lambeth, Southwark and Lewisham AHA in 1979 indicates. The AHA was suspended by the Secretary of State for threatening to overspend its budget, and a team of commissioners were appointed in its place. Twenty years later the Secretary of State removed the non-executive directors of the Guild Community Health Care NHS trust in Lancashire because of concerns about the management of the trust. Nevertheless, Brown's underlying point is valid, and the reason why these powers are used so rarely is that only very occasionally do they need to be invoked. The DH is able to maintain general oversight of the NHS through the other instruments already described, and through bargaining and negotiation rather than legal sanctions.

The balance of power between the centre and the periphery in the NHS has been viewed in various ways. Enoch Powell, Minister of Health from 1960 to 1963, argued that the centre had almost total control (Powell, 1966). Richard Crossman, Secretary of State from 1968 to 1970, maintained that the centre was weak and the periphery strong (Crossman, 1972); and Barbara Castle, Secretary of State from 1974 to 1976, likened Regional Health Authorities to:

a fifth wheel on the coach. They neither speak as elected representatives nor do they have the expertise of their own officials. And their attitude to the Secretary of State and department is necessarily pretty subservient – they want to keep their jobs! (Castle, 1980, p. 315)

The subservience noted by Castle was not much in evidence in a report on the workings of the DHSS prepared by three Regional Health Authority chairmen in 1976 (Regional Chairmen's Enquiry, 1976). The report resulted from an invitation by the Minister of State for Health, Dr David Owen, to the chairmen to examine the functions of the DHSS and its relationship with RHAs. The report was highly critical of the DHSS, and argued, perhaps not surprisingly, that more powers should be delegated to health authorities. In the chairmen's view too much control, and too many detailed decisions, were vested in the DHSS. These points were echoed in the Griffiths Inquiry into NHS Management. Griffiths argued 'The centre is still too much involved in too many of the wrong things and too little involved in some that really matter' (Griffiths Report, 1983, p. 12). The establishment of the Health Services Supervisory Board and the NHS Management Board in the DHSS were an attempt to meet these criticisms.

One point made in the regional chairmen's enquiry was that there should be a greater interchange of staff between the NHS and the DHSS as a way of improving understanding and communication. In fact, this has happened on an increasing scale in recent years, with a number of civil servants undertaking secondments in the NHS, and a number of health service managers and other staff being seconded into the Department. The process was taken a stage further in 1988 with the appointment of a regional general manager as Chief Executive of the NHS Management Executive. As we noted in Chapter 6, the NHS Executive often works through joint groups of civil servants and NHS staff. In addition, the Chief Executive uses meetings of regional directors as a key mechanism for explaining national policies and receiving feedback on the impact of these policies in practice.

It is apparent from this discussion that neither the DH nor NHS bodies can act independently of one another. The reason for this is that underlying the relationship between the different tiers of management in the NHS is the dependence of one tier on the other for resources of various kinds: finance, manpower, information and so on. As a result of this dependence, a process of exchange develops through which policies are implemented (Rhodes, 1979). An alternative way of viewing the interaction between management tiers is not as a system of exchange, but rather as a negotiating process in which policy is evolved as it is implemented (Barrett and Fudge, 1981). Whichever conceptualisation is adopted, a key factor in the implementation of health policy is the link between members of the same profession at different levels. Of particular importance is the position of the medical profession, and we now turn to an examination of its influence on the implementation of health policy.

Professional influences on policy implementation

The medical profession is involved in the management of the NHS at all levels. In the DH, doctors are represented at the very top of the Department through the Chief Medical Officer and they also contribute to policy making lower down the organisation. The NHS Executive board includes a medical director and each regional office has a director of public health who receives support from other medical colleagues. Within the NHS, the boards of health authorities and trusts almost invariably include at least one senior manager from a medical background. Their contributions are supplemented by advice received from medical advisory committees and from individual clinicians whose views will often carry considerable weight in the policy-making process. The establishment of primary care groups in 1999 exemplifies the influence of doctors in the new NHS with GPs usually in a majority on the boards of these groups and therefore in a position to exert considerable influence over resource allocation.

As well as having access to the DH, health authorities and trusts, the medical profession is in an influential position because of the role of doctors as the direct providers of services. In the case of GPs, this is reflected in their status as independent contractors within the NHS. Family doctors have for a long time resisted political or managerial interference in their work and have preferred to contract with the NHS to provide a service to patients rather than to be employed by health authorities. As independent contractors, GPs have been free to deliver care in the way they consider appropriate and only since the late 1980s have governments sought to monitor standards in general practice and give health authorities more influence over primary care. This has entailed the use of funds to improve premises and staffing levels and the employment of professional advisers to review prescribing patterns. There have also been moves to encourage GPs to take part in clinical audit. The introduction of personal medical services contracts under the 1997 Primary Care Act is particularly significant in this context as it entails health authorities negotiating contracts for the provision of primary care directly with GPs. While GPs retain a good deal of freedom to organise their work and determine how services should be provided, the effect of these developments has been to strengthen arrangements for accountability.

Hospital doctors are salaried employees of the NHS, but again their actions cannot be directly controlled by managers and NHS trusts. The reason for this, as the DHSS has explained, is that:

> At the inception of the NHS, the Government made clear that its intention was to provide a framework within which the health professions could provide treatment and care for patients according to their own independent professional judgement of the patient's needs. This independence has continued to be a central feature of the organisation and management of health services. Thus hospital consultants have clinical autonomy and are fully responsible for the treatment they prescribe for their patients. They are required to act within broad limits of acceptable medical practice and within policy for the use of resources, but they are not held accountable to NHS authorities for their clinical judgements. (Normansfield Report, 1978, pp. 424–5)

Consequently, hospital doctors determine what is best for their patients, including the place and length of treatment, and the kinds of investigation to be carried out. Medicine is one of the clearest examples of an occupation which has achieved the status of a profession, and a key feature of professions is the autonomy of their members to determine the content of their work. A central issue in the implementation of health policy is therefore how to persuade doctors to organise their work in a way which is consistent with central and local policies. Because doctors have a major influence on the use of resources in the NHS, it is ultimately their behaviour which determines patterns of resource allocation and service development. And because doctors are not managed by NHS trusts, there is no guarantee that policies will be carried out.

Nevertheless, attempts are made to influence medical practices, as in the consultative document on *Priorities* (DHSS, 1976b), which contained a bibliography of reports concerned with alternative ways of providing services. The reports drew the attention of doctors to innovations in clinical practices, including methods of treating patients on an out-patient basis rather than as in-patients, and ways of reducing the number of unnecessary x-rays carried out. As the consultative document noted, 'decisions on clinical practice concerning individual patients are and must continue to be the responsibility of the clinicians concerned. But it is hoped that this document would encourage further scrutiny by the profession of the resources used by different treatment regimes'. (DHSS, 1976b, p. 28). This attempt to influence professional behaviour suggested that more attention might be given to the important part played by doctors in determining the use of resources. In fact, the successors to the consultative document on *Priorities* placed less emphasis on this issue, and *Care in Action*, published in 1981, stressed instead the scope for improving the efficiency of non-medical services (DHSS, 1981c). In practice, most attempts to change professional practices originate within the profession, and indeed one of the characteristics of professions generally is that control is exercised through self-regulation from within. Thus publications in medical journals, conferences organised by professional associations, and discussion with peers are the main means by which change is facilitated. In this context, the role of the DH has traditionally been, wherever possible, to put the profession in the position of moving in the direction desired by both central and local agencies.

This has begun to change as resources have become constrained and attention has focused on the efficiency with which these resources are used. Particular attention has been paid to the involvement of doctors in management. In the past, the main vehicle for achieving greater medical participation in management was the so-called 'cogwheel' system. This system derived its name from three reports on the organisation of medical work in hospitals which were published between 1967 and 1974 with a cogwheel design on their covers (see Ministry of Health, 1967). The cogwheel system involved clinicians in associated specialities coming together in divisions and these divisions forming a medical executive committee to examine hospital services as a whole. The Griffiths Report into NHS management suggested that the cogwheel system provided a basis for clinicians to participate in decisions about priorities in the use of resources. More specifically, Griffiths proposed that a system of management budgeting should be developed involving clinicians and relating workload and service objectives to financial and manpower allocations.

In 1986, management budgeting was superseded by the resource management initiative. Resource management seeks to improve patient care by giving doctors and nurses a bigger role in the management of resources, devolving budgetary responsibility to clinical teams within hospitals, enabling managers to negotiate workload agreements with these clinical teams, and improving information systems to provide staff with better data about their services. There are various ways of achieving these objectives but in many hospitals services are increasingly run by clinical directors (usually doctors) with support from a nurse manager and a business manager. Initially, resource management operated at six acute hospital sites established as pilot projects. Following the Ministerial Review of the NHS in 1988, the government decided to extend resource management rapidly to other hospitals. Central funds were set aside to support implementation and a strong emphasis was placed on training and organisational development.

Despite the enthusiasm of the DH, evidence from the six pilot sites indicated that the costs of implementing resource management were underestimated, and that the process of involving doctors in management was more complex and time consuming than had been assumed. Research also suggested that there were few tangible benefits in terms of better services for patients and improved value for money. Although disappointing to the proponents of resource management, these conclusions were hardly surprising in view of the major changes in behaviour expected of doctors and managers. Nevertheless, doctors and nurses remained positive about resource management (Packwood, Keen and Buxton, 1991) and government policy throughout the 1990s continued to support moves to involve doctors in management in both hospitals and general practice. By the end of that decade, the principles of resource management had become widely established throughout the NHS, albeit with continuing variation in the detailed arrangements that were adopted.

In parallel, successive governments promoted the use of clinical audit in the hospital and community health services. Until 1998 this was done on a voluntary basis with resources being earmarked by the DH to provide the support needed to introduce audit arrangements and to encourage doctors and other health care professionals to participate. Participation in clinical audit became compulsory following a series of cases which identified failures in clinical performance within the NHS. The most serious of these cases arose in Bristol where a number of children died during or after heart surgery because of inadequacies in specialist services. The action taken by the Blair government in response to Bristol and related examples, including the establishment of the National Institute for Clinical Excellence and the Commission for Health Improvement and the introduction of clinical governance, heralded the beginnings of a new era in medical accountability. Not least, these initiatives sent out a clear signal that self-regulation was no longer seen as sufficient to safeguard standards and patients. The adoption of these policies was possible because of the accumulation of evidence that existing arrangements for ensuring quality were inadequate and this created a policy window (Kingdon, 1995) for politicians to push through changes which had previously been ruled off the agenda because of anticipated opposition from the medical profession.

Policy-making in NHS bodies

From the point of view of the DH and NHS bodies, clinical freedom may appear to be entirely negative, an obstacle to the implementation of national policies. However, the definition of policy adopted in Chapter 5, emphasising the idea that policy involves actions and decisions, drew attention to what might be called a bottom-up as well as a top-down perspective on policy. From a bottom-up perspective, the local autonomy of both NHS bodies and the medical profession is a positive feature in that it permits the development of policies which are appropriate to local circumstances, or at least local preferences. Indeed, local autonomy may lead to innovations which might not occur in a highly centralised system. In the final part of the chapter we therefore examine the local sources of policy change and development, and the micro politics of the NHS.

We have argued that, subject to broad guidance on policy from the DH, NHS bodies have some freedom to determine what policies to pursue in their areas. However, it is important to recognise that NHS bodies, like the DH, are not wholly or even mainly concerned with making new policies or initiating developments. As studies of policy-making in health bodies have shown, policy maintenance is more prevalent than policy-making, and any changes that do occur are likely to involve marginal adjustments to the status quo. The reason for this is that within the NHS various interests are competing for scarce resources, and in the absence of any one dominant group, bargaining between these interests tends to result in incremental change. As the author has argued elsewhere

> In policy systems where there are many different interests and where power is not concentrated in any individual or group, it is easier to prevent change than to achieve it. Successful policy promotion in such systems is dependent on the winning of a coalition of support by an active individual or 'interest'. (Ham, 1981, p. 153)

With this in mind, what interests contribute to health policy-making at the local level? Hunter, in a study of resource allocation in two Scottish health boards, suggests that decisions were influenced by a policy triad, comprising health board members, managers, and professional and lay advisory bodies (Hunter, 1980). Hunter argues that the influence of health board members on resource allocation was minimal. This confirms evidence from other sources indicating that the appointed members of health authorities experience difficulties with their role. Studies of DHAs have pointed to the constraints under which members operate (Haywood, 1983; Ham, 1984) and have highlighted the fact that members were often in the position of approving proposals put forward by their managers rather than making decisions themselves. This does not apply to authority chairmen who tended to be much more closely involved than members in the work of their authorities and who were better placed to influence decisions.

Hunter goes on to note that health board managers, although active and visible in the resource allocation process, were not themselves dominant. Like their counterparts in DHAs, managers appeared to be in control of the business of their authorities, but were constrained by inherited commitments and established patterns of service provision. Managers were able to exert some influence but their freedom of manoeuvre was limited by history and, more particularly, by the power of the medical profession. As we noted earlier in the chapter, this power derives as much from the profession's key position as the direct provider of services, as from its involvement in advisory committees. Hunter expresses the point in the following way:

> allocations . . . did not always reflect directly the wishes and wants of doctors; nor did they arise from some conspiracy on the part of the medical profession to win for itself the biggest share of available resources, so depriving other groups in need of them. The process was altogether more subtle . . . in their present established position as leaders of the health care team and as the primary decision-makers, doctors' decisions to treat patients commit resources . . . and impose additional pressures on administrators charged with allocating resources. (Hunter, 1980, p. 195)

The author's own work on policy-making in the Leeds Regional Hospital Board (RHB) came to similar conclusions. Through a variety of channels, medical interests were able to influence what was decided, and overall 'the distribution of power was weighted heavily in favour of the professional monopolists' (Ham, 1981, p. 198). The terminology used here is derived from the work of Alford, who argues that health politics are characterised by three sets of structural interests: professional monopolists, who are the dominant interests; corporate rationalisers, who are the challenging interests; and the community population, who are repressed interests (Alford, 1975a). Applying these concepts to the Leeds RHB suggested that 'the history of hospital planning between 1948 and 1974 can be seen as the history of corporate rationalisers. represented by regional board planners, trying to challenge the established interests of the medical profession, with the community hardly in earshot' (Ham, 1981, p. 75). A key point to appreciate is that because the medical profession is in an established position, small changes do not seriously threaten professional dominance. In other words, policy maintenance benefits medical interests by preserving the existing pattern of services within which the profession is predominant.

Further light is shed on local health policy-making by a study of two DHAs carried out between 1981 and 1985 (Ham, 1986). The study examined how a number of issues were handled in the two authorities. In the case of issues which were initiated at a national level, the Griffiths Report on general management and policy on competitive tendering, the study showed that a range of interests were involved in the implementation process. The most influential of these interests were DHSS ministers supported by RHA chairmen. Within the constraints imposed from above, DHA chairmen and managers had some influence over how the issues were taken forward, but authority members were only marginally involved.

In the case of issues which were initiated at a local level, the decision to acquire a CT scanner in one authority and the siting of orthopaedic services in the other, a large number of actors again participated in the policy-making process. However, no one group or interest emerged as most influential. The medical profession was actively involved and undoubtedly exerted influence but this was mediated by the views of DHA managers and chairmen. Also significant were the RHAs, particularly in shaping the financial context within which local issues were debated and resolved. DHA members played some part in policy-making but were important mainly in lending support to chairmen and managers.

Although the configuration of interests involved in policy-making and the individuals, groups or organisations who held power varied between issues, the overall picture to emerge from this study is of DHAs faced with pressure from above in the shape of national and regional policies, and pressure from below in the form of demands from hospital medical staff. DHA chairmen and senior managers played the major part in responding to these pressures and in articulating their own views in the policy process. This does not mean to say that managers have replaced doctors as the dominant interest in the NHS, even though the Griffiths Report undoubtedly served to consolidate and strengthen the position of managers. In neither of the two DHAs was the dominant value system seriously questioned and doctors were therefore able to maintain their influence.

As Hunter found in his study, the power of the medical profession was manifested not so much through formal bids for development considered by health authorities as through the continual process of innovation which preempted resources for development. This was well illustrated by the way in which growth money was taken up by creeping development resulting from doctors deciding to use particular drugs and introduce new methods of treatment with significant implications for supplies and equipment. Put another way, the influence of doctors was exercised through decisionless decisions (Bachrach and Baratz, 1970). The clinical freedom of doctors to do the best for their patients, and the consequent power of clinicians over resource allocation, was thus an important factor limiting the role of health authorities. This was reinforced by the influence of the medical profession at other levels, as in the requirements imposed by the medical royal colleges on the training and staffing of hospitals. These requirements define the parameters within which policies are formulated at a local level and constrain health authorities in the planning of specialist services by forcing compliance with professionally determined standards.

What is also apparent both from Hunter's study and others is that community interests do not carry a great deal of weight in the policy-making process of health authorities. Certainly, in the period between 1948 and 1974 organisations representing community or patient interests played little part in the deliberations of the Leeds RHB, although since 1974 the introduction of Community Health Councils (CHCs) at district level in the NHS in England and Wales has strengthened the consumer voice in health care. Hunter's study, which was carried out between 1974 and 1976, found that 'the influence of lay advisory bodies on the allocation process was practically non-existent' (Hunter, 1980, p. 198), but at the time Local Health Councils, the Scottish equivalent of CHCs, were in the process of being established. Since then, CHCs have become more in evidence, and in a number of areas have had a demonstrable impact on decision-making. Like consumer interests at central government level, however, CHCs are in a weak position compared with producer interests and they have to use their limited financial and manpower resources as effectively as possible if they are to influence NHS bodies. Nevertheless, CHCs have increased the accountability of health service managers (Brown, 1979) and some have helped to bring about policy changes in their areas.

Studies of policy-making in NHS bodies since the implementation of general management and the White Paper, *Working for Patients*, have sought to analyse whether established relationships have been altered by the reforms initiated by the Thatcher government. These studies point to some evidence of change with the members of NHS boards appearing to have increased their influence in certain cases and the balance of power within the medical profession shifting away from hospital doctors towards GPs. In parallel, hospital doctors who took on management responsibilities as a consequence of resource management became more prominent and there was evidence of managers gaining some influence in relation to the medical profession (Ferlie, Ashburner, Fitzgerald and Pettigrew, 1996). Researchers who in an earlier study had found strategic change taking place in some areas but not others (Pettigrew, Ferlie and McKee, 1992), concluded in their later analysis that there was evidence of transformational changes in the NHS, while adding that many of these changes were not well-embedded (Ferlie, Ashburner, Fitzgerald, and Pettigrew, 1996). Notwithstanding this, the same analysis contended that the dominance of the medical profession remained largely intact. The important conclusion this suggests is that while the decline of corporatism may have weakened the influence of the medical profession in negotiations over national policy, the power of doctors within the NHS remains significant. In Alford's terms, the medical profession continues to be dominant and the challenge of corporate rationalisers, especially politicians and managers, has not seriously threatened this dominance at the micro level.

Conclusion

It can be seen that policy-making in NHS bodies involves a range of interests each seeking to influence what is decided. This chapter has sought to describe the relationship between NHS bodies and the DH without oversimplifying what the Fallon Inquiry has described as 'an extraordinarily complex network of relationships, power and influence at the top of a very large public service' (Fallon Inquiry, 1999, p. 336). From a policy-implementation perspective, the guidelines and advice offered by the DH are fed into a policy arena where they have to compete with the demands of the various agencies and interests discussed in the preceding paragraphs.

In assessing the strength of these agencies and interests, the powerful position occupied by the medical profession is again apparent. DH policies which challenge the interests of key groups within the profession are likely to be resisted. An example was Richard Crossman's attempt to shift resources from acute hospital services to the long-stay sector after the Ely Report. Crossman failed in his attempt because of opposition from the medical profession, and he was forced to earmark additional funds in order to give greater priority to long-stay services (Crossman, 1977). Twenty years later, the Blair government was able to introduce changes to the regulation of the medical profession because of the accumulation of evidence about failures in clinical performance, although the time taken to make clinical audit compulsory and to introduce a greater measure of independent scrutiny into the assessment of quality and standards speaks volumes about the ability of the profession to resist policies which threaten clinical autonomy.

While it is difficult to overemphasise the strength of medical interests, it should be noted that in some areas of service provision other interests may also be important. For example, policies for mentally-ill people and people with learning difficulties may be more open to lay and community influences than policies for other client groups. It is, of course, particularly in these areas that the medical contribution is at its weakest. Again, for similar reasons innovations in community health services and prevention may arise among consumer groups and may develop through non-medical interests. Increasingly too managers and board chairmen are playing a bigger part in policy-making. Granted these qualifications, the general conclusion of this discussion is that nationally determined health policies are mediated by a range of interests at the local level, among which the medical profession is the most influential.

The picture that emerges, then, is of a complex series of interactions between the centre and periphery, through which each attempts to influence the other. While the existence of parliamentary accountability gives the appearance of centralisation in the NHS, the reality is rather different. Recognising that the stance taken by the centre tends to change over time, it can be said that the DH is able to exercise control over total health service spending and its distribution, but has less control over the uses to which funds are put. Circulars, consultative documents and White Papers, and guidelines on priorities are the main instruments the Department uses to attempt to influence the decisions of NHS bodies, but the advisory nature of these documents, and often their ambiguity, leaves scope for local interpretation of national policy. The accountability review process is a significant innovation and has led to greater central involvement and in some cases central control over policy-making and this has been reinforced by the strengthening of performance management and the earmarking of funds for specific purposes. Overall, though, as a mechanism for influencing NHS bodies, persuasion is more important than are statutory controls, necessarily so perhaps in a Service where considerable discretion is accorded to those who provide services.

8
Monitoring and Evaluating Health Policy

The aim of this chapter is to examine the monitoring and evaluation of health policy and the way in which the results of monitoring feed back into policy-making. The chapter begins by tracing the evolution of interest in monitoring and evaluation and it describes the variety of audit arrangements that currently exist. The discussion then moves on to the performance of the NHS in relation to health improvement and access to health care. The chapter concludes by assessing the achievements of the United Kingdom in relation to other countries, offering an overall judgement on the strengths and weaknesses of the NHS model.

The audit explosion

Monitoring the implementation of policy and evaluating impact and outcome are continuing activities. Both the Department of Health and NHS bodies play a part in monitoring and evaluation, and their work is supplemented by *ad hoc* inquiries and investigations and reviews undertaken by parliamentary committees and bodies like the Audit Commission. Increasingly, too, researchers are contributing to this process through studies commissioned both by government and independent foundations. A wide variety of what are best described as audit arrangements are currently in place but this has not always been the case. Historically, the capacity for monitoring and evaluation was not well-developed, and the current emphasis placed on audit and performance management needs to be located in its historical context.

As far as the DH is concerned, for many years the Department lacked the means to undertake a sustained review and analysis of health policies. Brown has noted that part of the reason for this was that 'until 1956 the Ministry

176

had no statistician, no economists and no research staff or management experts apart from a small group of work study officers' (Brown, 1979, p. 12). Although there were moves to make greater use of statistical information and economic analysis during the 1960s, the most significant changes did not occur until the reorganisation of the DHSS in 1972 and the parallel development of the Department's policy analysis capability. A number of innovations resulted from these developments, including the use of programme budgeting to analyse expenditure on health and personal social services, and the publication of studies of policies on the acute hospital sector (DHSS, 1981e), community care (DHSS, 1981a and 1981d), and the respective role of the general acute and geriatric sectors in the care of elderly hospital patients (DHSS, 1981f). In addition, reports were prepared on the progress made in implementing policies for mentally-handicapped people (DHSS, 1980c), and on NHS capital and buildings (DHSS, 1979b). The DHSS also published a review of the performance of the NHS over the decade to 1981 (DHSS, 1983a). These were all indications that the Department's monitoring role was being given greater priority.

Yet it remains the case that monitoring and evaluation are difficult tasks to perform within the NHS. This was noted in a memorandum submitted by the DHSS to the House of Commons Expenditure Committee in 1972 on services for the elderly. The Department argued that general aims could be formulated for services, such as 'to enable the elderly to maintain their independence and self respect', but measuring the extent to which these aims were achieved was problematic (Expenditure Committee, 1972, p. 3). Nevertheless, the Department noted that:

> this is not to say that the problems are wholly insoluble. It may, for instance, be possible in time to devise means of measuring the condition of individuals against agreed scales of, for example, mobility or social participation and correlating changes in different areas over time with the pattern of services provided; or to establish indicators of the health and social wellbeing of the elderly in particular communities or areas and to undertake similar correlations . . . But it will take many years to develop and test agreed measures, to establish a methodology for applying and interpreting them and to collect the necessary information. (Expenditure Committee, 1972, p. 4)

Many of these points apply to other areas of the NHS. The objectives of service provision can often be stated only in general terms, and they may not be entirely consistent with one another. Devising measures in order to assess whether objectives have been met is beset with difficulties, and as a result many of the indicators used concern either inputs into health care, for example expenditure and staffing levels, or activity levels, such as the number of beds occupied or patients treated. Outcome indicators, for example on mortality or morbidity rates, are rarely employed, and it is therefore difficult to judge whether policy is having an impact on the health of the population.

The area of service provision in which performance indicators have been applied most consistently in the past is that of hospital services for the mentally ill and people with learning difficulties. A series of reports published by the DHSS in the 1960s and early 1970s identified those hospitals falling within the lowest tenth of all hospitals for these patients for certain grades of staff and services (see for example DHSS, 1972). Thereafter, the reports measured progress made in achieving minimum standards of staffing and patients' amenities (see for example DHSS, 1974). More recently, considerable effort has gone into the production of a set of performance indicators covering the core services provided by district health authorities. The stimulus behind this initiative was an investigation by the Public Accounts Committee in 1981 during which two RHA chairmen acknowledged that there was scope for improving the quality of the information available for comparing the performance of services in different regions. The Committee urged the DHSS to give greater priority to its monitoring role, and subsequently officials from the Department developed an initial set of performance indicators in collaboration with staff of the Northern RHA. These were used on a trial basis in 1982 and a complete set of indicators relating to 1981 was published in 1983.

The indicators covered clinical activity, finance, manpower and estate management functions. They drew on routinely available statistical information and enabled health authorities to examine performance in areas such as the length of stay of patients in hospital, the costs per case of treating patients, the costs of providing services such as laundry and catering, and the number of staff employed. It has been emphasised that while comparisons of performance in different authorities may be helpful, the published reports were not intended to be league tables. Rather, they provided a starting point for analysis, and it was expected that exceptional performance as revealed by performance indicators would lead to further investigation. As well as providing a tool for use by local managers, performance indicators were examined during the accountability review process and enabled the DH to question RHAs, and RHAs to question DHAs on the provision of their services.

Performance indicators formed one part of a series of initiatives promulgated by the DHSS in the search for greater efficiency in the NHS (see Chapter 2). The indicators published in 1983 were seen as experimental and a Joint NHS/DHSS Group was established to advise on future developments. The Group's Report, issued in 1985, made a number of suggestions for improving the coverage and presentation of the indicators. These suggestions were incorporated in the second set of indicators. Subsequently, performance indicators were renamed health service indicators and greater emphasis was placed on their publication in a user-friendly form. The importance attached to the indicators by ministers was indicated in a speech made by the

Secretary of State to accompany publication of the 1986/7 indicators. The Secretary of State highlighted the fact that there were:

> considerable variations in performance between districts. For example, some districts treat only 25 patients a year in each surgical bed whilst others manage 53. Even when adjusted to take into account differences between the patients treated, some districts are still treating 14 per cent fewer patients than would be expected, whilst others are treating 27 per cent more.
>
> Similarly there are districts with an average length of stay 13 per cent longer than expected, whilst others manage a length of stay almost 22 per cent less than expected.
>
> And if we turn to costs we again find large variations. Costs within any one group of similar districts can vary by as much as 50 per cent. Even when adjusted for different types of patients, some districts are 15 per cent more costly than expected, others 15 per cent less. In other words, £1 spent on health care in one place might buy £1.15 worth of product, whereas somewhere else it might buy only 85 pence worth.
>
> So despite the Health Service's unquestionable achievements in boosting efficiency, I am convinced there is room for yet more improvements in performance. (Moore, 1988)

The importance of monitoring was emphasised by the House of Commons Social Services Committee as well as the Public Accounts Committee. As the Social Services Committee commented, 'the DHSS should continue to seek to develop ways of assessing quality independently of the input of resources; this is already the role of the Health Advisory Service and could usefully become a responsibility of any new Management Advisory Service' (Social Services Committee, 1981, p. xiii). The view of the DHSS at that time was that there were two kinds of monitoring: strategic monitoring, which examined whether services were developing in line with agreed policies and strategies; and efficiency monitoring, which assessed whether resources were being used to the best advantage (DHSS, 1980d). Both types of monitoring were the responsibility of the Management Advisory Service (MAS), described by Sir Patrick Nairne, a former Permanent Secretary at the DHSS, as 'an external, critical inspectorial eye translated into the NHS' (Public Accounts Committee, 1981, p. 69). The MAS was taken forward in two regional initiatives between 1982 and 1985 and was an indication that monitoring was receiving greater attention. Even more significant was the introduction of the accountability review process as a mechanism for monitoring the performance of health authorities throughout the NHS on a routine basis. This process enabled the DHSS to exercise greater oversight of developments in the NHS and was a means of increasing central control over performance and ensuring compliance with national objectives. The accountability review process formed the basis, as we noted in Chapter 7, of current arrangements for performance management within the NHS and was the first systematic attempt since the establishment of the NHS to monitor the implementation of policy.

Notwithstanding the MAS, the development of performance indicators and the accountability review process, the Griffiths Report commented in 1983:

> The NHS . . . still lacks any real continuous evaluation of its performance . . . Rarely are precise management objectives set; there is little measurement of health output; clinical evaluation of particular practices is by no means common and economic evaluation of these practices extremely rare. Nor can the NHS display a ready assessment of the effectiveness with which it is meeting the needs and expectations of the people it serves. (Griffiths Report, 1983, p. 19)

Some of the reasons why monitoring and evaluation are underdeveloped in the NHS have been identified by Klein, a former specialist adviser to the Social Services Committee. As Klein (1982) has noted, the health policy arena is characterised by complexity, heterogeneity, uncertainty and ambiguity. Complexity is evident in the wide range of occupations involved in providing services; heterogeneity in the variety of services provided; uncertainty in the absence of a clear relationship between inputs and outputs; and ambiguity in the meaning of the information which is available. Given these factors, Klein concluded that performance evaluation is most usefully seen as a process of argument.

If this is the case, what territory should the argument cover? Most attempts to monitor performance in the NHS have made use of measures of the input of resources and activity levels. Doll (1974) has suggested that these measures of economic efficiency need to be considered alongside indicators of medical outcome and social acceptability. Doll's analysis has been developed by Maxwell (1984) who has identified six dimensions of the quality of health care: access to services, relevance to need, effectiveness, equality, social acceptability, and efficiency and economy. There is considerable overlap between Maxwell's dimensions of quality and the framework for assessing performance proposed by the Blair government in its plans for the future of the NHS. This framework also contained six areas of assessment and these are displayed in Table 8.1. In proposing this approach, the government announced that an annual survey of patient and user experience was being established to collect data about the social acceptability of services.

In taking this line, the Blair government was extending the approach initiated under the Major government through publication of the *Patient's Charter* in 1991 and performance tables analysing the achievement of NHS trusts in terms of the standards included in the *Charter*. In so doing, it was accepting not only the need for effective monitoring, but also the importance of moving the results out of the committee room and into the public domain. A key component of the Blair government's approach was a commitment to go beyond the indicators of access and convenience contained in the *Patient's Charter* to assess clinical performance and the outcome of treatment. This

Table 8.1 *NHS performance assessment framework*

Areas	Aspects of performance
(i) *Health improvement*	The overall health of populations, reflecting social and environmental factors and individual behaviour as well as care provided by the NHS and other agencies
(ii) *Fair access*	The fairness of the provision of services in relation to need on various dimensions: • geographical • socioeconomic • demographic (age, ethnicity, sex) • care groups (for example, people with learning difficulties)
(iii) *Effective delivery of appropriate healthcare*	The extent to which services are: • clinically effective (interventions or care packages are evidence-based) • appropriate to need • timely • in line with agreed standards • provided according to best-practice service organisation • delivered by appropriately trained and educated staff
(iv) *Efficiency*	The extent to which the NHS provides efficient services, including: • cost per unit of care/outcome • productivity of capital estate • labour productivity
(v) *Patient/carer experience*	The patient/carer perceptions on the delivery of services including: • responsiveness to individual need and preferences • the skill, care and continuity of service provision • patient involvement, good information and choice • waiting and accessibility • the physical environment; the organisation and courtesy of administration arrangements
(vi) *Health outcomes of NHS care*	NHS success in using its resources to: • reduce levels of risk factors • reduce levels of disease, impairment and complications of treatment • improvement in quality of life for patients and carers • reduce premature deaths

Source: Secretary of State for Health (1998b).

took forward work that had been started by the Major government and was given added impetus by evidence of failures of clinical performance within the NHS which came to light after the 1997 general election.

These failures were also instrumental in the establishment of the Commission for Health Improvement as a statutory body at arm's length from government to:

- provide national leadership to develop and disseminate clinical governance principles;
- independently scrutinise local clinical governance arrangements to support, promote and deliver high-quality services, through a rolling programme of local reviews of service providers;
- undertake a programme of service reviews to monitor national implementation of National Service Frameworks, and review progress locally on implementation of these frameworks and NICE guidance;
- help identify and tackle serious or persistent clinical problems. The Commission will have the capacity for rapid investigation and intervention to help put these right; and
- over time, increasingly take on responsibility for overseeing and assisting with external incident inquiries (Secretary of State for Health, 1998b, p. 52).

The Commission, which was expected to begin work in 2000, builds on the experience of the NHS Health Advisory Service and its predecessor, the Hospital Advisory Service, established by Richard Crossman following the Ely Report of 1969 to visit long-stay hospitals and advise on how standards could be raised (see below). The particular significance of the Commission was that its remit covered all NHS trusts and primary care trusts, and its powers to monitor quality and act on its findings were considerably greater than those of the Health Advisory Service.

The work of the Commission for Health Improvement is intended to be complementary to that of the Audit Commission and the National Audit Office. Both of these bodies engage in independent monitoring of the activities of the DH and performance within the NHS. The NAO has conducted a series of value for money studies in the NHS and its reports are often used as a basis for enquiries by the Public Accounts Committee. For its part, the Audit Commission has carried out a number of investigations in the field of health policy. Topics covered include GP fundholding, the commissioning of specialised services, and care of the elderly.

In recent years the NAO and the Audit Commission have made a significant contribution to monitoring and evaluation, and their studies have been supplemented by the work of the Health Services Commissioner or Ombudsman in relation to complaints. The Ombudsman publishes an annual report identifying trends and issues arising in his work as well as reports into selected investigations. An example of the latter which was particularly influential in shaping policy was the report published in 1994 into the failure of the NHS in Leeds to fund the continuing care of a patient. This led directly to the DH issuing revised guidance requiring health authorities and local authorities to review local policies and services to ensure that statutory obligations were being fulfilled.

As these comments indicate, there has been a considerable expansion of monitoring activity both within the NHS and by statutory bodies and related organisations. This reflects the 'audit explosion' (Power, 1994) across government as a whole in the 1980s and 1990s, and the particular concern in the case of health services to strengthen existing forms of regulation including the regulation of medical work (Allsop and Mulcahy, 1996). The growth of monitoring derived in part from reductions in the rate of increase in NHS spending in the wake of the oil crises of the 1970s and the subsequent search for efficiencies in existing budgets, and in part it emerged out of the application by the Thatcher government of the techniques of the new public management to health care. The coming together of economic pressures and political values created the circumstances in which services like the NHS were opened up to greater scrutiny and were expected to account more systematically for their performance. The extension of monitoring into the quality of medical care marks a further stage in the development of audit within the NHS, building on self-regulation and peer review by clinicians and introducing new mechanisms for promoting high standards of care.

Alongside the expansion of monitoring, there has also been an increasing interest in the evaluation of health policy. Of particular importance in this context has been the establishment of the NHS research and development programme which has provided funding and support not only for the evaluation of clinical interventions, but also for studies of the implementation and impact of policy. Recent examples of policy evaluations commissioned by the DH include studies of the introduction of total purchasing within the NHS (Mays, Goodwin, Killoran and Malbon, 1998) and of the implementation of *The Health of the Nation* (DH, 1998b). Indeed, after a period at the beginning of the 1990s when ministers were reluctant to evaluate health policy, many major initiatives are now launched in association with independent assessments funded by government. In parallel, there are examples of evaluations conducted by researchers with the support of research councils and independent foundations. There is, of course, no guarantee that the results of evaluations will be acted upon, and initiatives ostensibly launched as trials to be assessed before being implemented nationally are often taken forward before the findings of evaluations are known. Nevertheless, there is some evidence to suggest that the contribution of ideas and research to policy-making, one of the themes addressed in Chapter 6, is increasing, albeit at the margins.

To return to the systems model of the policy process, monitoring and evaluation provide feedback on the impact of health policy and in so doing may influence policy-making. As we have emphasised throughout this book, the policy process is complex and is subject to a range of political and other influences. Those involved in monitoring and evaluation, whether within the NHS or outside, are only one set of actors in this process, and there is no guarantee that the results of their work will make a difference. In Kingdon's terms, much depends on the coming together of problems, politics and participants at a time when there are opportunities to influence policy (Kingdon, 1995). The results of monitoring and evaluation contribute to the development of policy by identifying problems that demand attention, and linking these problems with participants in a position to influence the outcome.

Against this background, we now turn to an examination of the performance of the NHS. This is a large topic and it is one that may be approached in a number of ways. For the purposes of this chapter, and given the space available, the focus is on health improvement and access to health care. This is followed by an assessment of the performance of the NHS in the context of the experience of other countries. In this way, it is hoped to offer a summary of the achievements of the NHS over 50 years after its establishment

Health improvement

The available evidence indicates that the health of the population has improved steadily not just in the lifetime of the NHS but over the last 150 years. This is most apparent from trends in mortality in Britain which have been reviewed by the Office of National Statistics (Charlton and Murphy, 1997). Table 8.2 shows that in the period from 1841–1991, the expectation of life increased at all ages and was particularly pronounced in the younger age groups. A boy born in 1841 could expect to live until 41 years and a girl until 43 years; by 1991 the comparable figures were 73 years for boys and 79 years for girls.

Another way of examining improvements in health is to examine trends in death rates by age. This illustrates declining death rates at all ages with the decline again being greatest in the younger age groups. Charlton's analysis has shown that improvements in survival in the ninenteenth century were in fact confined to children and young adults (Charlton, 1997). These improvements extended to other age groups in the twentieth century, although life expectancy for people aged 75 and over only increased from around 1950. Between 1984 and 1994 the greatest improvement in health occurred among adults aged 15–19 and 45–64, and the least improvement among adults aged 20–44 (Dunnell, 1997).

Table 8.2   *Life expectancy, England and Wales, 1841–1991*

Year	*Expected further years of life at ages:*											
	0		5		15		35		55		75	
	M	*F*	*M*	*F*	*M*	*F*	*M*	*F*	*M*	*F*	*M*	*F*
1841	41	43	51	52	44	45	30	32	17	18	6	7
1901	45	49	54	56	46	48	29	32	16	18	6	7
1931	58	62	60	62	51	54	33	36	18	20	6	7
1961	68	74	65	71	55	61	36	41	19	23	7	9
1991	73	79	69	74	59	65	40	45	22	26	9	11

Source: Charlton (1997).

In the case of infants, there was a marked acceleration in the decline of infant deaths after the Second World War. Figure 8.1 shows the improved survival of children at different ages in England and Wales since 1950. For boys born in 1950, 96.6 per cent survived at age 1 compared with 99.1 per cent of those born in 1990. For girls the figures were 97.4 per cent in 1950 and 99.3 per cent in 1990. These improvements in health have been associated with changes in the causes of death. As we noted in Chapter 1, public health measures taken in the nineteenth century played a major part in tackling infectious diseases which at that time accounted for one death in every three . In place of infectious diseases there have been marked increases in mortality from cancers, heart attacks and stroke. There is also some evidence that the decline in mortality has been accompanied by an increase in morbidity as measured by patient consultations with GPs and self-reported illness (Dunnell, 1997). It has been suggested that this increase may reflect rising expectations on the part of patients as well as increased survival time following initial diagnosis. Put another way, if medical science has contributed to the decline in mortality it may have done so at least in part by turning fatal conditions into treatable (or at least containable) illnesses. This is supported by evidence that the number of years of healthy life have not increased in line with the overall improvement in life expectancy (Bebbington and Darton, 1996).

Yet to make this point is to raise an even more fundamental question about the contribution of the NHS to health improvement. The gains made in the last 50 years may have been associated with the introduction of a health services available free at the point of use to patients, but this is not the same as demonstrating that they have been caused by the NHS. Just as in the nineteenth century when public health legislation and the provision of pure water supplies and better housing were instrumental in the fight against infectious diseases, so too in the twentieth century factors outside the NHS

186

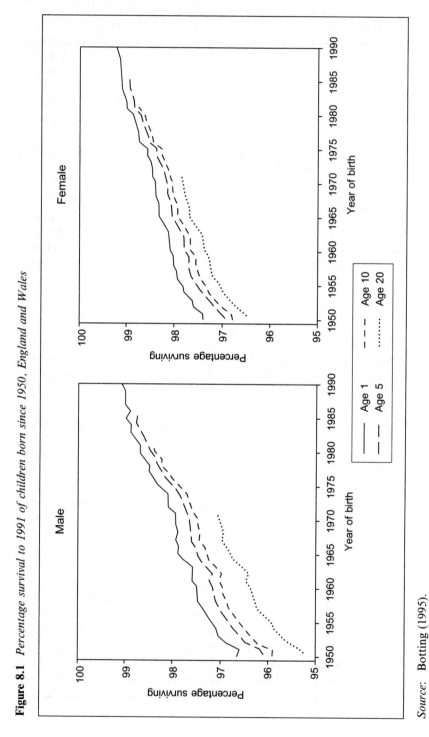

Figure 8.1 *Percentage survival to 1991 of children born since 1950, England and Wales*

Source: Botting (1995).

exert an important influence on the health of the population. This is demonstrated by the existence of inequalities in health between social groups. The extent of health inequalities was documented in the 1980 Black Report and the findings of this report have been updated and confirmed by later analyses.

Social class inequalities are usually analysed using the classification of occupations employed by the Registrar-General. This divides occupations into five main groupings varying from social class I, which contains professional occupations such as accountants and teachers, to social class V, which contains unskilled manual occupations like labourers and office cleaners. An analysis of death rates reveals evidence of social class differences in all age groups, and these are shown in Table 8.3. Class differences in morbidity are displayed in Figure 8.2. Of particular concern in recent times has been the long-term trend in class differences in health. The evidence indicates a widening in inequality between the 1970s and 1990s in the adult population, and a narrowing of differences in the case of infants (Drever and Whitehead, 1997).

The argument of the Black Report was that 'differences in the material conditions of life' (Black Report, 1980, p. 357) were mainly responsible for health inequalities, although the Report acknowledged that the causes were complex and multiple. The implication that followed was that steps to reduce inequalities needed to focus on tackling these material conditions. This entailed action in a range of areas of public policy, including, in the view

Table 8.3   *Age-specific mortality rates, by social class, men aged 20–64, all causes, England and Wales, 1991–93*

Social Class	Mortality rate per 100 000								
	20–24	*25–29*	*30–34*	*35–39*	*40–44*	*45–49*	*50–54*	*55–59*	*60–64*
I – Professional	98	91	142	228	373	704	1186	2057	3735
II – Managerial & Technical	139	146	197	279	380	722	1230	2148	3992
IIIN – Skilled (non-manual)	158	181	319	448	600	1125	1773	2975	5414
IIIM – Skilled (manual)	219	221	279	429	619	1141	1989	3521	6736
IV – Partly skilled	195	260	325	485	681	1244	2020	3491	6227
V – Unskilled	368	489	660	950	1334	2047	3430	5534	9341
England & Wales	246	250	307	425	579	1035	1745	2966	5181

Source: Drever and Bunting (1997).

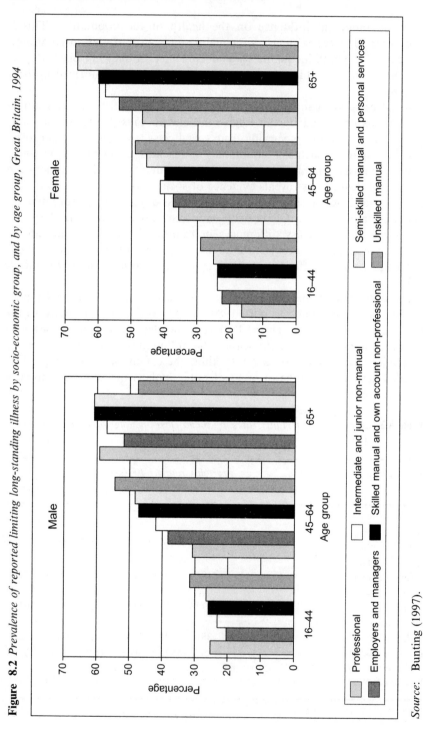

Figure 8.2 *Prevalence of reported limiting long-standing illness by socio-economic group, and by age group, Great Britain, 1994*

Source: Bunting (1997).

of the Black Report, increases in child benefit, the introduction of a child-care allowance, improvements to housing conditions, and free school meals for children. These proposals were rejected by the Thatcher government which disputed both the explanation of health inequalities offered in the Black Report, and the proposal that additional public expenditure was required to address these inequalities. This meant that the issues raised in the Report were largely ignored in central government despite evidence that inequalities in the 1980s not only persisted but also increased (Whitehead, 1987).

It took the election of the Blair government in 1997 to refocus attention on health inequalities. The Acheson Report was commissioned by the government to update the findings of the Black Report and particularly to advise on priorities for policy development. In so doing, the Report emphasised the importance of measures to reduce poverty, improve education, increase work opportunities, and strengthen access to housing. It also noted that action in the NHS should be concentrated on the prevention of ill-health and premature mortality. In this area, the proposals of the Acheson Report included ensuring equitable access to effective health care and the development of partnerships between the NHS and other agencies. Like the Black Report, the Acheson Report stressed the need to improve the health of families and children and consistent with its brief it examined inequalities between the genders and those affecting minority ethnic groups as well as between social classes.

Thinking on health inequalities has moved on since the Black Report to emphasise not only the relationship between absolute poverty and ill-health but also the importance of relative deprivation. As the work of Wilkinson has shown, inequalities are greater in countries where there are wide disparities in income and wealth (Wilkinson, 1996). Along with other researchers, he maintains that the influence of material conditions is mediated by social relationships, suggesting a more complex explanation of the causes of inequalities than that offered in the Black Report. Nevertheless, the implication for policy is broadly similar in that tackling inequalities requires action to strengthen social relationships alongside policies to reduce income inequalities, rather than primarily measures within the NHS. What remains unclear, even under a Labour government, is whether these implications will be acted upon especially when the Acheson Report has been criticised for failing to cost and prioritise its recommendations.

What does this discussion tell us about the performance of the NHS? In relation to health improvement, it would be simplistic to give credit to the NHS for all the improvements in health that have occurred since the Second World War, in the same way that it would be wrong to blame the NHS for the persistence and widening of health inequalities. Recognising that the role of medicine in improving the population's health has been more significant in the twentieth century than the nineteenth century, but is still less important than the influence of other factors, it can be suggested that by making available medical advances to the population the NHS has contributed to the long-term trends we identified at the beginning of this section. The main gains have occurred from the prevention of ill-health, for example through vaccination, and also through the extension of life made available by new forms of treatment for cancer and heart disease. By comparing trends in mortality from avoidable causes and other causes between 1950 and 1994, Charlton and colleagues suggest that the application of medical advances has had a beneficial effect. This is illustrated in Table 8.4 which shows that the decline in mortality from conditions where effective treatments are available is around twice that for other conditions.

In the context of increases in life expectancy in the United Kingdom of around 30 years during the twentieth century, the estimate in relation to United States experience that medical advances have contributed around 5 years to life expectancy increases in that country (Bunker, Frazier and Mosteller, 1994), puts the impact of organised health care services into perspective. Nevertheless, given that access to effective health care explains some of the improvement in health that has occurred, it is important to understand the record of the NHS in relation to access. It is to this issue that we now turn.

Table 8.4 *Comparison of mortality rates per million population in England and Wales in 1950 and 1994*

Cause of death	1950	1994	% fall
All causes (all ages)	12 964	7771	40
Eight 'avoidable' causes (all ages)*	513	102	80
All other	12 451	7669	38
Tuberculosis (ages 5–64)	379	3	99
Hypertensive disease (ages 35–64)	282	20	93
Cerebrovascular disease (ages 35–64)	757	233	69
Chronic rheumatic heart disease (ages 5–64)	85	1	99
Appendicitis (ages 5–64)	22	1	96
Cholelithiasis and cholecystitis (ages 5–64)	12	1	92
Cervical cancer (ages 5–64)	46	20	56
Hodgkin's disease (ages 5–64)	15	4	73
Perinatal mortality**	37	8	79
Maternal mortality***	87	8	91

* Tuberculosis, hypertensive disease, cerebrovascular disease, chronic rheumatic heart disease, appendicitis, cholelithiasis and cholecystitis, cervical cancer, Hodgkin's disease.
** Perinatal mortality expressed as deaths per 1000 births.
*** Maternal motality expressed as deaths per 100 000 births.

Source: Charlton, Fraser and Murphy (1997).

Access to health care

The Bill which established the NHS stated:

All the Service or any part of it, is to be available to everyone in England and Wales. The Bill imposes no limitations on availability – e.g. limitations based on financial means, age, sex, employment or vocation, area of residence, or insurance qualification. (Ministry of Health, 1946, p. 3)

Over 50 years later, the NHS can claim considerable success in meeting this objective. Notwithstanding the introduction of charges for some services, the Royal Commission on the NHS argued in 1979 that 'one of the most significant achievements of the NHS has been to free people from fear of being unable to afford treatment for acute or chronic illness' (Royal Commission on the NHS, 1979, pp. 10–11). For a generation brought up on a health service largely free at the point of use, it is easy to overlook this achievement. Yet at a time when some other developed countries, such as the United States, have still to ensure access to health care for all citizens, it is salutary to remember that the United Kingdom takes this for granted and the population does not live in fear of bankruptcy in the event of contracting serious medical conditions. More positively, international comparisons indicate that funding health services through general taxation, as in the United Kingdom, is more equitable than other methods (van Doorslaer, Rutten and Wagstaff, 1993).

Despite this achievement, there remain a variety of inequities in access to health care. To begin with, there are differences between England, Northern Ireland, Scotland and Wales (Dixon, Inglis and Klein, 1999). These differences encompass the health of the population, funding levels, and the provision of services and show that expenditure per capita is lowest in England and highest in Scotland, whereas health indicators tend to be best in England and worst in Scotland. With the extra resources available, the Scottish NHS buys more hospital beds and staff per capita than the English NHS and has higher rates of both inpatient and outpatient activity than England. The position in Northern Ireland and Wales is generally between these extremes, indicating that even in advance of devolution there are important differences between the four countries that make up the United Kingdom.

Variations in health are also evident between the English regions. For example, in 1995 the infant mortality rate in England stood at 6.1, and within England the rate varied from 5.2 in Anglia and Oxford to 7.0 in the West Midlands. In the same year the perinatal mortality rate for England was 8.8, and within England the rate varied from 7.3 in Anglia and Oxford to 10.1 in West Midlands (Pullinger, 1997). Variations in funding levels and the provision of services also exist. These illustrate that in 1994, using the former RHAs as the units of analysis, the number of beds per 1000 population varied from 3.4 in the Oxford region to 5.5 in East Anglia. Similarly, the number of hospital medical staff per 100 000 population varied from 96 in the Trent and West Midlands regions to 122 in North East Thames. Allocations to RHAs ranged from £391 per capita in the Oxford region to £512 per capita in North East Thames (Office of Health Economics, 1997).

Differences in the allocation of resources to the English regions have been recognised since the early 1970s. An internal DHSS review led to the introduction of a new method of allocating revenue in 1971–72, and in 1975 the Resource Allocation Working Party (RAWP) was established to produce a formula:

> To reduce progressively, and as far as is feasible, the disparities between the different parts of the country in terms of opportunity for access to health care for people at equal risk; taking into account measures of health needs, and social and environmental factors which may affect the need for health care. (DHSS, 1975c)

The RAWP report recommended a formula based on the size of each region's population, weighted for age, sex and morbidity, with standardised mortality ratios being used as a proxy for morbidity (DHSS, 1976a). Using this approach, the Working Party found that some regions had allocations around 10 per cent below their target share of resources, and others had allocations more than 10 per cent above. In accepting the recommendations put forward, the Secretary of State recognised that they would have to be implemented in stages, and this continues to be the case. This is a source of frustration to health authorities below their weighted capitation target and was one of the reasons the Acheson Report recommended that there should be more rapid progress towards equity in resource allocation. The principles of the RAWP approach have been maintained even though the detail of its application have changed, sometimes quite significantly, in the light of research into the indicators that best reflect variations in need and alterations to the structure of the NHS. Figures show that by 1997–98, over 90 per cent of health authorities were within 5 per cent of their target allocation.

Alongside regional differences there are social class differences in access to health care. The significance of these was recognised by Titmuss writing in 1968:

> We have learnt from 15 years' experience of the Health Service that the higher income groups know how to make better use of the Service; they tend to receive more specialist attention; occupy more of the beds in better equipped and staffed hospitals; receive more elective surgery; have better maternity care; and are more likely to get psychiatric help and psychotherapy than low income groups – particularly the unskilled. (Titmuss, 1968, p. 196)

Support for Titmuss's analysis came from Alderson's examination of a number of mainly preventative services. This found underuse of services in relation to need, and Alderson commented:

The data presented are compatible with the hypothesis that there is a group in the community who are aware of the provisions of the health service and who obtain a higher proportion of the resources of the health service than would be expected by chance and a much higher proportion in relation to their needs when compared with others in the community. (Alderson, 1970, p. 52)

One of the explanations of variations in the utilisation of services by social class is that these services may not be equally available in different parts of the country. It is this observation that lies behind the inverse care law formulated by Julian Tudor-Hart which states that 'the availability of good medical care tends to vary inversely with the need of the population served' (Tudor-Hart, 1971, p. 412). Tudor-Hart's thesis is that areas of social deprivation containing high proportions of people from the lower social groups tend to have access to less good health services even though their need for these services is greater than that of higher social groups. This argument is reinforced by the work of Le Grand who combined data on the utilisation of services and need to demonstrate that higher social groups benefited more from the NHS than lower social groups (Le Grand, 1978).

More recent evidence has been reviewed and summarised by Propper (1998). Her analysis of data on utilisation and need, displayed in Table 8.5, reported much less systematic variation in the use of services in relation to need than was evident from Le Grand's study. On the other hand, research into the provision of specific interventions do demonstrate variation. For example, the use of GP services was related to social class, with people in the lower social groups making greater use of these services than those in higher social groups. There is a more mixed picture in relation to hospital services, with evidence of services being provided in proportion to deprivation in some areas but not in others. On the basis of its review of the evidence, the Acheson Report commented, 'For many . . . NHS hospital treatments, there

Table 8.5 *Percentage shares of NHS expenditure standardised for need, 1974–87*

Income quintile	1974	1982	1985	1987
Bottom	24.6	22.5	22.7	22.7
2nd	21.6	20.3	22.7	21.2
3rd	19.3	21.1	19.7	19.9
4th	17.9	21.7	18.9	19.8
5th	16.6	14.5	16.1	16.3
Concentration index	−0.083	−0.092	−0.070	−0.062

Note: The concentration index presented at the bottom of each column is a summary measure of the extent of departure from proportionality. It is bounded between −1 and 1, a positive value indicating a regressive distribution.

Source: Propper (1998).

is little evidence of systematic inequities in access between deprivation groups' (Acheson Report, 1998, p. 113), although it did note research pointing out that intervention rates for heart treatment were not higher in areas of greatest need.

A third area in which there are inequities in access concerns the care available to groups such as elderly people, people with learning difficulties and the mentally ill. We noted in Chapter 1 that concerns about the quality of care provided to these groups was one of the factors behind the reorganisation of the NHS in 1974. The issue was brought to prominence in 1967 when a pressure group known as Aid for the Elderly in Government Institutions published a book called *Sans Everything – A Case to Answer,* containing allegations of ill-treatment to elderly patients in psychiatric and geriatric care (Robb, 1967). The Minister of Health asked regional hospital boards to set up independent enquiries and the general conclusion of the enquiries was that the allegations were unfounded.

A rather different picture emerged from the report of the committee of enquiry set up to investigate conditions at Ely Hospital, a hospital for people with learning difficulties in Cardiff. The committee found that many of the allegations of ill-treatment of patients were true, and that there were serious deficiencies at Ely. A number of recommendations were made for improving standards at Ely and at long-stay hospitals generally, including the setting up of a system of inspection to ensure that the local managers of services were aware of what was required (Ely Report, 1969). The Secretary of State at the time of Ely, Richard Crossman, used the report to give greater priority to long-stay services. The Hospital Advisory Service (HAS) was set up to provide the system of inspection recommended by the committee of enquiry, although it was presented as a means of giving advice rather than an inspectorate. In addition, Crossman earmarked funds to be spent specifically on hospitals for people with learning difficulties. These earmarked funds were later extended to other long-stay services, although earmarking for this purpose came to an end in 1974. At the same time, the DHSS issued advice to hospital boards and committees on measures which could be taken at little cost to raise standards of care.

The momentum provided by Crossman was maintained through the publication of a series of further reports into conditions at long-stay hospitals. Partly in response to these inquiries, the DHSS published White Papers setting out the future direction in which services should move; and in terms of overall service development the Department gave priority to these services in the consultative document on *Priorities* published in 1976. These actions were an attempt to allocate a greater share of resources to an area of the NHS which it was recognised had fallen behind required standards (Martin, 1984).

Progress towards achieving the kinds of priorities set out in 1976 has been slow and uneven. Part of the difficulty of achieving national priorities is that health authorities may not share the objectives of the DH. The claims of other groups, particularly in the acute hospital sector, may be pressed strongly at the local level, and may push service development in a different direction from that desired by central government. As we noted in Chapter 7, the implementation of national priorities can therefore be problematic. This point can be illustrated in relation to services for people with a learning difficulty, where a review of progress made in implementing the policies set out in the White Paper, *Better Services for the Mentally Handicapped*, noted that the percentage of NHS revenue allocated to these services declined between 1974–75 and 1977–78. The review commented:

> the financial data for health services suggests that the constraints since 1974, together with demographic pressures and the need to rationalise acute services in order to release revenue for development, meant that health authorities could do little to sustain the previous increase in expenditure on mental handicap services other than their increasing contribution through Joint Finance. (DHSS, 1980c, p. 62)

Undoubtedly one of the reasons for this is that, despite the priority given by the DH, these services are relatively weak in the struggle for scarce resources that occurs in health authorities. Put another way, the micro politics of the NHS may run counter to the macro politics leading to a gap between intention and action.

A fourth area in which access to care has emerged as an issue is the time patients spend waiting for hospital treatment. Waiting lists have existed ever since the establishment of the NHS and their growth is illustrated in Figure 8.3. In examining these trends it is important to recognise that of patients admitted from waiting lists, half are admitted within six weeks, around two-thirds within three months, and only a small proportion wait as long as the 18 months period specified as the maximum waiting time in the *Patient's Charter*. Analysis has shown that five specialties account for around three-quarters of patients waiting, and at various times initiatives within the NHS have succeeded in cutting both waiting lists and waiting times, in some cases significantly. Although there are differences between areas in the experience of patients waiting for treatment, from an equity perspective a more important consideration is the ability of some patients to access treatment through the private sector rather than having to wait for an NHS operation.

As Yates (1987 and 1995) has shown, there is in fact a perverse incentive for hospital specialists in that their income from private practice is in part dependent on the existence of NHS waiting lists and the willingness of some people to pay for treatment to avoid waiting. This derives from the bargain struck between Bevan and the medical profession at the inception of the NHS after which Bevan famously claimed to have stuffed the mouths of specialists with gold to entice them into the NHS (see Chapter 1). The effects are still felt today with private practice coexisting with NHS work, and

Figure 8.3 *Waiting lists in England and Wales, 1948–96*

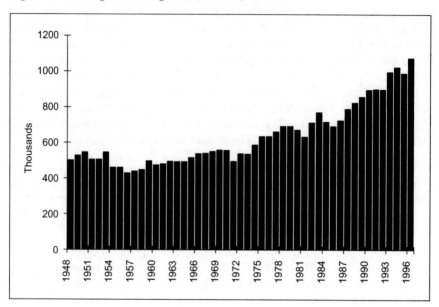

patients who are able to pay for treatment receiving this treatment in a matter of days as opposed to months. Only under the Labour Government in the 1970s did this issue become a matter of political controversy, and even then attention focused more on the existence of private beds in NHS hospitals than the employment contract of specialists. One of the consequences of the reforms to the NHS initiated by the Thatcher government was an expansion of private provision by NHS trusts and this means that paradoxically the NHS is currently a major provider of acute services to private patients. The consequence is to make even more stark the inequities in access that arise from the persistence of private practice within the NHS.

At the time of writing, reducing waiting lists is a high political priority as the Blair government seeks to fulfil its election pledge to cut the number of people on waiting lists by 100 000 in a context in which waiting lists increased immediately after the 1997 general election. One of the reasons that waiting lists have been singled out as a priority is a concern that an increasing number of people may choose to 'go private' if they are unable to receive treatment in the NHS in a reasonable time, and that this may undermine support for the NHS as a universal service. Achieving the targets that have been set is, however, proving difficult, with evidence of some reduction in inpatient waiting lists being matched by increases in the numbers waiting for outpatient appointments. Other NHS services may also be affected adversely by the overriding priority attached to cutting the number of people on waiting lists. To cite only the most obvious example, the aspiration to improve services for people with mental illness or learning difficulties may be more difficult to implement when acute services are receiving much of the attention.

The NHS in the international context

Throughout this book reference has been made to the performance of the NHS in relation to other countries. We noted in Chapter 4 that population health outcomes in the United Kingdom lag behind those of some other developed countries and comparative data on population health confirm this. Using OECD statistics on infant mortality and expectation of life, the United Kingdom appears consistently in the middle of the range. This is not confined to the OECD as demonstrated by Figure 8.4, which uses a composite index drawing on indicators such as life expectancy, infant mortality and immunisation coverage to show the position of the United Kingdom in the European context. We have also shown that expenditure on health services in the United Kingdom is relatively low by international standards, although it is close to what would be expected using economic performance as the predictor. The control over health services expenditure exercised by successive governments helps to explain the position of the United Kingdom in relation to other countries and is consistent with the findings of the OECD (1994b) that political commitment is an important factor in accounting for international differences in spending in health care.

The evidence on public attitudes indicates high levels of satisfaction with the NHS, notwithstanding the decline in the 1990s noted in Chapter 3. Again this is reinforced by recent international evidence comparing attitudes in Australia, Canada, New Zealand, the United Kingdom and the United States (Blendon, Donelan, Schoen, Davis and Binns, 1998). In the case of the United Kingdom, this generally found both higher levels of satisfaction in relation to the performance of health services and changes made by government, and lower levels of dissatisfaction when respondents were asked about difficulties in accessing services. Examples cited in the survey included 15 per cent of people in the United Kingdom reporting that they had experienced difficulties getting medical care compared with between 15 and 28 per cent in other countries, and 25 per cent of people in the United Kingdom reporting that the NHS worked well and required only minor change compared with between 9 and 20 per cent in other countries. The

Figure 8.4 *Health in Europe*

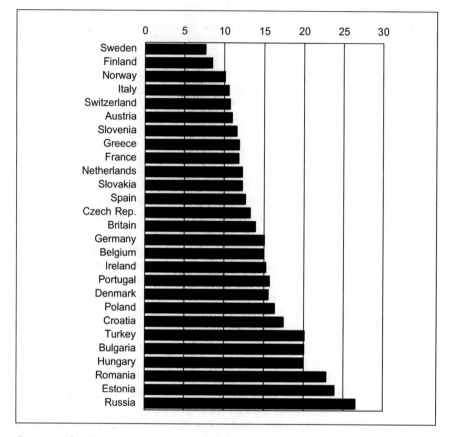

Source: *The Economist*, 12 December 1998.

most important problem cited by United Kingdom respondents was the lack of government funding. As the sponsors of the survey concluded:

> The National Health Service is turning 50 and appears to remain popular. UK families are the least concerned for their personal health care future and relatively low proportions voice support for major rebuilding. Families are well-protected financially. Although waiting times are often long, people in the United Kingdom appear more accepting of longer waiting times for nonemergency services than respondents in other countries. There is strong support for increased funding of the public health system. (Commonwealth Fund, 1998)

In relation to the reform of health care, there are again parallels with international developments. Many countries have introduced changes to the financing and delivery of health care in the 1980s and 1990s in response to perceived weaknesses in existing arrangements. The epidemic of reform that has resulted has included policies to strengthen the management of health services, the introduction of new ways of paying hospitals and doctors, and experiments with market-like mechanisms. Although the United Kingdom has been at the forefront of these developments, countries as diverse as the Netherlands, Sweden and the United States have also experienced significant change with ideas and innovations transferring rapidly between different systems. In this process, policy-makers from other countries have looked to the United Kingdom in the search for lessons both about the experience of reform and the performance of the system that gave its name to the Beveridge model (Ham, 1997b).

An overall judgement on the performance of the NHS in relation to other countries would be that the United Kingdom stands out because it is able to provide universal and more or less comprehensive health services at low cost. The evidence summarised in this chapter and reviewed more extensively elsewhere indicates that the NHS performs reasonably well in delivering its equity objectives, and it is also relatively efficient. Undoubtedly one of the reasons for this is the role of the government in controlling expenditure through its position as the main funder and near monopoly purchaser of health care. As Abel-Smith once commented, the NHS might no longer be the envy of the world but it is certainly the envy of the world's finance ministers (Abel-Smith, 1994). This lesson was not lost on the Thatcher government which flirted with radical options for the reform of health service funding but, as we have seen, concluded that tax funding was the preferred option.

Another reason why the NHS performs reasonably well is the strength of primary care within the United Kingdom. The existence of GPs as the first point of contact and as the gatekeepers between patients and specialists means that a high proportion of medical needs are met without the involvement of hospitals. Not only does this help to contain costs, but it also contributes to the high levels of satisfaction reported by the public (GP services are consistently rated more highly by the public than hospital services). There is also some evidence that countries with a strong primary care orientation tend to achieve better health outcomes. The key research in this field is the work of Starfield whose comparison of 11 systems in the 1980s demonstrated that primary care in the United Kingdom was both more prominent than in other countries and accounted for the ability of the United Kingdom to deliver comprehensive services for expenditure that was low in the comparative context (Starfield, 1992)

To make these points is not to ignore the weaknesses of the NHS. Throughout this book, including in this chapter, we have drawn attention to aspects of health care where there is room for improvement. In no particular order, these include lack of responsiveness and choice, especially in relation to hospital services, uneven performance in respect of the quality of care, and the continuing challenge of ensuring equity in health outcome and service delivery. To this list might be added the comparative neglect of capital expenditure as evidenced by the state of many NHS buildings, and pressures on staff recruitment in some areas, possibly as a consequence of success in containing costs, including wage costs. More fundamentally, and linked to the last point, the evidence on rationing reviewed in earlier chapters indicated that the NHS is struggling to maintain its commitment to deliver comprehensive services to the population, especially in the fields of long-term care and dentistry and in respect of the funding of new forms of treatment such as drugs.

The question that arises for the future is whether the NHS is sustainable in its present form? On this question, opinion is divided with mainstream Conservative and Labour politicians united in the view that the NHS can continue to offer comprehensive and universal services funded through general taxation, and many critics arguing that only with increased public or private funding will the NHS be able to survive. The force of the latter argument was recognised in the report of the Royal Commission on long-term care with its proposals that the costs of care should be shared by the government and individuals. By extension, it might be argued that the same should apply to the NHS, although the political costs for any government in opening up a debate about the use of private funds alongside government expenditure are likely to be high. It is for this reason, as Pierson (1994) has shown in his analysis of welfare reform in the United States and the United Kingdom, that changes are likely to occur indirectly rather than through open debate.

To raise these possibilities is to underline the inevitable trade offs that arise in the case of health policy. Fundamentally, the dilemma for policy-makers is the balance to be struck between objectives such as efficiency, equity, quality and cost control in circumstances in which it is increasingly difficult to score well on all indicators. It follows that the future direction of the NHS will be shaped by the relative value attached to these objectives. In the immediate future, under the Blair government, the focus has shifted towards equity and quality as can be seen from the commitment in *The New NHS* White Paper to reducing variations in performance and raising standards in the NHS as a whole. At the same time, the present Labour government appears to be just as committed to improving efficiency and controlling costs as its Conservative predecessors. The additional resources allocated to the NHS since the 1997 general election have not enabled the gaps in coverage that opened up in the 1980s and 1990s to be filled, nor have they insulated the NHS from recurrent crises. Indeed, the NHS under Labour appears just as vulnerable in this respect as the Conservatives, reflecting Enoch Powell's oft-quoted observation that:

> One of the most striking features of the National Health Service is the continual, deafening chorus of complaint which rises day and night from every part of it, a chorus only interrupted when someone suggests that a different system altogether

might be preferable, which would involve the money coming from some less (literally) palpable source. The universal Exchequer financing of the service endows everyone providing as well as using it with a vested interest in denigrating it, so that it presents what must be a unique spectacle of an undertaking that is run down by everyone engaged in it. (Powell, 1976, p. 16)

It is in this context that the Blair government's plan to modernise the NHS assumes particular importance. The government's reaffirmation of its commitment to the NHS and its apparent reluctance to encourage the growth of the private sector as a safety valve alongside the NHS means that the focus of attention will continue to be, in the language of economists, on how to increase allocative efficiency and technical efficiency within the NHS. The proponents of the third way claim that the eclectic mixture of policies and levers they have put in place will succeed where other options have failed, although this remains a hypothesis to be tested rather than a statement of fact. Fundamentally, the issue at stake is whether a health service that went through a series of efficiency drives under the Thatcher and Major governments and is internationally recognised as offering good value for money can continue to perform well in the face of rising demands and constrained resources. Even more challenging is the capacity of the NHS to improve its performance against a background of increasing expectations and changing social attitudes.

At least two scenarios are possible. Taking the optimistic view, the policy cocktail mixed by the Blair government will deliver the objectives that have been set enabling the NHS not only to survive but also to expand to meet the demands with which it is confronted. Support for this view comes from the priority attached to the NHS in the Comprehensive Spending Review and the obvious determination of the government to drive through the changes it has initiated. Taking the pessimistic view, there is no reason to believe that the reforms promoted by the government will make a bigger impact than the internal market, in relation to which the balance of evidence points to little change either positive or negative (see Chapter 2). If this is the case, then the NHS will struggle to fulfil professional and public expectations, and the mixed economy of health care in the United Kingdom will become even more diverse as patients who are able to exit to the private sector and staff become increasingly dissatisfied with working conditions in a public service unable to adapt to the challenge of increasing expectations and changing attitudes. In this scenario, the NHS risks becoming a safety net for those unable to access alternatives, although the transition from the current arrangement to this potential future is likely to be long drawn out and frequently painful.

A litmus test for the future is provided by the report of the Royal Commission on long-term care. The majority on the Royal Commission has thrown down a gauntlet in proposing significantly increased public spending alongside means-tested private expenditure to provide support for those in need. The cautious response of the government to the report indicates that even this proposal, which in itself fell short of compulsory social insurance funding of long-term care of the kind found in some other countries and advocated by a number of contributors to the debate about this issue, may not find favour. If this does indeed prove to be the case, then the implication is that the role of the private sector both in funding and provision will become more significant in long-term care, and by extension the same may apply to the NHS. This raises the possibility of a third scenario in which the government maintains a major role in the funding of services and the regulation of provision while accepting the likelihood of an increased role for the private sector alongside the public sector. Unlike in the pessimistic option described above, this would not entail the NHS becoming a safety net. Rather, it involves moving beyond the traditional and often unhelpful dichotomies that have dominated debate about the NHS in the quest for a new synthesis (Ham, 1996). Such a future is implied by the proposals of the minority on the Royal Commission which rejected the provision of free care for all and instead favoured a mixture of public and private funding, alongside tighter regulation of service providers.

Conclusion

In this chapter we have traced the evolution of the monitoring and evaluation of health policy. A wide range of arrangements are currently involved in the audit of health service performance in contrast to the early phases of the NHS when these functions were under-developed. We have seen how the results of monitoring feed back into policy-making, an example being the report by the Health Services Commissioner which led to changes of policy in relation to continuing care. We have also noted that for monitoring to influence policy-making, ministers and civil servants must be predisposed to act on the results. In this respect, the rejection of the recommendations of the Black Report by a Conservative government stands in contrast to the willingness of a Labour government to change the principles of NHS resource allocation in the light of evidence about continuing inequalities in the distribution of the budget between regions.

Data on the performance of the NHS demonstrate improvements in health and health care since its inception. Nevertheless, there are a number of inequities in access to services and these continue to pose a challenge. Viewed in the international context, the NHS performs reasonably well, notwithstanding concerns about uneven standards and the inequities that arise from the coexistence of public provision and private practice. Looking to the future, a number of scenarios can be identified, and in all of them the NHS faces a major challenge in improving its performance against a background of increasing expectations and changing social attitudes.

9

Power in Health Services

The examination of the monitoring and evaluation of health policy in Chapter 8 revealed various inequalities in health and health services. In seeking to explain these inequalities, it is necessary to analyse the distribution of power in health care systems. In other words, explaining the distribution of benefits within health services requires us to ask who controls those services and who influences the allocation of resources? There are a number of theoretical approaches to answering these questions, and three will be examined here: Marxist, pluralist and what, for want of a better term, we shall call structuralist.

Marxist approaches

Marxists argue that medical care in societies like Britain must be seen as part of the capitalist mode of production (Doyal, 1979). Within capitalism, Marxists contend that there is an important division between the owners of the means of production – the dominant class or the bourgeoisie – and those who have to sell their wage labour – the subordinate class or the proletariat. It is the capitalist mode of production which gives rise to class relations of production, and Marxists go on to argue that the economically dominant class is also politically dominant. The state therefore acts in the long-term interests of the bourgeoisie, and performs a number of functions.

In O'Connor's terms, the state assists in the process of capital accumulation, and also performs the function of legitimation (O'Connor, 1973). State expenditures are directed towards these ends, and are made up of social capital and social expenses. State expenditures on health services comprise partly social capital, in so far as health services involve the reproduction of a healthy labour force, and partly they comprise social expenses, in so far as health services help to maintain non-working groups and promote social harmony. State involvement in the provision of health services stems from two sources: action by the bourgeoisie to reduce the costs of labour power and to prevent social unrest; and action by the proletariat through the class struggle to win concessions from the bourgeoisie. However, Marxists argue that there may develop a fiscal crisis for the state when the demand for expenditure on health services outstrips the ability of the state to fund that expenditure. At this point a restructuring of public expenditure may occur to the disadvantage of state health services. Marxists would interpret this as an attack on the interests of the subordinate class, even though health services are seen as a form of social control (Gough, 1979).

Within this theoretical perspective, inequalities in service provision between client groups are explained in terms of the lack of productivity of the mentally ill, people with learning difficulties and the elderly. It is suggested that because these groups cannot make a significant contribution to the development of the economy and of profit, they will receive a lower quality service than productive groups. Similarly, social class inequalities in health are interpreted by Marxists as evidence of the continuing influence of economic factors on health and the persistence of class divisions within society. The distribution of benefits within health services is therefore explained by reference to class conflict and the dominance of the bourgeoisie.

At a macro level of analysis a number of authors have used Marxist theory to explain developments in health policy. Yet a convincing theory of power must also be able to explain the processes of policy-making and implementation described in Chapters 6 and 7. Marxist approaches are much weaker at this level of analysis, and Marxist studies of particular decisions, issues or health care organisations are little developed. In contrast, pluralist theories, with their focus on the role of pressure groups and bargaining and negotiation within policy communities, offer a range of insights into the dynamics of health policy-making, and we will now consider the utility of these theories.

Pluralism

The essence of the pluralist democratic theory of power is that the resources which contribute to power are widely distributed among different groups. As we noted in Chapter 5, pluralists argue that no one group is dominant, and each is able to exercise some influence (see for example Dahl, 1961). Power is in fact shared between official groups in governmental agencies and outside interests exerting pressure on these agencies. This helps to ensure there is no consistent bias in the allocation of values, although pluralists would recognise that groups vary in their ability to exercise power. Developments in health services and health policy are explained in terms of the interplay between pressure groups. Since there is no dominant interest, pluralists analyse the distribution of power in relation to particular issues, studying who wins and who loses through often detailed examination of the preferences of different interests and the extent to which decisions match up with expressed preferences. The question of who has power is for the pluralists an empirical question, to be answered by means of case studies of particular policy areas. A range of factors may be important, including party manifestos, key individuals, official reports and the activities of pressure groups, but their relative influence must be studied in specific cases.

Examples of studies of the NHS which have their roots in the pluralist democratic tradition are Willcocks's (1967) examination of the creation of the NHS and Eckstein's (1960) analysis of the operation of the BMA. Each author analyses the way in which decisions are arrived at in a system of pressure group politics, and each is able to show how the outcomes were the result of compromise between the various interests involved. Professional interests vie with consumer interests, and civil servants with politicians, but alliances change, leading to the fragmentation of power which pluralists observe. The strength of pluralist theory is the richness of detail provided about decision-making and the high degree of sophistication which has often been achieved in the analysis of individual, group and organisational influences on policy processes.

Like Marxism, though, pluralism does not provide a completely adequate theory of power. For example, in earlier chapters we noted the key position occupied by the medical profession in the organisation of health services, and our discussion of how policies are made and implemented in the NHS suggests certain inadequacies in the pluralist position. In particular, the strength of producer groups and the relative weakness of consumer groups cast doubt on the pluralists' argument that any group can make itself heard effectively at some stage in the decision-making process, and that no group is dominant (Ham, 1977). Accordingly, as we argued in Chapter 7, attention needs to be paid to the work of Alford, who has maintained that it is important to analyse the nature of structural interests within health services. We will now examine Alford's thesis in greater detail.

Structuralist approaches

Alford argues that structural interests are those interests which gain or lose from the form of organisation of health services (Alford, 1975a). There are three sets of structural interests: dominant, challenging and repressed. Dominant interests are the professional monopolists; challenging interests are the corporate rationalisers; and repressed interests are the community population. Dominant interests are served by existing social, economic and political institutions, and therefore only need to be active when their interests are challenged. Alford argues that the medical profession is dominant in health services, but the profession may be challenged by corporate rationalisers such as health planners and administrators. Again, patient and consumer groups representing the community population may seek to move out of their repressed position by organising to articulate their interests. These struggles between structural interests are not the same as the competition for power between pressure groups. Pressure group competition may well take place within structural interests, as between, for example, different groups of doctors. These conflicts are important, but they leave unchallenged the principle of professional monopoly and dominance. Pressure group politics coexist with struggles between structural interests, and may explain how particular issues are resolved. Structural interests are, however, more significant in influencing the overall distribution of benefits, and in shaping the main contours of power relationships.

The value of Alford's framework has been demonstrated in a study of policy-making in the NHS (Ham, 1981), and the inequalities in power he points to indicate a position close to elitist interpretations of the power structure. In the health sector, professional control of knowledge, recruitment and training, as well as claims to professional autonomy over the content of work, provide the basis of the medical profession's power. Its organisation through powerful pressure groups in continuous contact with governmental agencies, coupled with involvement at all stages in the system of administration, enhance this power. In emphasising elite power based on professional position, the above analysis offers an alternative to both pluralism and Marxism.

Structuralist approaches recognise the existence of pressure group politics but contend that studies which remain at the level of groups are incomplete. Equally, while structuralists acknowledge the importance of economic and class factors, they maintain that class divisions are less important in explaining the development and organisation of health services than divisions between structural interests. The two are by no means synonymous. In particular, the growth of intermediate groups between the bourgeoisie and the proletariat requires some modification of the straightforward Marxist position, and highlights the need for a framework able to take account of the complexities of social divisions within contemporary society.

This suggests that what is required is an approach which builds on the strength of each of the theoretical positions discussed here. We have argued that all three positions have some merits, but none provides an adequate account by itself. Rather than seeking to develop one theory to the point where it furnishes a complete explanation in its own right, it may be preferable to attempt to search for links between the different theories. An investment of effort in this direction holds out the prospect of high returns, not least because the three positions we have discussed tend to focus on different levels of analysis.

Put another way, these theories are complementary rather than alternative and each is able to offer insights into the dynamics of the policy process. The key issue, then, is to develop 'mediating frameworks to connect macro-theory with specific policy issues' (Dunleavy, 1981, p. 4). One approach to this is through the examination of dominant value systems in particular policy areas and their influence on policy. More specifically, by analysing the operation of professional ideologies in health services, it may be possible to establish links between the way issues are defined and resources allocated, the nature of structural interests and the distribution of power, and macro theories of the state (Ham, 1980). The difficulties of doing this are considerable, but a start can be made by exploring the role of the medical profession and the way in which the profession's view of health has come to occupy a dominant position.

Concepts of health

There are many different concepts of health. Margaret Stacey has identified three dimensions along which these concepts vary: individual or collective; functional fitness or welfare; preventive or curative (Stacey, 1977). Stacey notes that in Western societies the individualistic concept of health tends to dominate, and it is usually associated with ideas of functional fitness and curative approaches. This concept seeks the causes of illness within the biological systems of individuals, and it attempts to provide a specific cure for illness in order to make individuals fit for work. Alongside the individualistic concept of health, Stacey notes the existence of a collective concept which emphasises the importance of prevention. The collective concept seeks the causes of illnesses within the environmental, economic and social systems in which people live, and attempts to prevent illness arising by tackling the unhealthy aspects of those systems. Stacey also notes the existence of a welfare concept of health, emphasising the importance of relieving pain and providing care.

While these concepts coexist, it is the individualistic, functional fitness, curative approach which is the most influential. This approach has been characterised as the medical model of health, a model in which doctors have a central role and hospitals play a major part. It has been suggested that the model has two components: a disease component, which holds that illness results from pathological processes in the biochemical functions of the body; and an engineering component, which sees the body as a machine to be repaired by technical means (Illsley, 1977). The medical model emphasises specific, individual causes of illness and searches for specific individual cures for these illnesses. Acceptance of the medical model is important, first, in justifying the preeminent position of the medical profession in health matters, and second, in helping to explain the pattern of investment in health services. Within the NHS, the bulk of resources is allocated to personally orientated, general and acute hospital services. Much less importance has been attached to collective, preventive and welfare approaches to health.

Using an historical perspective, Fox (1986) has shown how the medical model replaced the collective concept of health in the early decades of the twentieth century. As a consequence, the focus of health policy shifted from public health measures and the relief of poverty to the organisation of medical services. Fox uses the phrase 'hierarchical regionalism' to describe the principles on which health policy evolved. These principles include the view that the causes of illness and disease are discovered in medical schools. For most of the twentieth century, a key aim of policy has been to ensure that the results of medical science are made available to the population through hierarchies of services organised on a regional basis. In these hierarchies, specialist hospital services play a major part.

Alternative approaches, such as those emphasising the social and environmental influences on health, have received less attention. However, this may be changing as the medical model comes under increasing attack. The attack on medical dominance in the health field has been spearheaded by writers such as McKeown, who have questioned the significance of the medical contribution in bringing about improvements in health. McKeown's work has demonstrated that improved nutrition, purer water supplies, behavioural changes limiting family size and leading to the better spacing of births, and improved methods of sewage disposal, have been mainly responsible for the advances in health which have occurred in the last 200 years. These factors contributed to the decline in infectious diseases, and assisted in reducing death rates and increasing life expectancy. In contrast, medical science had very little impact until the introduction of vaccines and certain drugs in the twentieth century. Yet McKeown argues that even these interventions came at a time when overall death rates were already in decline as a result of earlier environmental and behavioural changes. On the basis of his analysis, McKeown contends that:

> medical science and services are misdirected, and society's investment in health is not well used, because they rest on an erroneous assumption about the basis of human health. It is assumed that the body can be regarded as a machine whose protection from disease and its effects depends primarily on internal intervention. The approach has led to indifference to the external influences and personal behaviour which are the predominant determinants of health. (McKeown, 1976, p. xiv)

McKeown's work has had a major influence in the development of the health field concept articulated by Lalonde (1974). This concept analyses illness and disease in terms of four elements: human biology, the environment, life-style and health care organisation. Human biology includes aspects of health, such as ageing, which are developed within the body as a result of the basic biology of man. The environment comprises matters relating to health external to the body, over which the individual has little or no control. Life-style refers to the decisions by individuals which affect health and over which they have control. And health care organisation consists of the arrangements made to provide organised health services to individuals. Like McKeown, Lalonde suggests that while most efforts to improve health have centred on medical interventions through health care organisation, it is the other three elements which are more important in identifying the causes of sickness and death. In particular, Lalonde points to the need for people to adopt healthy life-styles in order to prevent illness arising.

This is very much in line with the policy on public health adopted by the DH. As we noted in Chapter 4, the Department has used the work of people like McKeown to argue that greater emphasis should be given to prevention, and that individuals should look after themselves by giving up smoking, adopting an appropriate diet, taking exercise, and so on. This individualistic approach to prevention does not seriously threaten the medical model, and it has been criticised for 'blaming the victim'. A growing body of research indicates that life-style may be less significant than the environment (defined in its widest sense) in influencing illness and disease and that a collective approach to health is needed if progress is to be made in tackling contemporary health problems. This was the argument of the Black Working Group on Inequalities in Health, and other studies have drawn attention to the industrial and environmental causes of cancer (Doyal *et al.*, 1983), the impact of unemployment on health (Brenner, 1979), and to the various ways in which the processes of production, distribution and consumption contribute to illness and disease (Draper, Best and Dennis, 1977). These studies constitute a significant challenge to the medical model, not least because they imply a much reduced role for doctors, and they have begun to influence health policy (see Chapter 4). It must be added, though, that medicine has remained remarkably resilient in the face of criticism, and continues to provide the dominant explanation of health problems in contemporary Western societies.

What are the implications of this analysis for the earlier discussion of power in health care systems? What we hope to have shown is that the medical model, as the dominant (though not the only) value system in the health field, exercises a key influence on the definition of issues and the allocation of resources. The question this raises is whose interests are served by the medical model? Stacey (1977) has reminded us that concepts do not stand alone, they must be understood in terms of the power of different groups. Let us then return to the examination of theories of power for help in explaining the dominance of the medical model.

Power, interests and ideology

In the pluralist framework, concepts of health and the role of medicine are not seen as having special significance. The medical profession is viewed as one interest among many, albeit in most studies a key interest; and concepts of health are implicitly assumed to have emerged out of the underlying consensus on which pluralist theories are based. Within this consensus, prevailing concepts of health are no more than a reflection of the shifting balance of power between interests. The fact that they have remained the same over time is seen by pluralists as an indication of the large measure of agreement between these interests on the meaning of health and the manner in which services should be provided. The question that needs to be asked about this interpretation is whether the consensus which pluralists observe is genuine or false. In other words, is the consensus the result of spontaneous agreement among different groups in the population, or does it derive from manipulation by dominant groups?

This question is not easily resolved. Pluralists would argue that people's expressed preferences are the only reliable guide to their interests, and the fact that these preferences demonstrate strong support for the medical profession is in itself sufficient to show that the consensus on values is genuine. In contrast, critics of pluralism would argue that people's real interests may differ from their expressed preferences, in which case the possibility of a false consensus being manipulated by dominant groups cannot be ruled out. The problem with this approach is how to establish the existence of real interests which are different from expressed preferences (Saunders, 1979). One line of analysis in the health field would be to develop McKeown's work, which, as we have noted, has suggested that society's investment in health is not well-used because it is based on the medical model. What this indicates is that people's real interests might be better served by an alternative pattern of investment. That is, improved health might result from a reorientation away from personally orientated, hospital-based health care towards a system in which more emphasis was given to the social causes of illness and disease. If this could be demonstrated, then a rather different explanation of the interests served by dominant concepts of health would be needed.

Such an explanation is provided by structuralists. For structuralists, dominant concepts of health serve the interests of the medical profession because they legitimate the profession's claim to control in health services. In other words, prevailing concepts of health are explained by the position of the medical profession as a dominant structural interest and its success in getting individualistic definitions of illness and disease accepted. The dominance of medicine is in turn accounted for historically in terms of the success of physicians, surgeons and apothecaries in winning state approval for their position, and in turning their occupations into professions having exclusive control over their area of work (Wilding, 1982). Medical dominance does not imply a conspiracy against subordinate groups. Rather, it reflects the power of doctors, their control of key resources such as expertise and knowledge, and their ability to achieve acceptance for their own concept of health. This concept of health makes sense to groups in the population other than doctors, but as we have shown, it is not the only concept, and it is not necessarily the concept which best serves the interests of the population.

Like structuralists, Marxists would challenge the pluralists' position that consensus is genuine, but would see dominant concepts of health not as an indication of the power of the medical profession, but as evidence of the dominance of the bourgeoisie. In particular, Marxists argue that the individual, disease-based model of curative medicine helps to maintain the position of dominant groups by masking the real causes of illness which lie within the social and economic system of capitalism. As Navarro has put it:

> the social utility of medicine is measured primarily in the arena of legitimation. Medicine is indeed socially useful to the degree that the majority of people believe and accept the proposition that what are actually politically caused conditions can be individually solved by medical intervention. From the point of view of the capitalist system, this is the actual utility of medicine – it contributes to the legitimation of capitalism. (Navarro, 1976, p. 208)

For Marxists, the medical model is a key linking concept explaining not only how issues are defined and benefits distributed in the policy process, but also highlighting underlying class divisions within society. The conclusion to be drawn from the Marxist analysis is that the prevailing concept of health serves class interests, that power is weighted heavily in favour of those interests, and that doctors, although seemingly in a powerful position, merely administer the health care system on behalf of dominant groups.

It thus emerges that Marxists and structuralists see different interests being served by dominant concepts of health. Structuralists argue that the medical profession has power in its own right, not simply power deriving from its utility to dominant groups. In contrast, Marxists argue that medical power results from class power. The Marxist position is well summarised by Navarro, who criticises writers such as Alford for:

> their failure to recognise that those elites (for example medicine) are in reality segments of a dominant class and that, when they are considered in a systemic and not just a sectorial fashion, they are found to possess a high degree of cohesion and solidarity, with common interests and common purposes for transcending their specific differences and disagreements. (Navarro, 1976, pp. 189–90)

The question which needs to be raised about this argument is whether all conflicts are 'in reality' class conflicts, and if so how disagreements between the state and the medical profession can be explained. A key theme of this book has been the challenge to medical dominance in the NHS during the 1980s and 1990s as politicians have questioned the autonomy of doctors and have pursued policies which have been strongly opposed by the BMA and other interest groups. In the final section of this chapter we analyse the significance of these developments and what they tell us about power in health services.

Theories and practice

The underlying determinism of Marxist approaches has increasingly been challenged by writers who have pointed to developments in policy and practice which cannot adequately be explained by these approaches. Saunders, for example, has argued that state expenditure on health services may be dysfuntional rather than automatically serving the interests of dominant groups (Saunders, 1981). The fiscal crisis of the state that began in the 1970s has illustrated the importance of Saunders's criticism, and has indicated that while expenditure on areas of collective consumption like the NHS may benefit professional interests, it may be against the interests of dominant groups, whose main purpose is to maintain capital accumulation. A similar point is made by Cawson (1982) who argues that the growth of public expenditure has been fuelled by the bargaining processes between the state and producer groups. Cawson explains this in terms of the development of a corporate sector in the British political system in which producer groups like the BMA are intimately involved both in the making of policy and its implementation. Cawson predicts that expenditure cuts will be resisted by producer groups and that governments faced with a fiscal crisis will seek to reduce the burden of public expenditure by privatising services.

Although this has happened in some policy areas, a comparative study of welfare reform in the USA and the UK (Pierson, 1994) has highlighted the political difficulties in cutting back public services, including health care, and has shown how governments used a variety of indirect strategies to bring about change rather than risk confrontation and electoral unpopularity. These strategies were pursued in part because of the strength of existing bureaucratic and professional institutions and their ability to resist change. Health policy in Britain in the 1980s and 1990s exemplifies this and demonstrates that the response to the fiscal crisis that developed at that time was mediated by the influence of pressure groups and other interests. While there was some growth in the contribution of the private health sector in the this period, privatisation of NHS services was limited to non-clinical areas such as catering, cleaning and laundry services which were opened up to competitive tendering, and increases in charges for prescriptions, dental care and ophthalmic services. The indirect strategies pursued were of greater significance and included the use of private finance to pay for new capital projects, the unannounced transfer of long-term care from the NHS to social services and to private funders and providers, and the use of private hospitals for the treatment of some NHS patients. These policies all stemmed from a concern to control public expenditure at a time when changes in the economy and in political alignments undermined the post war consensus on the expansion of the welfare state and led to the examination of more radical alternatives.

Yet, in making this point, it should also be noted that the Thatcher government considered but rejected moving away from tax funding of the NHS to private funding both because of the political costs associated with such a move and evidence that alternative methods of funding appeared to offer little benefit. In other words, the fiscal crisis that prompted a review of policy did not lead automatically to the response predicted by some analysts. Rather, the eventual outcome represented a compromise between the ideological instincts of politicians in power and their assessment of what was feasible and desirable. It was this that led the Thatcher government to focus on ways of increasing efficiency and of curtailing professional power. In so doing, the government had to overcome the resistance of the BMA and related organisations and it had to persuade civil servants in the Department of Health to support policies that unsettled established routines in the health policy community. To this extent, corporatist relationships in the health sector made it more difficult for a reforming government of the centre-right to pursue those policies that it instinctively favoured.

In relation to health services, the reforms initiated since the Griffiths Report can be seen as an attempt to strengthen the hand of managers in their challenge to medical dominance. The appointment of general managers, and the call for doctors to be more closely involved in management, were both designed to introduce greater control over the activities of the medical profession and to influence the behaviour of consultants in their position as the key influencers of resources in the NHS. What is more, the recommendation in the Griffiths Report that arrangements for public consultation on decisions should be streamlined was interpreted by some observers as an attempt to maintain community interests in their repressed position. As Day and Klein noted at the time, one of the implications was that conflict between managers and professionals was more likely to occur, particularly if clinical freedom was questioned and challenged (Day and Klein, 1993). Coincidentally, publication of the Griffiths Report occurred within days of a claim that clinical freedom had died, 'crushed between the rising costs of new forms of investigation and treatment and the financial limits inevitable in an economy that cannot expand indefinitely' (Hampton, 1983, p. 1238). While this obituary appeared premature, the medical profession was not slow to recognise the threat posed by Griffiths and to argue that doctors should take on the general management role whenever possible.

In practice, the appointment of doctors as general managers was the exception rather than the rule, and the introduction of general management did lead to a more active management style in which managers were increasingly involved in questioning medical priorities (Flynn, 1991). The extent to which this resulted in a shift in the frontier of control between managers and doctors is disputed with the balance of evidence maintaining that change was limited. To quote Harrison, who has made an extensive study of general management:

> the basic sources of (in Alford's terms) the doctors' structural monopoly remain unchanged. It is still general practitioners who provide the selection for consultants to work on. It is still consultants who decide which, and how many patients to see, and how to diagnose and treat them. . . The prime determinant of the pattern of the health services is still, just as before Griffiths, what doctors choose to do. (Harrison, 1988, p. 123)

The Griffiths reforms were taken a stage further by *Working for Patients*. The White Paper built on the introduction of general management and sought to reinforce measures already taken to increase the accountability of the medical profession. As a consequence, general managers took part in the appointment of hospital consultants, negotiated job plans with each consultant, and participated in deciding which consultants should receive distinction awards. In parallel, new disciplinary procedures were introduced for hospital doctors, the resource management initiative was extended throughout the NHS, and clinical audit received higher priority. In the case of GPs, the Family Health Services Authorities established following the White Paper were given increased powers to monitor the performance of GPs in relation to the new contract introduced in 1990.

The separation of purchaser and provider responsibilities and the introduction of contracts posed a challenge to medical dominance. The establishment of health authorities and GP fundholders as purchasers created a countervailing power to established interests in NHS trusts, and over time this had some impact on priority-setting and resource allocation. To some degree, the effect was to shift influence within the medical profession, for example between hospital doctors and GPs, and to some degree it enhanced the role of managers in relation to doctors. Again, though, the impact of these changes should not be exaggerated. Just as with the introduction of general management, the effect on roles and relationships within the NHS was complex as patterns of pluralistic bargaining among doctors mediated the implementation of these changes and defeated attempts to explain their impact from any single perspective. Put another way, while the relative position of structural interests changed only at the margins, there were shifts *within* each set of interests which had an influence on policy-making, as in the enhanced priority attached to public health and primary care.

The policies pursued by the Blair government elected in 1997 take a stage further the search for ways of making doctors more accountable for their performance. These policies build on both general management and the separation of purchaser and provider responsibilities and focus particularly on the introduction of new forms of regulation to raise standards within the NHS. Specifically, doctors are required to take part in clinical audit and to work within the guidelines set at a national level by the National Institute for Clinical Excellence. The establishment of the Commission for Health Improvement provides a means of independent examination of clinical performance, and the publication of comparative data on clinical outcomes marks the beginning of an attempt to open up variations in standards to public scrutiny. The genesis of these policies lies in part in examples of failures of clinical performance within the NHS, but it is also the latest manifestation of a long-term trend to enhance professional accountability.

To summarise this argument, it is clear that developments such as the appointment of general managers into the NHS, the challenge to the professions and the separation of purchaser and provider responsibilities cannot be explained simply in terms of the internal dynamics of the Service. Policies in the health field are constrained by a wider set of factors, particularly the approach taken by government to the management of the economy and public expenditure. The value of the perspective offered by writers such as Cawson is precisely that it draws attention to the economic context within which social policies are developed. Cawson's analysis of corporatism and welfare is closely linked to the structuralist analysis of power, and both Cawson and Alford recognise the significance of the process of capital accumulation and the role played by the state in promoting economic activity. At the same time, they reject Marxist models of political analysis which reduce all conflicts to class conflicts. Alford in particular maintains that the way in which the accumulation process influences structural interests and policy development in the health field is highly complex. While health policy cannot be adequately understood without reference to economic policy, it cannot be explained solely or even mainly in terms of class analysis. As Alford has written, 'The translation of class interests (or a cultural consensus) into organisational form and then into action is problematic and contingent' (Alford, 1975b, p. 153). Our analysis underlines the importance of this observation and indicates the futility of attempting to read off policy responses from any of the traditions outlined in this chapter.

The implication that follows is not only that no single theoretical perspective is able to offer an adequate explanation, but also that some perspectives are more useful than others. Furthermore, the extent to which each perspective is useful will depend on the focus of analysis. As the evidence presented in this book shows, the dynamics surrounding particular policy initiatives are often best illuminated by ideas drawn from the pluralist tradition, supplemented by concepts developed by political scientists to study agenda-setting, the role of political institutions and the functioning of policy communities and networks. Analysis of patterns of policy development over time and the changing nature of power and influence need to be informed by the insights offered by the theory of structural interests, recognising that the outcome of bargaining and negotiation on individual issues will be shaped by the way in which some interests systematically gain or lose.

In turn, explanations of major changes in the content of the policy agenda must relate these changes to developments in the economy and society, given the influence of events such as war on the creation of the NHS and fiscal crises on the introduction of the internal market. This latter insight is the most valuable contribution of Marxist perspectives even though these perspectives are often overly deterministic and fail to reflect the complexities of social divisions in contemporary society. In short, as Klein has demonstrated in seeking to explain the origins of *Working for Patients,* a variety of interpretations need to be invoked to account for major policy change (Klein, 1995, p. 176).

Conclusion

At first sight, pluralist theories offer a convincing explanation of the distribution of power within health services. After all, the NHS comprises a large number of different groups competing for resources, and most decisions result from bargaining between these groups. Furthermore, health policies tend to involve small adjustments to what has gone before, and a variety of interests are often involved in policy-making. This is in part the picture which has emerged from the discussion of health policy-making and implementation in earlier chapters, and it fits the description of political activity put forward in the pluralist model.

However, Marxist theories challenge the assumptions behind pluralism and provide an alternative explanation. Instead of focusing on immediate conflicts between pressure groups, Marxists seek to relate health care systems to the economic systems within which they are located. By analysing the underlying processes at work, Marxists argue that health services are shaped by dominant groups, whose interests are served by prevailing concepts of health and illness. Health services help to legitimate capitalism and to promote capital accumulation. Pluralists are unable to perceive this because they concentrate on surface struggles and neglect deeper class conflicts. Furthermore, pluralists take dominant concepts of health for granted, and do not question seriously the beneficial impact of medicine or the possibility that conflict may be limited to a narrow range of issues through ideological domination.

In contrast to both approaches, Alford's theory of structural interests looks beyond the surface politics of pressure group conflicts and finds not class struggle but professional dominance. This approach recognises that the world of everyday politics may well approximate to pluralist theories, but it goes further to identify wide discrepancies in power in relation to dominant, challenging and repressed structural interests. Alternative concepts of health are acknowledged to exist, and prevailing concepts reflect the ability of dominant groups to get their definitions accepted. Within this framework, it is possible to encompass both the strengths of pluralist theory, recognising the diversity and variety of pressure group behaviour, and some of the insights of the Marxist analysis, acknowledging that what appears to be going on may obscure underlying conflicts between key interests.

It is suggested, then, that future work might usefully build on this framework and seek to further explicate the 'problematic and contingent' nature of relationships between individual and group action on particular issues of health policy, the role of structural interests, and the characteristics of the state. Our earlier analysis of professional ideologies in the health care system provided some hints on how this might be done, and further empirical studies are required. Above all, it is the interaction of the different levels of analysis which is in need of further investigation. Sophisticated studies of specific policy issues need to be related to the action and inaction of structural interests and the changing role and functions of the state if a complete understanding of the complexities of health policy is to be obtained.

Too often in the past, research at one level has occurred in isolation from research at other levels. The challenge now facing students of health policy and politics is to develop mediating frameworks to link different levels of analysis. Harrison's analysis of the introduction of general management into the NHS (Harrison, 1994) has illustrated how a variety of theoretical perspectives can help to explain particular initiatives, thereby paving the way for other studies. As we argued at the beginning of the book, individuals and groups may have an impact on policy, but under conditions not of their own choosing. This has been demonstrated by Smith (1999) in his analysis of power within government and Smith's contention that actors are central but are constrained by context and structure reinforces these arguments. Articulating the relationship between action and structure is therefore of the utmost importance, and the discussion in this chapter has pointed to some directions in which work might proceed.

Guide to Further Reading

Chapter 1

Further reading suggestions on the development of health services and health policy must necessarily be highly selective. Useful general accounts of the evolution of the welfare state in Britain are provided by Bruce (1968), Fraser (1973), Gilbert (1966, 1970) and Timmins (1995). Studies which look more specifically at the history of the medical profession and health services include those by Abel-Smith (1964), Cartwright (1971) and Stevens (1966). Eckstein (1958), Lindsey (1962) and Webster (1988; 1996) provide a wealth of material on the period before and after the creation of the National Health Service. Levitt (1979) describes the reorganised structure of the NHS introduced in 1974, and Brown (1979) analyses the impact of the 1974 changes. Klein (1995) offers a good overview of the politics of health services in the period since 1939.

Chapter 2

The background to the Ministerial Review of the NHS is traced in Timmins (1995) and Butler (1992). A summary of the debate which took place during the Review is contained in Ham, Robinson and Benzeval (1990). The government's proposals were contained in three White Papers, *Working for Patients, Caring for People* and *Promoting Better Health* (Secretary of State for Health and others, 1989a, 1989b; Secretary of State for Social Services and others, 1987). Klein's account of the politics of the NHS (Klein, 1995) contains a useful analysis of the events which led up to the Review and the outcome. Ham (1997a) describes the implementation of the reforms, while Le Grand, Mays and Mulligan (1998) review the evidence on the impact of the internal market.

Chapter 3

The Blair government's proposals are set out in a White Paper, *The New NHS* (Secretary of State for Health, 1997), a Green Paper on public health, *Our Healthier Nation* (Secretary of State for Health, 1998a), and a consultation document on quality in the new NHS, *A First Class Service* (Secretary of State for Health, 1998b). Early commentaries on the government's plans are provided in Klein (1998) and Ham (1999). The results of the comprehensive spending review set out plans for the future of NHS spending (Chancellor of the Exchequer, 1998), and the experience of primary care groups is foreshadowed in Regen, Smith and Shapiro (1999). The implications of devolution are reviewed in Hazell and Jervis (1998).

Chapter 4

Useful summaries of contemporary issues in health policy are provided in the annual reports of the Department of Health (for example, DH 1998a) and the annual guidance on planning and priorities. Information on expenditure trends and the performance of the NHS since its establishment is contained in the compendium of statistics produced by the Office of Health Economics (1997). More specific information is best tracked by consulting circulars, White Papers and other policy statements issued by the Department of Health. Examples include the Green Paper on public health (Secretary of State for Health, 1998a), the consultation paper on quality in the new NHS (Secretary of State for Health, 1998b), and the paper on the development of partnership working (Department of Health, 1998c). Reports from other organisations, like the Audit Commission's review of services for older people, offer a commentary on particular initiatives (Audit Commission, 1997). Experience of rationing in the NHS is analysed by Klein, Day and Redmayne (1996).

Chapter 5

More detailed information on the nature of policy and political systems can be found in Easton's work (Easton, 1953, 1965a, 1965b). Jenkins (1978) examines policy analysis using a political and organisational perspective and makes use of an amended systems model, and Parsons (1995) offers an overview of different perspectives on policy analysis. The Crossman and Castle Diaries (Crossman, 1975, 1976, 1977; Castle, 1980) give inside views of the organisation of British central government. Beer (1969) provides an important interpretation of the evolution of politics in Britain; and Smith (1976) describes central government from a policy perspective. Brown and Steel (1979) analyse changes in the civil service and the machinery of government, while Norton (1981) discusses the role of the House of Commons and Richardson and Jordan (1979) focus on the part played by pressure groups in the policy process. Jordan and Richardson (1987) examine the policy process in Britain, and Hennessy (1986; 1989; 1995) analyses the role of the Cabinet, civil service and other institutions. Dunleavy and others (1997) assess recent developments in British politics. Smith (1999) reviews the role of the core executive.

Chapter 6

Brown (1975) has written a good, general account of the workings of the DHSS and the part it played in the management of the NHS, personal social services and social security until the mid-1970s. Detailed information on the organisation of the DHSS, particularly in relation to health services, is provided by Butts and colleagues (Butts, Irving and Whitt, 1981) and Razell (1980). The Griffiths Report (1983) and the Regional Chairmen's Enquiry (1976) indicate some of the reasons why a change in the organisation of the DHSS was necessary. The Crossman and Castle Diaries give valuable insights into the politician's view of health policy-making in central government (Crossman, 1977; Castle, 1980). Studies of policies on hospital planning (Allen, 1979) and smoking (Popham, 1981) have illustrated the role of ministers, civil servants and pressure groups in the policy process. The Banks review (1994) summarises developments in the 1980s and 1990s. More recent accounts of the internal workings of the DH are few and far between, and Day and Klein's assessment is probably the best (Day and Klein, 1997).

Chapter 7

Brown (1975, 1977) discusses in general terms the relationship between the DHSS and health authorities, while Haywood and Alaszewski (1980) analyse the extent to which the NHS Planning System has been an effective vehicle for the implementation of central policies. Hunter (1980) explores the dynamics of policy-making in health authorities, and identifies a number of phases in centre–periphery relationships (Hunter, 1983). The author's own examination of policy-making in the NHS between 1948 and 1974 (Ham, 1981) covers similar territory. Klein's (1995) work on the politics of the NHS contains much that is relevant to the student of health policy implementation, as does the author's study of health authorities in the period 1981–85 (Ham, 1986). Harrison (1988; 1994) assesses the impact of the Griffiths Report on general management and the effect this had on the role of managers. Ferlie and colleagues (1996) offer an interpretation of the impact of the new public management on the NHS.

Chapter 8

The *Report of the Royal Commission on the NHS* (1979) contains a general review of the impact of the NHS. The RAWP report (DHSS, 1976a) describes the method used to allocate resources on an equitable geographical basis, and its implementation and impact are reviewed by Mays and Bevan (1987). The Black Report, *Inequalities in Health* (1980), brings together information on social class differences in health and the use of health services, and makes proposals for reducing these differences, and more recent evidence is reviewed by Drever and Whitehead (1997). The Acheson Report (1998) focuses on the policy options for addressing health inequalities. The series of inquiries into long-stay hospitals provide powerful evidence of client-group inequalities. Examples are the Ely and Normansfield reports (Ely Report, 1969; Normansfield Report, 1978). Martin (1984) has summarised the reports and has analysed the nature of the problems that exist in this area. Yates (1987 and 1995) has examined waiting lists and the role of private practice. Charlton and Murphy (1997) summarise and discuss the evidence on population health. The reports of the Social Services Committee (1980, 1981) and the DHSS response (1980d) discuss the difficulties of monitoring and evaluating health services. Evidence on comparative health care can be found in OECD (1992; 1994b) and Ham (1997b).

Chapter 9

The Marxist perspective has been most fully developed by Navarro (1976) and Doyal (1979). The structuralist argument has been set out by Alford (1975a), and applied to the NHS by the author (Ham, 1981). Pluralist ideas have been applied in the work of Eckstein (1960) and Willcocks (1967). Stacey (1977b) and Illsley (1977) review different concepts of health and the way these concepts have influenced service provision. Outside the health field, Saunders (1979) has written a major study of theories of power and the role of ideology which is of considerable relevance to the student attempting to understand the complexities of health policy-making. Smith's (1999) analysis examines the interplay between actors, institutions, context and structure. Harrison (1994) applies a range of theoretical perspectives to the study of health policy.

Bibliography

Abel, L. A. and Lewin, W. (1959) 'Report on Hospital Building', *British Medical Journal Supplement,* 4 April, 109–14.

Abel-Smith, B. (1964) *The Hospitals 1800–1948* (Heinemann).

Abel-Smith, B. (1994) *How to Contain Health Care Costs: An International Dilemma* (University of London).

Acheson Report (1998) *Independent Inquiry into Inequalities and Health* (The Stationery Office).

Alderson, M. R. (1970) 'Social Class and the Health Service', *The Medical Officer*, 17 July, 50–2.

Alford, R. (1975a) *Health Care Politics* (University of Chicago Press).

Alford, R. (1975b) 'Paradigms of Relations between State and Society', in Lindberg, L. N., Alford, R., Crouch, C. and Offe, C. (eds), *Stress and Contradiction in Modern Capitalism* (Lexington Books).

Allen, D. (1979) *Hospital Planning* (Pitman Medical).

Allsop, J. and Mulcahy, L. (1996) *Regulating Medical Work* (Open Univeristy Press).

Ashton, J. and Seymour, H. (1988) *The New Public Health* (Open University Press).

Audit Commission (1996) *What the Doctor Ordered* (HMSO).

Audit Commission (1997) *The Coming of Age* (Audit Commission).

Bachrach, P. and Baratz, M. S. (1970) *Power and Poverty* (Oxford University Press).

Bagehot, W. (1963) [1867] *The English Constitution*, new edn (Fontana).

Baggott, R. (1986) 'Alcohol, Politics and Social Policy', *Journal of Social Policy*, vol. 15 (4), 467–88.

Banks, G. T. (1979) 'Programme Budgeting in the DHSS', in Booth, T. A. (ed.), *Planning for Welfare* (Blackwell).

Banks Review (1994) *Review of the Wider Department of Health* (DH).

Banting, K. (1979) *Poverty, Politics and Policy* (Macmillan).

Barrett, S. and Fudge, C. (eds) (1981) *Policy and Action* (Methuen).

Bebbington, A. and Darton, R. (1996) *Healthy Life Expectancy in England and Wales: Recent Evidence* (University of Kent).

Becker, H. (ed.) (1967) *Social Problems: A Modern Approach* (Wiley).

Beer, S. H. (1969) *Modern British Politics*, 2nd edn (Faber).

Best, G. (1987) *The Future of NHS General Management: Where Next?* (King's Fund).

Bevan, G., Copeman, H., Perrin, J. and Rosser, R. (1980) *Health Care Priorities and Management* (Croom Helm).

Birch, R. (1983) 'Policy Analysis in the DHSS: Some Reflections', *Public Administration Bulletin*, no. 43.

Black Report (1980) *Inequalities and Health* (DHSS).

Blackstone, T. (1979) 'Helping Ministers do a Better Job', *New Society,* 19 July, 131–2.

Blendon, R., Donelan, K., Schoen, C., Davis, K. and Binns, K. (1998) *1998 Commonwealth Fund International Health Policy Survey* (Commonwealth Fund).

Bloor, K. and Maynard, A. (1993*)* *Expenditure on the NHS during and after the Thatcher Years* (Centre for Health Economics).

Bloor, K. and Maynard, A. (1994) 'An Outsider's View of the NHS Reforms', *British Medical Journal*, vol. 309, 352–3.

Botting, B. (ed) (1995) *The Health of Our Children* (HMSO).

Botting, B. (1997) 'Mortality in Childhood', in Drever, F. and Whitehead, M. (eds), *Health Inequalities, op. cit.*

Bottomley, V. (1995) *The NHS: Continuity and Change* (DH).

Bower, H. (1998) 'Staff Cuts would leave CMO Stranded in a Crisis', *British Medical Journal*, vol. 317, 25 July, 232.

Brenner, H. (1979) 'Mortality and the National Economy', *The Lancet,* 15 September, 586–73.

Brown, R. G. S. (1975) *The Management of Welfare* (Fontana).

Brown, R. G. S. (1979) *Reorganising the National Health Service* (Blackwell & Robinson).

Bruce, M. (1968) *The Coming of the Welfare State,* 4th edn (Batsford).

Bunker, J. B., Frazier, H. S. and Mosteller, F. (1994) 'Improving Health: Measuring Effects of Medical Care', *The Milbank Quarterly*, vol. 72 (2), 225–58.

Bunting, J. (1997) 'Morbidity and Health-related Behaviour of Adults – a Review', in Drever, F. and Whitehead, M. (eds), *Health Inequalities, op. cit.*

Butler, J. (1992) *Patients, Policies and Politics* (Open University Press).

Butler, J. R. with Bevan, J. M. and Taylor, R. C. (1973) *Family Doctors and Public Policy* (Routledge & Kegan Paul).

Butts, M., Irving, D. and Whitt, C. (1998) *From Principles to Practice* (Nuffield Principal Hospital Trust).

Calman-Hine (1995) *A Policy Framework for Commissioning Cancer Services* (DH).

Cannon, G. (1984) 'The Cover-up that Kills', *The Times*, 12 June, 13.

Cartwright, F. (1971) *A Social History of Medicine* (Longman).

Castle, B. (1980) *The Castle Diaries 1974–76* (Weidenfeld & Nicolson).

Cawson, A. (1982) *Corporatism and Welfare* (Heinemann).

Central Health Services Council (1969) *The Functions of the District General Hospital* (HMSO).

Central Policy Review Staff (1975) *A Joint Framework for Social Policies* (HMSO).

Chancellor of the Exchequer (1998) *Modern Public Services in Britain*, Cm 4011 (The Stationery Office).

Charlton, J. and Murphy, M. (eds) (1997) *The Health of Adult Britain 1841–1994*, Vols 1 and 2 (The Stationery Office).

Charlton, J. (1997) 'Trends in all-cause mortality: 1841–1994', in Charlton and Murphy (eds), Vol 1, *op. cit.*

Charlton, J., Fraser, P. and Murphy, M. (1997) 'Medical Advances and Iatrogenesis', in Charlton and Murphy (eds), Vol. 1, *op. cit.*

Clode, D. (1977) 'Plans aren't Worth the Paper they are Written on', *Health and Social Services Journal,* 16 September, 1314–16.

Cmnd 9058 (1983) *Financial Management in Government Departments* (HMSO).

Commonwealth Fund (1998) *Nations Face Public Discontent with Health Care* (Commonwealth Fund).

Crossman, R. H. S. (1963) Introduction to Bagehot, W., *The English Constitution* (Fontana) *op. cit.*

Crossman, R. H. S. (1972) *A Politician's View of Health Service Planning* (University of Glasgow Press).

Crossman, R. H. S. (1975) *The Diaries of a Cabinet Minister*: Vol 1, *Minister of Housing 1964–66* (Hamilton & Cape).

Crossman, R. H. S. (1976) *The Diaries of a Cabinet Minister:* Vol 2, *Lord President of the Council and Leader of the House of Commons 1966–68* (Hamilton & Cape).

Crossman, R. H. S. (1977) *The Diaries of a Cabinet Minister:* Vol 3, *Secretary of State for Social Services 1968–70* (Hamilton & Cape).

Dahl, R. (1961) *Who Governs?* (Yale University Press).

Day, P. and Klein, R. (1983) 'The Mobilisation of Consent versus the Management of Conflict: Decoding the Griffiths Report', *British Medical Journal*, vol. 287, 1813–16.

Day, P. and Klein, R. (1997) *Steering but not Rowing?* (The Policy Press).

DH (1991) *The Patient's Charter*.

DH (1994) *The Operation of the NHS Internal Market: Local Freedoms, National Responsibilities*.

DH (1997) *Statement of Responsibilities and Accountabilities*.

DH (1998a) *The Government's Expenditure Plans 1998–99. Departmental Report* (The Stationery Office).

DH (1998b) *The Health of the Nation – a Policy Assessed* (The Stationery Office).

DH (1998c) *Partnership In Action*.

DHSS (1971) *Better Services for the Mentally Handicapped*, Cmnd 4683 (HMSO).

DHSS (1972) *The Facilities and Services of Psychiatric Hospitals in England and Wales 1970*, Statistical and Research Report Series no. 2 (HMSO).

DHSS (1974) *The Facilities and Services of Mental Illness and Mental Handicap Hospitals in England and Wales 1972*, Statistical and Research Report Series no. 8 (HMSO).

DHSS (1975a) *Better Services for the Mentally Ill*, Cmnd 6223 (HMSO).

DHSS (1975b) *Draft Guide to Planning in the NHS*.

DHSS (1975c) *First Interim Report of the Resource Allocation Working Party*.

DHSS (1976a) *Sharing Resources for Health in England* (HMSO).

DHSS (1976b) *Priorities for Health and Personal Social Services in England* (HMSO).

DHSS (1976c) *The NHS Planning System*.

DHSS (1976d) *Prevention and Health: Everybody's Business* (HMSO).

DHSS (1977a) *Prevention and Health*, Cmnd 7047 (HMSO).

DHSS (1977b) *The Way Forward* (HMSO).

DHSS (1979a) *Patients First* (HMSO).

DHSS (1979b) *Review of Health Capital*.

DHSS (1980a) Health Circular (80) 8, *Health Service Development Structure and Management*.

DHSS (1980b) *Hospital Services: The Future Pattern of Hospital Provision in England*.

DHSS (1980c) *Mental Handicap: Progress, Problems and Priorities*.

DHSS (1980d) *Reply by the Government to the Third Report from the Social Services Committee, Session 1979–80*, Cmnd 8086 (HMSO).

DHSS (1981a) *Report of a Study on Community Care*.

DHSS (1981b) *Growing Older*, Cmnd 8173 (HMSO).

DHSS (1981c) *Care in Action* (HMSO).

DHSS (1981d) *Care in the Community*.

DHSS (1981e) *Report on a Study of the Acute Hospital Sector* (HMSO).

DHSS (1981f) *Report on a Study of the Respective Roles of the General Acute and Geriatric Sectors in Care of the Elderly Hospital Patient*.

DHSS (1983a) *Health Care and its Cost* (HMSO).

Dixon, J., Inglis, S. and Klein, R. (1999) 'Is the English NHS Underfunded?' *British Medical Journal*, vol. 318, 20 February, 522–6.

Doll, R. (1974) *To Measure NHS Progress* (Fabian Society).

Doyal, L. with Pennell, I. (1979) *The Political Economy of Health* (Pluto Press).

Doyal, L. *et al.* (1983) *Cancer in Britain* (Pluto Press).

Draper, P., Best, G. and Dennis, J. (1977) 'Health and Wealth', *Royal Society of Health Journal*, 97, 65–70.

Drever, F. and Bunting, J. (1997) 'Patterns and Trends in Male Mortality', in Drever, F. and Whitehead, M. (eds), *Health Inequalities, op. cit.*

Drever, F. and Whitehead, M. (eds) (1997) *Health Inequalities* (The Stationery Office).

Dunleavy, P. (1981) 'Professions and Policy Change: Notes Towards a Model of Ideological Corporatism', *Public Administration Bulletin*, no. 36, 3–16.

Dunleavy, P., Gamble, A., Holliday, I. and Peele, G. (eds) (1997), *Developments in British Politics*, Vol. 5 (Macmillan).

Dunnell, K. (1997) 'Are we Healthier', in Charlton and Murphy (eds), Vol 2, *op. cit.*

Easton, D. (1953) *The Political System* (Knopf).

Easton, D. (1965a) *A Systems Analysis of Political Life* (Wiley).

Easton, D. (1965b) *A Framework for Political Analysis* (Prentice-Hall).

Eckstein, H. (1958) *The English Health Service* (Harvard University Press).

Eckstein, H. (1960) *Pressure Group Politics* (Allen & Unwin).

Edelman, M. (1971) *Politics as Symbolic Action* (Markham).

Edelman, M. (1977) *Political Language* (Academic Press).

Ely Report (1969) *Report of the Committee of Enquiry into Allegations of Ill-treatment of Patients and Other Irregularities at the Ely Hospital, Cardiff*, Cmnd 3975 (HMSO).

Enthoven, A. (1985) *Reflections on the Management of the NHS* (Nuffield Provincial Hospitals Trusts).

Expenditure Committee (1971) Employment and Social Services Sub-Committee, *Minutes of Evidence*, 31 March 1971, session 1970–1, HC 323ii (HMSO).

Expenditure Committee (1972) *Relationship of Expenditure to Needs*, eighth report from the Expenditure Committee, session 1971–2 (HMSO).

Fallon Inquiry (1999) *Report of the Committee of Inquiry into the Personality Disorder Unit*, Ashworth Special Hospital, Vol. 1, Cm 4191–11 (The Stationery Office).

Ferlie, E., Ashburner, L., Fitzgerald, L. and Pettigrew, A. (1996) *The New Public Management in Action* (Oxford University Press).

Flynn, R. (1991) 'Coping with Cutbacks and Managing Retrenchment in Health', *Journal of Social Policy*, 20 (2), 215–36.

Fowler, N. (1991) *Ministers Decide* (Chapmans).

Fox, D. (1986) *Health Policies Health Politics* (Princeton University Press).

Fraser, D. (1973) *The Evolution of the British Welfare State* (Macmillan).

Gilbert, B. B. (1966) *The Evolution of National Insurance in Great Britain* (Michael Joseph).

Gilbert, B. B. (1970) *British Social Policy 1914–39* (Batsford).

Godber, G. (1975) *The Health Service: Past, Present and Future* (Athlone Press).

Godber, G. (1981) 'Doctors in Government', *Health Trends*, vol. 13.

Godber, G. (1998) 'Role of Chief Medical Officer has indeed Diminished', *British Medical Journal*, vol. 317, 28 November, 1521.

Gough, I. (1979) *The Political Economy of the Welfare State* (Macmillan).

Griffiths, R. (1992) 'Seven Years of Progress – General Management in the NHS', *Health Economics*, 1(1), 61–70.

Griffiths Report (1983) *NHS Management Inquiry* (DHSS).

Griffiths Report (1988) *Community Care: Agenda for Action* (HMSO).

Guillebaud Committee (1956) *Report of the Committee of Enquiry into the Cost of the National Health Service,* Cmd 9663 (HMSO).

Hall, P., Land, H., Parker, R. and Webb, A. (1975) *Change, Choice and Conflict in Social Policy* (Heinemann).

Halper, T. (1989) *The Misfortunes of Others: End-Stage Renal Disease in the United Kingdom* (Cambridge University Press).

Ham, C. J. (1977) 'Power, Patients and Pluralism', in Barnard, K. and Lee, K. (eds), *Conflicts in the NHS* (Croom Helm).

Ham, C. J. (1980) 'Approaches to the Study of Social Policy Making', *Policy and Politics,* vol. 8(1), 55–71.

Ham, C. J. (1981) *Policy Making in the National Health Service* (Macmillan).

Ham, C. J. (1984) 'Members in Search of an Identity', *Health and Social Service Journal,* 23 February, 222–3.

Ham, C. J. (1986) *Managing Health Services* (School for Advanced Urban Studies, University of Bristol).

Ham, C. J. (1988) 'The NHS – Travelling without Map or Compass', *The Health Service Journal,* April, 412–13.

Ham, C. J. (1993) 'Priority Setting in the NHS: Reports from Six Districts', *British Medical Journal,* vol. 367, 435–8.

Ham, C. J. (1996) *Public, Private or Community? What Next for the NHS* (DEMOS).

Ham, C. J. (1997a) *Management and Competition in the NHS* (Radcliffe Medical Press).

Ham, C. J. (ed) (1997b) *Health Care Reform: Learning from International Experience* (Open University Press).

Ham, C. J. (1999) 'The Third Way in Health Care Reform: Does the Emperor have any Clothes?' *Journal of Health Services Research and Policy,* vol. 4(3), 1–6.

Ham, C. J., Robinson, R. and Benzeval, M. (1990) *Health Check* (King's Fund Institute).

Ham, C. J., Smith, J. and Temple, J. (1998) *Hubs, Spokes and Policy Cycles* (King's Fund).

Hampton, J. R. (1983) 'The End of Clinical Freedom', *British Medical Journal,* vol. 287, 1237–8.

Hansard (1986) 'NHS (General Managers)', written answers, 26 June, col. 298.

Harrison, S. (1988) *Managing the National Health Service* (Chapman & Hall).

Harrison, S. (1994) *National Health Service Management in the 1980s* (Avebury).

Haywood, S. (1983) *District Health Authorities in Action* (University of Birmingham).

Haywood, S. and Alaszewski, A. (1980) *Crisis in the Health Service* (Croom Helm).

Haywood, S. and Hunter, D. (1982) 'Consultative Processes in Health Policy in the United Kingdom: A View from the Centre', *Public Administration,* vol. 69, 143–62.

Hazell, R. and Jervis, P. (1998) *Devolution and Health* (The Nuffield Trust).

Heclo, H. (1974) *Modern Social Politics in Britain and Sweden* (Yale University Press).

Heclo, H. (1978) 'Issue Networks and the Executive Establishment', in King, A. (ed.), *The New American Political System* (American Enterprise Institute).

Heclo, H. and Wildavsky, A. (1981) *The Private Government of Public Money,* 2nd edn (Macmillan).

Hennessy, P. (1986) *Cabinet* (Basil Blackwell).

Hennessy, P. (1989) *Whitehall* (Secker & Warburg).

Hennessy, P. (1995) *The Hidden Wiring* (Victor Gollancz).

Hood, C. (1991) 'A Public Management for All Seasons', *Public Administration,* 69, 3–19.

Hood, C. and James, O. (1997) 'The Central Executive', in Dunleavy, P. *et al.* (eds), *Developments in British* Politics, Vol. 5, *op. cit.*

Hunter, D. (1980) *Coping with Uncertainty* (Research Studies Press).

Hunter, D. (1983) 'Centre–Periphery Relations in the National Health Service: Facilitators or Inhibitors of Innovation?', in Young, K. (ed.), *National Interests and Local Governments* (Heinemann).

Illsley, R. (1977) 'Everybody's Business? Concepts of Health and Illness', in Social Science Research Council, *Health and Health Policy Priorities for Research* (SSRC).

Ingle, S. and Tether, P. (1981) *Parliament and Health Policy: The Role of MPs 1970–75* (Gower).

James, J. (1983) 'Some Aspects of Policy Analysis and Policy Units in the Health Field', in Gray, A. and Jenkins, W. (eds), *Policy Analysis and Evaluation in British Government* (Royal Institute of Public Administration).

Jenkins, W. I. (1978) *Policy Analysis* (Martin Robertson).

Jones, K. (1972) *A History of the Mental Health Services* (Routledge & Kegan Paul).

Jordan, A. G. and Richardson, J. J. (1987) *British Politics and the Policy Process* (Unwin Hyman).

Judge, K., Mulligan, J. and New, B. (1997) 'The NHS: New Prescriptions Needed?' in Jowell, R. *et al.* (eds), *British Social Attitudes: The 14th Report* (Social and Community Planning Research).

Kaye, V. (1977) 'The Team Spirit', *Health and Social Services Journal*, 16 September.

Kingdon, J. W. (1995) *Agendas, Alternatives and Public Policies*, 2nd edn (Harper Collins).

King's Fund Institute (1988) *Health Finance: Assessing the Options* (King's Fund Institute).

Klein, R. (1982) 'Performance Evaluation and the NHS: A Case Study in Conceptual Perplexity and Organisational Complexity', *Public Administration*, vol. 60, Winter, 385–404.

Klein, R. (1983) *The Politics of the National Health Service* (Longman, 2nd edn 1989).

Klein, R. (1984) 'The Politics of Ideology vs. the Reality of Politics: The Case of Britain's National Health Service in the 1980s', *Milbank Memorial Fund Quarterly/ Health and Society*, vol. 62(1), 82–109.

Klein, R. (1995) *The New Politics of the NHS*, 3rd edn (Longman).

Klein, R., Day, P. and Redmayne, S. (1996) *Managing Scarcity* (Open University Press).

Klein, R. (1998) 'Why Britain is Reorganising its National Health Service – Yet Again', *Health Affairs*, 17, 111–25.

Labour Party (1995) *Renewing the NHS* (The Labour Party).

Laing, W. (1990) *Laing's Review of Private Health Care 1990/91* (Laing-Buisson Publications).

Lalonde, M. (1974) *A New Perspective on the Health of Canadians* (Government of Canada).

Lawson, N. (1992) *The View from No. 11* (Bantam Press).

Le Grand, J., Mays, N. and Mulligan, J. (eds) (1998) *Learning from the NHS Internal Market* (King's Fund).

Le Grand, J. (1978) 'The Distribution of Public Expenditure: The Case of Health Care', *Economica*, vol. 45, 125–42.

Lee-Potter, J. (1997) *A Damn Bad Business* (Gollancz).

Levitt, R. (1979) *The Reorganised National Health Service*, 3rd edn (Croom Helm).

Lewis, J. (1986) *What Price Community Medicine?* (Wheatsheaf Books).

Likierman, A. (1988) *Public Expenditure* (Penguin Books).

Lindblom, C. E. (1965) *The Intelligence of Democracy* (The Free Press).

Lindblom. C. E. (1977) *Politics and Markets* (Basic Books).

Lindsey, A. (1962) *Socialized Medicine in England and Wales* (University of North Carolina Press).

Mackintosh, J. P. (1974) *The Government and Politics of Britain,* 3rd revised edn (Hutchinson).

Malone-Lee. M. (1981) 'Where Loyalties Differ', *Health and Social Services Journal,* 26 November, 1448–9.

March, J. and Olsen, J. (1989) *Rediscovering Institutions: The Organisational Basis of Politics* (Free Press).

Martin, J. P. (1984) *Hospitals in Trouble* (Blackwell).

Maxwell, R. (1984) 'Quality Assessment in Health', *British Medical Journal,* vol. 288. 12 May, 1470–2.

Maxwell, R. (1987) 'Private Medicine and Public Policy', in Harrison, A. and Gretton, J. (eds), *Health Care in the UK 1987* (Policy Journals).

Maynard, A. and Bloor, K. (1996) 'Introducing a Market to the United Kingdom's National Health Service', *The New England Journal of Medicine,* 334, 604–8.

Mays, N. and Bevan, G. (1987) *Resource Allocation in the Health Service* (Bedford Square Press).

Mays, N., Goodwin, N., Killoran, A. and Malbon, G. (1998) *Total Purchasing. A step towards Primary Care Groups* (King's Fund).

McKeown. T. (1976) *The Role of Medicine* (Nuffield Provincial Hospitals Trust).

Middlemas, K. (1979) *Politics in Industrial Society* (André Deutsch).

Ministry of Health (1946) *NHS Bill. Summary of the Proposed New Service,* Cmd 6761 (HMSO).

Ministry of Health (1967) *First Report of the Joint Working Party on the Organisation of Medical Work in Hospitals* (HMSO).

Moore, J. (1988) *Protecting the Nation's Health.* Issued under cover of DHSS press release 88/97.

NAHA (1987) *Autumn Survey 1987* (NAHA).

Nairne, P. (1983) 'Managing the DHSS Elephant: Reflections on a Giant Department', *Political Quarterly,* 243–56.

National Audit Office (1989) *The NHS and Independent Hospitals* (HMSO).

National Audit Office (1995) *Contracting for Acute Health Care* (HMSO).

Navarro, V. (1976) *Medicine Under Capitalism* (Prodist).

NHS Executive (1996) *Seeing the Wood, Sparing the Trees.*

NHSME (1991) *A Review of the Functions and Organisation of the Management Executive.*

Nicholl, J. P., Beeby, W. R. and Williams, B. T. (1989) 'Roles of the Private Sector in Elective Surgery in England and Wales, 1986', *British Medical Journal,* 298, 243–7.

Nixon, J. and Nixon, N. (1983) 'The Social Services Committee: A Forum for Policy Review and Policy Reform', *Journal of Social Policy,* vol. 12 (3), 331–55.

Normansfield Report (1978) *Report of the Committee of Inquiry into Normansfield Hospital,* Cmnd 7357 (HMSO).

Norton, P. (1981) *The Commons in Perspective* (Martin Robertson).

Norton, P. (1997) 'Parliamentary Oversight', in Dunleavy, P.*et al.* (eds), *Developments in British Politics,* 5, *op. cit.*

Nuffield Provincial Hospitals Trust (1946) *The Hospital Surveys: The Domesday Book of the Hospital Services* (Oxford University Press).

O'Connor, J. (1973) *The Fiscal Crisis of the State* (St Martin's Press: also Macmillan, 1981).

OECD (1992) *The Reform of Health Care: A Comparative Analysis of Seven OECD Countries* (OECD).

OECD (1994a) *OECD Economic Surveys: United Kingdom 1994* (OECD).

OECD (1994b) *The Reform of Health Care Systems: A Review of Seventeen OECD Countries* (OECD).

OECD (1998) *OECD Health Data 98* (OECD).

Office of Health Economics (1989) *Compendium of Health Statistics,* 7th edn (OHE).

Office of Health Economics (1997) *Compendium of Health Statistics,* 10th edn (OHE).

Owen, D. (1992) *Time to Declare* (Michael Joseph).

Packwood, T., Keen, J. and Buxton, M. (1991) *Hospitals in Transition* (Open University Press).

Paige, V. (1987) 'The Development of General Management within the NHS', *The Health Summary,* June, 6–8.

Parsons, W. (1995) *Public Policy* (Edward Elgar).

Pater, J. E. (1981) *The Making of the NHS* (King's Fund).

Pettigrew, A., Ferlie, E. and McKee, L. (1992) *Shaping Strategic Change* (Sage).

Pierson, P. (1994) *Dismantling the Welfare State?* (Cambridge University Press).

Popham, G. T. (1981) 'Government and Smoking: Policy Making and Pressure Groups', *Policy and Politics,* vol. 9(3), 331–47.

Powell, J. E. (1966) *A New Look at Medicine and Politics* (Pitman).

Powell, J. E. (1976) *Medicine and Politics: 1975 and After* (Pitman).

Power, M. (1994) *The Audit Explosion* (DEMOS).

Propper, C. (1998*)* *Who Pays For and Who Gets Health Care?* (The Nuffield Trust).

Public Accounts Committee (1977) *Ninth Report from the Public Accounts Committee Session 1976–77,* HC 532 (HMSO).

Public Accounts Committee (1981) *Seventeenth Report from the Public Accounts Committee Session 1980–81: Financial Control and Accountability in the NHS,* HC 255 (HMSO).

Pullinger, J. (1997) *Regional Trends 32* (The Stationery Office).

Razell, E. (1980) *Improving Policy Analysis in the DHSS,* Civil Service College Working Paper no. 19.

Regen, E., Smith, J, and Shapiro, J. (1999*)* *First off the Starting Blocks: Lessons from GP Commissioning Pilots for PCGs* (University of Birmingham).

Regional Chairmen's Enquiry (1976) *Regional Chairmen's Enquiry into the Working of the DHSS in Relation to Regional Health Authorities* (DHSS).

Rhodes, R. A. W. (1979) 'Research into Central–Local Relations in Britain. A Framework for Analysis', appendix 1, in Social Science Research Council, *Central–Local Relationships* (SSRC).

Richardson, J. J. and Jordan, A. G. (1979) *Governing under Pressure* (Martin Robertson).

Robb. B. (ed.) (1967) *Sans Everything – A Case to Answer* (Nelson).

Roberts. J. (1990) 'Kenneth Clarke: Hatchet Man or Remoulder?', *British Medical Journal,* vol. 301. 1383–6.

Robinson, R. and Le Grand, J. (eds) (1994) *Evaluating the NHS Reforms* (King's Fund Institute).

Robinson, R. and Judge, K. (1987) *Public Expenditure and the NHS: Trends and Prospects* (King's Fund Institute).

Royal Commission on the National Health Service (1979) *Report,* Cmnd 7615 (HMSO).

RIPA (Royal Institute of Public Administration) (1980) *Policy and Practice: The Experience of Government* (RIPA).

Saunders, P. (1979) *Urban Politics* (Hutchinson).

Saunders, P. (1981) 'Notes on the Specificity of the Local State', in Boddy, M. and

Fudge, C. (eds). *The Local State: Theory and Practice* (University of Bristol, School for Advanced Urban Studies).

Secretary of State for Health and others (1989a) *Working for Patients* (HMSO).

Secretary of State for Health and others (1989b) *Caring for People* (HMSO).

Secretary of State for Health (1992) *The Health of the Nation*, Cm. 1986 (HMSO).

Secretary of State for Health (1996) *The National Health Service: A Service With Ambitions*, Cm 3425 (The Stationery Office).

Secretary of State for Health (1997) *The New NHS. Modern. Dependable* (The Stationery Office).

Secretary of State for Health (1998a) *Our Healthier Nation*, Cm 3852 (The Stationery Office).

Secretary of State for Health (1998b) *A First Class Service* (The Stationery Office).

Secretary of State for Scotland (1997) *Designed to Care* (The Stationery Office).

Secretary of State for Social Services and others (1987) *Promoting Better Health* (HMSO).

Smee, C. (1995) 'Self-governing Trusts and GP Fundholders: the British Experience', in Saltman, R. and von Otter, C. (eds), *Implementing Planned Markets in Health Care* (Open University Press).

Smith, B. (1976) *Policy Making in British Government* (Martin Robertson).

Smith, C. (1996) *A Health Service for a New Century*.

Smith, J., Bamford, M., Ham, C., Scrivens, E. and Shapiro, J. (1997) *Beyond Fundholding: A Mosaic of Primary Care Led Commissioning and Provision in the West Midlands* (Universities of Birmingham and Keele).

Smith, M. (1999) *The Core Executive in Britain* (Macmillan).

Smith, R. (1991) 'William Waldegrave: Thinking beyond the New NHS', *British Medical Journal*, vol. 302, 711–14.

Social Services Committee (1980) *The Government's White Papers on Public Expenditure: The Social Services, Third Report from the Social Services Committee, Session 1979–80*, HC 701–2 (HMSO): vol. 1, *Report*; vol. 2 *Minutes of Evidence and Appendices*.

Social Services Committee (1981) *Public Expenditure on the Social Services, Third Report from the Social Services Committee, Session 1980–81*, HC 324–1 (HMSO): vol. I, *Report*; vol. II, *Minutes of Evidence and Appendices*.

Social Services Committee (1984) *Griffiths NHS Management Inquiry Report, First Report from the Social Services Committee, Session 1983–4*, HC 209 (HMSO).

Social Services Committee (1990) *Public Expenditure on Health Matters, Session 1989–90*, HC 484 (HMSO).

Solesbury, W. (1976) 'The Environmental Agenda', *Public Administration*, Winter, 379–97.

Stacey. M. (1977) 'Concepts of Health and Illness: A Working Paper on the Concepts and their Relevance for Research', in Social Science Research Council, *Health and Health Policy – Priorities for Research* (SSRC).

Starfield, B. (1992) *Primary Care: Concept, Evaluation and Policy* (Oxford University Press).

Stevens, R. (1966) *Medical Practice in Modern England* (Yale University Press).

Stowe, K. (1989) *On Caring for the National Health* (The Nuffield Provincial Hospitals Trust).

Taylor, P. (1984) *The Smoke Ring* (The Bodley Head).

Thwaites, B. (1987) *The NHS: The End of the Rainbow* (The Institute of Health Policy Studies, University of Southampton).

Timmins, N. (1995) *The Five Giants* (HarperCollins).

Titmuss, R. (1968) *Commitment to Welfare* (Allen & Unwin).

Tudor-Hart, J. (1971) 'The Inverse Care Law', *The Lancet*, 27 February, 405–12.

van Doorslaer, E., Rutten, F. and Wagstaff, A. (1993) *Equity in the Finance and Delivery of Health Care: An International Perspective* (Oxford University Press).

Warden, J. (1998) 'Role of Chief Medical Officer has been Eroded', *British Medical Journal*, vol. 317, 14 November, 1340.

Warner, M. and Riley, C. (1994) *Closer to Home. Healthcare in the 21st Century* (National Association of Health Authorities and Trusts).

Webster, C. (1988) *The Health Services Since the War*, Vol. 1 (HMSO).

Webster, C. (1996) *The Health Services Since The War*, Vol. 2 (The Stationery Office).

Webster, C. (1998) *The National Health Service: A Political History* (Oxford University Press).

Whitehead, M. (1987) *The Health Divide* (Health Education Council).

Wilding, P. (1982) *Professional Power and Social Welfare* (Routledge & Kegan Paul).

Wilkinson, R. (1996) *Unhealthy Societies: The Afflictions of Inequality* (Routledge).

Willcocks, A. J. (1967) *The Creation of the National Health Service* (Routledge & Kegan Paul).

Willetts, D. (1987) 'The Role of the Prime Minister's Policy Unit', *Public Administration*, vol. 65, 443–54.

Yates, J. (1987) *Why Are We Waiting?* (Oxford University Press).

Yates, J. (1995) *Private Eye, Heart and Hip* (Churchill Livingstone).

Young, H. (1989) *One of Us* (Macmillan).

Young, H. and Sloman, A. (1982) *No, Minister* (BBC).

Index